THE ESSENTIAL GUIDE
CAPTAIN MARVEL

CW00507321

WELCOME!

Who is Captain Marvel? The short answer is Carol Danvers – a former air force pilot granted amazing powers by an exploding piece of alien tech. It's certainly a succinct answer, but one that doesn't do justice to her incredible comic history – which is a lot more complicated! Both her history, and the history of the Captain Marvel moniker itself, is an intriguing tapestry of different characters, costumes and comic creators that stretches back over 50 years.

After a quick recap of how she gained her powers, we begin our journey with a trio of tales from the hero's debut *Ms. Marvel* series. Written by Chris Claremont with art by Carmine Infantino and Dave Cockrum, this is an early turning point for Carol, as the confusion around her new super-hero situation is finally laid to rest. We follow up with *Uncanny X-Men #164* – another tale that sees a startling transformation for Carol as she battles alongside Marvel's mutant heroes.

We then jump forwards to modern day and the former-Ms. Marvel's rebirth as Captain Marvel. First, we have the debut issue from her 2012 series, written by Kelly Sue DeConnick and illustrated by Dexter Soy, which firmly established the new status quo for Carol Danvers. Finally, we round things up with a two-parter from 2014, as Cap, her pet cat Chewie and Rocket Raccoon face an extra-terrestrial threat that's all teeth and tentacles, and looking to take a bite out of all three of them!

Along the way you can find out writer Chris Claremont and Kelly Sue DeConnick's thoughts on Carol's comic adventures, get the inside scoop from artist Jamie McKelvie on Captain Marvel's modern redesign, take a look back at some of her other costumes and get the lowdown on some of her allies and enemies. By the end of this book you should hopefully have a pretty good idea of just who Carol is – and, more importantly, why she's become one of Marvel's most iconic heroes! Enjoy!

Ed Hammond
Marvel Editor, Panini UK
2019

ARVEL SELECT THE ESSENTIAL GUIDE TO CAPTAIN MARVEL Contains material originally published in magazine form as Ms. Marvel #19-21, Uncanny X-Men
64, Captain Marvel #1 and Captain Marvel #7-8. First printing 2019. Published by Panini Publishing, a division of Panini UK Limited. All rights reserved. ke Riddell, Managing Director. Alan O'Keefe, Managing Editor. Mark Irvine, Production Manager. Marco M. Lupoi, Publishing Director Europe. Simon Frith, nior Editor. Ed Hammond, Reprint Editor. Alex Foot & Angela Hart, Designers. Seb Patrick, Additional Content. Office of publication: Brockbourne House, 77 Mount Ephraim, Tunbridge Wells, Kent TN4 8BS. Distributed by Marketforce (UK) Ltd, Marketforce (UK) Ltd., 2nd Floor, 5 Churchill Place, Canary Wharf, London, E14 5HU. Enquiries: 020 3787 9001. Licensed by Marvel Characters B.V. www.marvel.com. All rights reserved.

2019 MARVEL

MIX
Paper from
responsible sources
FSC® C010353

THE LIFE AND TIMES OF...
CAROL DANVERS

IMBUED WITH THE POWER OF AN ALIEN KREE WARRIOR, CAPTAIN MARVEL IS A HERO WHOSE SUPERHUMAN ABILITIES ARE ON A TRULY COSMIC SCALE. BUT WHO IS THE WOMAN BEHIND THE MASK – AND HOW DID SHE ACQUIRE THESE INCREDIBLE GIFTS? READ ON AS WE DELVE INTO CAROL DANVERS' PAST.

SPREADING HER WINGS

Fighter pilot, spy, head of security for NASA, best-selling author and finally, a super hero… you certainly can't say that Carol Danvers' career path has been a predictable one. She's come a long way from her early years in Boston, growing up in a staunchly traditional household and fighting to be treated equally by an over-bearing, chauvinistic father. It could've all been so different for Carol. Unlike her two brothers, her father refused to pay for Carol's college tuition, thinking that all she needed was a good husband to look after her. Appalled by her father's old-fashioned attitude, the fiercely independent Carol joined the air force after leaving high school – much to her father's disapproval.

ENTER... THE KREE

Grounded, but still with one eye on the skies, Carol took up a position as head of security at NASA headquarters, Cape Canaveral. It was here she met Dr. Walter Lawson, a scientist with an incredible secret – he was in fact an alien Kree warrior by the name of Captain Mar-Vell. Sent to Earth to spy on humanity's blossoming space programme, Mar-Vell had instead become the planet's protector. Carol soon became embroiled in Mar-Vell's battle with his arch-enemy Yon-Rogg. It was at this time Carol was caught in the explosion of a Kree device dubbed the Psyche-Magnitron, an event with consequences no one could've foreseen…

SO YOU WANT TO HIRE ME. AND YOU WANT ME TO EDIT A WOMAN'S MAGAZINE *YOUR* WAY-- INCLUDING A FEATURE ON THIS *SUPER-WOMAN.*

OKAY, MR. JAMESON-- WHAT ABOUT MY *SALARY?*

SALARY?

SURE--AS IN WEEKLY PAYCHECK?

HMMMM...

NOVEL AMBITIONS

Unfairly demoted for her apparent inability to combat superhuman threats, Carol left NASA and wrote an explosive exposé about her former employers. The book was a hit and she soon found a new career as a writer. Eventually moving to New York, she took up a position as the editor of *Woman*, a new magazine published by the *Daily Bugle*.

TWENTY THOUSAND?

THIRTY.

TWENTY-TWO?

THIRTY!

TWENTY-FIVE?

THIRTY!

BLAST IT! HOW CAN I ARGUE MONEY WITH A *WOMAN?*

ALL RIGHT, ALL RIGHT-- THIRTY!

AND ONE THING *MORE*, JONAH... MY NAME IS *MS.* CAROL DANVERS.

AND AS FAR AS *DIETS* AND *RECIPES* GO--

FORGET IT.

HURRUMPH!

DOUBLE LIFE

Soon after, Carol began suffering from blackouts. Little did she know that she had developed a dual personality due to the Psyche-Magnitron explosion. During moments of stress, Carol would transform into Ms. Marvel, donning a new costume and gaining the powers of a Kree warrior. Over time, her two personalities began to merge and Carol came to the realisation that she and Ms. Marvel were one and the same. With the mystery of her duelling personalities solved, Carol was ready to truly embrace her new role as a super hero!

"I CAN FEEL THE *FLOOR* UNDER MY BACK, *WATER* UNDER MY LEFT ARM..."

"AND DEEP *WITHIN* ME-- I FEEL THE *CHANGE.*"

"MY BODY'S *GLOWING,* BECOMING LARGER, STRONGER --DIFFERENT.

"DEAR GOD, CAROL DANVERS IS *DISAPPEARING.* NOW THERE'S SOMEONE *ELSE,* SOMEONE *BETTER* THAN I AM--"

HER OWN HERO!
MS. MARVEL'S EARLY YEARS

BEFORE SHE WAS CAPTAIN MARVEL, CAROL DANVERS FIRST BLAZED A TRAIL AS MS. MARVEL. WE SAT DOWN WITH CHRIS CLAREMONT, THE WRITER RESPONSIBLE FOR HER EARLY ADVENTURES, FOR A QUICK CHAT.

DANVERS' DEBUT

First appearing as a support character in the original Captain Marvel's adventures, Carol Danvers entered the Marvel Universe in 1968's *Marvel Super Heroes #13*. Her relationship with Dr. Walter Lawson (Marvel's human alias) meant she would become a recurring guest-star, though after her run-in with the exploding Psyche-Magnitron in 1969's *Captain Marvel #18* her appearances would become far more sporadic.

Fast-forward to 1977 and Marvel were looking for a new female hero to headline her own book – preferably one who could also utilise the Marvel name. Writer **Gerry Conway** rescued Carol from comicbook oblivion, giving her a new super-hero identity. For the character's moniker, they steered clear of 'Marvel Girl' which they felt was too juvenile and settled on Ms. Marvel. But two issues in, Conway stepped down from the title, leaving one of Marvel's rising star writers, **Chris Claremont** to take over the book – not that he minded. "Gerry left with issue two," explained Claremont. "I needed the work and **Archie** (editor **Archie Goodwin**) gave it to me. And I thought it was a lot of fun, you know, I liked Carol as a character."

Only two issues in, not much of Ms. Marvel's origin had been established thus far, giving Claremont pretty much a blank slate to work from: "There was an interaction with Captain Marvel and the Psyche-Magnitron, and it turned out to be infectious. I think it might have been something he [Conway] would have gone in to later down the line, but it all got caught up in his brief tenure as editor-in-chief and then his brief tenure as writer. It was all basically left up in the air. So I had to ask myself, 'How can I find a way to make this make sense, and how can I make her her own person?'"

CHANGE OF STYLE

However, there was one thing Chris felt needed changing – her wardrobe: "The costume itself was always a challenge. **Jim Starlin**'s costume for Captain Marvel was brilliant. It was the ideal visual exemplification of the male paradigm. You have these broad blue shoulders and then a red arrow going straight down – the perfect reverse pyramid. And then you have the trunks, the blue point of the arrow at the base. And you look at it like, 'Woah – this guy is cool!' The female form doesn't do that. So what you end up with is a costume that doesn't really work on a woman's form and is incredibly difficult to draw in action, in a comic.

"If you look at any sort of modern dance, the leotards are always solid because when the body twists, there is no way the straps don't move – the same was true for Ms. Marvel. So what you have to ask when drawing her is, where does the fabric go? And if you think of it realistically then it's going to get incredibly inappropriate, pretty fast.

"So the first thing we ended up doing was sealing the holes and just making it a straight leotard and hoping that would work, but... my ongoing goal was always to try and find a way to redefine her visually, that would make her unique and make her absolutely kick-ass cool."

entice female readers as much as male readers. I wanted the women and girls to think of her as, 'Oh, this is someone I could be.'"

To further avoid her appearing derivative of Captain Marvel, Claremont made an effort to give Ms. Marvel a slew of new villains to help define her: "I was trying to build a catalogue of characters, a cast, but especially a catalogue of adversaries that were worthy of her." The series cancellation with issue #23 curtailed his plans, but, just as it didn't mean the end for Carol, neither did it mean an end for her villains. "The irony for me is that Mystique and Deathbird, and to a small extent Rogue, started out as Ms. Marvel characters, then Avengers characters. It always cracked me up that they only ended up in the X-Men because Ms. Marvel got cancelled," said Claremont.

EN VOGUE

But it wasn't just Ms. Marvel who needed to have an aspirational appearance – the writer made every effort to ensure Carol Danvers was just as modern and relatable to readers too. "I'd literally go to the newsagents and pick up copies of *Vogue* and every fashion magazine I could get my hands on for reference," revealed Claremont. "And I'd leaf through it and clip out anything that looked contemporary and cool to give to the artist. Versace would look cool… Italian designers galore. Because the idea is that this is comics and she needs to look cutting edge. We were certainly trying to reach and

INDEPENDENT HERO

With his 21 issues, Claremont, along with artists **John Buscema**, **Jim Mooney**, **Keith Pollard**, **Sal Buscema**, **Carmine Infantino**, **Dave Cockrum** and **Mike Vosburg**, set the groundwork for her later popularity. As to whether he had a favourite issue during this time, Claremont said, "I suppose there are two issues – one being *Ms. Marvel #19*, the Carmine Infantino issue where I went full-tilt into her backstory, to establish the 'what' and 'why' of her past. The other, for obvious reasons, is the first Dave Cockrum issue with her new look. Dave came up with one of his best costumes ever. It was simple, it was dynamic and the splash page of issue 18 said it all – "I look great!" – and finally she did. For both Dave and I, this was what Carol should have been all about from the kick-off, establishing her visually right from the start as her own woman."

MARVEL® COMICS GROUP
APPROVED BY THE COMICS CODE AUTHORITY
Ms. MARVEL TM
35¢
19
AUG
02198
©1978 MARVEL COMICS GROUP
Ms. MARVEL TM
THIS ISSUE--AT LAST--
THE FEMALE FURY MEETS
CAPTAIN MARVEL!
AT THE MERCY OF RONAN!

THIS IS *CRAZY!* A LIGHTNING BOLT-- HITTING OUT OF A *CLOUDLESS* SKY?!?

MAC-RONN-- YOU *OKAY?!*

SHAKEN UP, MY FRIEND. BUT OTHER-WISE *UN-HURT.*

LIZZIE-HONEY, ARE YOU--?!

I'M... *FINE,* ETHAN. I THINK. MAC-RONN, HOW'S *MINERVA?*

STUNNED, BUT *COMING AROUND.*

IT'S A *MIRACLE* WE'RE STILL ALIVE, IF WE'D BEEN *INSIDE* THE HOUSE...

INSIDE THE HOUSE--?!? BY THE GREAT PAMA-- *RONAN!*

HE WAS IN THE *KITCHEN* WHEN THE BOLT *HIT!*

MAC-RONN-- *NO!*

LET ME *GO!* I MUST GET TO HIM BEFORE IT'S *TOO LATE--!*

IT'S *ALREADY* TOO LATE, MAN! THE HOUSE IS AN *INFERNO.* NO ONE COULD HAVE *SURVIVED,* NOT EVEN RONAN!

MAC-RONN, ETHAN-- *LOOK!*

"*SOMETHING'S MOVING* IN THE FIRE!"

SMOKE'S TOO *THICK*--CAN'T QUITE MAKE OUT *WHAT* IT--!

BY THE GREAT PAMA!

RONAN.

ETHAN-- ALL OF A SUDDEN, I'M... *AFRAID.*

NEW YORK, NEW YORK-- FOR BETTER OR WORSE, THE **MEDIA** CAPITAL OF THE WORLD AND HOME OF "**WOMAN**" MAGAZINE,

ITS HOTSHOT EDITOR, **CAROL DANVERS**, DOESN'T **KNOW** IT YET...

...BUT **TODAY** IS GOING TO CHANGE HER LIFE, **FOREVER.**

HM, COFFEE'S COLD.

BETTER GRAB A **REFILL.** I COULD USE A **BREAK** ANYWAY.

I'M GETTING **NOWHERE** WITH THIS EDITORIAL.

I.... I...

KBASH!

IN HER **MIND'S-EYE,** SHE'S NO LONGER ON EARTH, BUT IN THE CHAMBER OF THE **SUPREME INTELLIGENCE** ON KREE-LAR...

...A PLACE SHE'S **NEVER** SEEN, YET ONE SHE SOMEHOW **KNOWS.**

BEFORE SHE REALIZES WHAT'S **HAPPEN-ING--**

--THE SUPREMOR **REACHES** OUT FROM HIS HOLOGRAM TANK AND **GRABS** HER.

CAROL DANVERS! THE TIME HAS **COME** FOR YOU TO **SERVE** THE IMPERIAL KREE!

HER MIND SCREAMS THIS IS IM-**POSSIBLE,** YET IT'S HAPPENING JUST THE SAME. HE'S SQUEEZING THE **LIFE** OUT OF HER!

AND THEN, AS **SUDDENLY** AS THE PRESCIENT SEVENTH-SENSE TRANCE BEGAN, IT **ENDS.**

WOW.

WHERE'D **THAT** COME FROM? AND AM I REALLY SURE I WANT TO **KNOW?**

BE **NICE** IF THIS WAS NO MORE THAN A **BAD DREAM--!**

CAROL DANVERS-- YOU WHO CALL YOUR-SELF **MS. MARVEL--**

HAH?!?

--IN THE NAME OF THE **IMPERIAL KREE,** I HAVE **COME** FOR YOU!

RESIST ME AT YOUR **PERIL!**

THKOW!

WHAT WAS **THAT**?! SOUNDED LIKE AN **EXPLOSION.**

JONAH, THE **ELEVATOR!** IT'S **FALLING!**

DON'T **PANIC,** MARLA. I'LL HIT THE **EMERGENCY STOP!**

OH, **NO!** THE BLASTED SWITCH ISN'T **WORKING!** I CAN'T STOP THE CAR--AND IT'S AN **ELEVEN FLOOR** DROP TO THE **STREET!**

HALA! I CUT THE ELEVATOR CABLES!

I'VE GOT TO **CATCH** IT-- **FAST!**

GOT IT!

NOW IF I CAN ONLY **BRAKE** IT IN TIME--!

SKREEAAKT!

MARLA! THE STRAIN WAS **TOO MUCH** FOR HER--SHE'S **FAINTED.**

YOU! MS. **MARVEL!!**

I **KNEW** ONE OF YOU SUPER-CREEPS WAS **RESPONSIBLE** FOR THIS! GOOD OR BAD, IT DOESN'T **MATTER**--YOU'RE ALL THE **SAME!** YOU'RE LIKE **TERRORISTS,** DANGEROUS SIMPLY BECAUSE YOU **EXIST.**

YOU'VE GOT TO BE **STAMPED OUT**--NO MATTER WHAT THE **COST!** AND IF **J. JONAH JAMESON** HAS ANYTHING TO SAY ABOUT IT, LADY, YOU **WILL** BE!

I *HEAR* YOU, JONAH, AND I'D LOVE TO *ARGUE* THE POINT, IF I HAD THE *TIME*...

...BUT I *DON'T*. I DOUBT YOU'D *LISTEN* ANYWAY.

STILL, THAT'LL PROBABLY BECOME ONE MORE EDITORIAL *HASSLE* CAROL DANVERS DOESN'T *NEED*. SOONER OR LATER, JONAH AND I ARE GONNA COME TO *BLOWS*...

...AND THAT FRACAS WILL *NOT* BE PLEASANT.

ASSUMING, OF COURSE, I *LIVE* TO SEE IT.

HEAR ME, *WOMAN!* I AM *RONAN*-- *PUBLIC ACCUSER* OF THE *KREE*.

ON THE ORDERS OF THE *SUPREME INTELLIGENCE*-- AND FOR THE *GOOD* OF THE *EMPIRE*--

--YOU *WILL ACCOMPANY* ME TO KREE- LAR.

NOT *WITHOUT* A FIGHT, I *WON'T!*

SO BE IT.

MY *UNIVERSAL WEAPON* HAS MORE THAN ENOUGH POWER TO *DEAL* WITH *YOU*.

KANG!

I SURE...*WALKED* INTO THAT ONE. I'VE A FEELING THAT, *COMPARED* TO THIS...

...MY TUSSLE WITH *CENTURION* WAS A *PILLOW FIGHT*. I CAN'T AFFORD A SINGLE *MISTAKE*.

YOU FIGHT *WELL*, WARRIOR.

HALA! ELECTRICAL *CHARGE* SHOOTING THROUGH MY BODY! NERVES ON *FIRE*--SO MUCH *PAIN!*

THOUGH YOU WERE *BORN* A TERRAN, YOUR *COURAGE* WOULD BRING HONOR TO A *KREE.*

BUT *COURAGE* COUNTS FOR *LITTLE* AGAINST RONAN.

MANAGED TO TWIST LOOSE-- *BLAST!* HE CAUGHT MY PUNCH, WITH SUCH *EASE!* HE'S BEEN *STRINGING* ME ALONG...

...*TEST-ING* ME TO FIND MY *LIMITS.*

MY-- *ARM!!*

RONAN IS *POWER PERSONIFIED*, WOMAN. DO NOT *RESIST.* MY *FRIGI-GRIP* WILL LOCK YOU IN *CRYOGENIC STASIS* IN SECONDS.

NO!!

SHATTERED ...ICE CASING...

...BUT MY ARM....IS *FROZEN* TO THE MARROW. THIS--ON TOP OF THE *PUNISHMENT* IT TOOK FROM CENTURION*-- MAKES MY RIGHT SIDE... PRETTY MUCH *USE-LESS!*

*LAST ISH--ROG.

HAVE TO *BLOCK* OUT THE *PAIN.*

IF I CAN ONLY *REACH* RONAN'S WEAPON, THIS'LL BE A *WHOLE NEW BALLGAME!*

FOR *YOU*, MS. MARVEL, THE BATTLE IS *OVER.*

NO POWER ON EARTH CAN *SAVE* YOU NOW.

NOT SO, ACCUSER! YOU'VE OBVIOUSLY FORGOTTEN THE POWER OF--

--CAPTAIN MARVEL!

MAR-VELL?!

I ALWAYS ASSUMED THAT WE'D MEET AGAIN SOMEDAY. BUT NOW THAT IT'S HAPPENING--

--I'M... SCARED.

DID YOU THINK YOUR RESURRECTION WOULD GO UNNOTICED BY ONE WHO IS COSMICALLY AWARE?!

SHOK!

BRAK!

I SENSED THE SUBTLE SHIFT IN THE EARTH'S PSYCHIC FIELD WHEN YOUR MEMORY WAS RESTORED--

--AND A QUICK TRIP TO THE WILFORD RANCH CONFIRMED MY WORST FEARS.

THANK THE STARS YOU LEFT THEM ALL UNHARMED, ACCUSER, FOR I'D HAVE MADE YOU PAY FOR THEIR LIVES!

I DON'T KNOW WHY YOU'VE ATTACKED THIS WOMAN--

--BUT AS OF THIS MOMENT, THE BATTLE IS ENDED!

SK ZAK!

TIME PASSES...

...AND WHEN AT LAST MAR-VELL RE-OPENS HIS EYES...

...HE FINDS HIMSELF ON THE **COMMAND DECK** OF AN IMPERIAL **STARSHIP.**

GREETINGS, CAPTAIN. WE WERE **BEGINNING** TO THINK YOU WOULDN'T **WAKE UP.**

WHAT'S THIS ALL **ABOUT,** RONAN? I CAN UNDERSTAND YOUR COMING AFTER **ME**--

--BUT WHY THE WOMAN?!

I'M **SURPRISED** AT YOU, MAR-VELL. I THOUGHT THAT BY NOW YOU'D HAVE **GUESSED.**

SUPRE-MOR!

OF COURSE. WHAT OTHER **MIND** COULD HAVE CONCEIVED OF SO BRILLIANT-- YET SO **SIMPLE**-- A PLAN?

WITHIN MS. MARVEL ARE **COMBINED** THE GENETIC HERITAGE OF THE **FINEST KREE** WARRIOR EVER BORN-- **YOU,** CAPTAIN MAR-VELL--

--AND THE LATENT **PSIONIC TALENTS** COMMON TO ALL TERRANS,

THE **POWER** I ONCE SOUGHT FROM YOU AND **RIK-JONZZ** POSSESSED BY A SINGLE **FEMALE.**

IT IS HER **DESTINY** TO BECOME THE **MOTHER** TO A RACE OF NEW-KREE THAT NO FORCE IN THE UNIVERSE CAN **WITH-STAND.**

I WILL TAKE HER **SOUL** AS I ONCE THOUGHT TO TAKE YOURS, WITH THE **MILLENNIA BLOOM.** ITS SIREN-SONG WILL REACH INTO THE **CORE** OF HER BEING--

--AND TURN IT **INSIDE-OUT.** ALL THAT IS **HUMAN** WITHIN HER WILL BE EXPUNGED, AND WHAT IS KREE WILL BE A **TABULA RASA**--

TEK!

--A **BLANK PAGE**-- FORMLESS CLAY WHICH I WILL **SHAPE** AS I CHOOSE.

BEGIN, RONAN.

DOORS **OPEN** SILENTLY, AND THE MILLENNIA BLOOM-- LOCKED IN **STASIS** BY THE SUPREMOR SINCE HIS LAST **FATEFUL** CONFRONTATION WITH MAR-VELL*-- FLARES TO LIFE WITHIN THE **CRYSTAL CELL**...

...IT'S GENTLE, CORUSCATING LIGHT PAINTING MS. MARVEL IN **RAINBOW** COLORS.

*CAPTAIN MARVEL #46--R.S.

SLOWLY, STEADILY, THE LIGHTS GROW TO NEAR-*SOLAR* BRILLIANCE, MS. MARVEL CRYING OUT AS THE WORLD AROUND HER *DISSOLVES* UNDER THEIR ONSLAUGHT.

AND THEN, IT'S *HER* TURN, THE CHROMATIC SYMPHONY HITTING HER ON *EVERY* LEVEL OF PERCEPTION AT ONCE.

SHE'S *CAUGHT*, MIND AND BODY AND SOUL, UNABLE--*UNWILLING*--TO BREAK FREE AS THE LIGHT SHOW BUILDS TO A *THUNDERING* CRESCENDO.

TIME STOPS, REALITY LOSES ALL *MEANING* AND, SUDDENLY, SHE'S IN THE *SUPREMOR'S* CHAMBER--

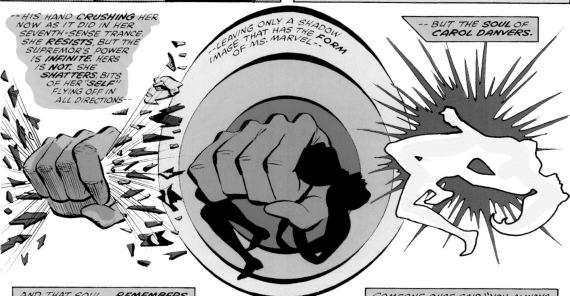

--HIS HAND *CRUSHING* HER NOW AS IT DID IN HER SEVENTH-SENSE TRANCE. SHE *RESISTS*, BUT THE SUPREMOR'S POWER IS *INFINITE*. HERS IS *NOT*. SHE *SHATTERS*, BITS OF HER "*SELF*" FLYING OFF IN ALL DIRECTIONS--

--LEAVING ONLY A SHADOW IMAGE THAT HAS THE *FORM* OF MS. MARVEL--

-- BUT THE *SOUL* OF *CAROL DANVERS.*

AND THAT SOUL...*REMEMBERS.* THE IMAGES FLASH THROUGH HER MIND LIKE A *SENSORAL MOVIE* AS SHE FINDS HERSELF BOTH *APART* FROM THE ACTION AND A *PART* OF IT.

JUST LIKE SHE WAS BOTH A PART OF HER *FAMILY*... AND *APART* FROM IT.

SOMEONE ONCE SAID, "YOU ALWAYS *HURT* THE ONE YOU *LOVE.*" IF SO, HER FATHER MUST HAVE LOVED HER *VERY MUCH.* EVEN NOW, SHE CAN'T REMEMBER A TIME THEY WEREN'T *FIGHTING.*

...THIS DISCUSSION IS *OVER*, CAROL, MY DECISION IS *FINAL.*

NOT BEFORE YOU TELL ME *WHY*, DAD. YOU OWE ME *THAT* MUCH, AT LEAST.

AFTER BASIC TRAINING, SHE FOUND HERSELF ASSIGNED TO **STRATEGIC OPERATIONS**, AND PARTNERED WITH **COLONEL MICHAEL ROSSI** WHO WAS FIRST HER TEACHER, THEN HER FRIEND, AND FINALLY HER **FIRST LOVE**. THEY SOON BECAME SOMETHING OF A **LEGEND**.

AT **NASA'S** REQUEST, SHE WAS ASSIGNED TO CAPE CANAVERAL AS **SECURITY CHIEF**. IT WAS THERE THAT SHE FIRST MET **CAPTAIN MARVEL**...

...AND FOUND HERSELF CAUGHT IN THE **MIDDLE** OF A GAME OF **INTER-STELLAR VENGEANCE**.

SHE REMEMBERS LYING SEMI-CONSCIOUS BENEATH THE **PSYCHE-MAGNITRON**, WISHING SHE HAD THE **POWER** TO STAND WITH MAR-VELL AS AN **EQUAL**.

AND THE KREE **MIRACLE MACHINE** HAD TURNED HER WISH INTO **REALITY**, DRAWING ENERGY FROM MAR-VELL'S **NEGA-BANDS** AND USING IT TO LITERALLY **REBUILD** CAROL CELL-BY-CELL...

...COMBINING IN HER THE **BEST** ELEMENTS OF KREE AND HUMAN. BUT THE PROCESS -- A COMPLETE **GENETIC RECONSTRUCTION** -- WOULD TAKE **TIME**.

SO, TO **BRIDGE** THAT NECESSARY GAP THE MACHINE CREATED A **COSTUME** THAT WOULD ELECTRONICALLY **MIMIC** MANY OF CAROL'S NASCENT POWERS AND SUMMONED HER BACK TO THE CAVE, WEEKS LATER, TO **FIND** IT.

UNFORTUNATELY THE PSYCHE-MAGNITRON HAD DONE ITS WORK **TOO WELL**. IT HAD GIVEN CAROL NOT ONLY THE **POWER** OF A KREE, BUT THE **MIND** OF ONE AS WELL. THE RESULTANT CONFLICT HAD **SPLIT** HER PERSONALITY IN **HALF**.

IN TIME, CAROL HAD MADE HER OWN *PEACE* WITH HERSELF, BUT NOW THE MILLENNIA BLOOM HAS *UNDONE* ALL THAT...

MY REFLECTION-- IT'S *CAROL DANVERS!*

HALA! SHE'S TURNING INTO A *DEMON*--! SHE WANTS ME *DEAD!*

NO, MONSTER! IF *ANYONE* DIES IN THIS NIGHTMARE--

--IT WILL *NOT* BE *MS. MARVEL!*

THERE'S NO *CRASH* AS THE MIRROR-MONSTER SHATTERS, ONLY THE WAIL OF A *LOST SOUL...*

...GIVING WAY TO THE *SOBS* OF A WOMAN PUSHED TO THE *LIMITS* OF HER SANITY, AND *FAR BEYOND.*

IT IS *DONE,* MAR-VELL. THE WOMAN IS *MINE.*

OH, CAROL.

WE ALL *EXPERIENCED* SOME OF WHAT YOU WENT THROUGH. I FEEL SOMEHOW... *RESPONSIBLE.*

AND NOW, THE SUPREMOR WILL *REMAKE* YOU IN HIS OWN IMAGE-- AS HE REMADE *RONAN*-- AND I AM *HELPLESS* TO STOP...EH?

BY THE GREAT PAMA--!

I SENSE *NO CHANGE* IN HER!

IF THE *MILLENNIA BLOOM* HAD DONE WHAT THE SUPREMOR EXPECTED OF IT, MY *COSMIC AWARENESS* WOULD HAVE MARKED THE *"DEATH"* OF CAROL'S HUMAN PERSONALITY.

BUT I SENSE *NO* ALTERATION IN HER *PSYCHIC AURA.* HER MIND-- HER SOUL-- ARE *WHOLE!*

SHE'S STILL TERRIBLY **WEAK**, THOUGH. I HAVE TO BUY HER SOME **TIME**!

I TRUST YOU'RE **PROUD** OF YOURSELF, ACCUSER, SO **SCARED** OF A TERRAN-BORN **FEMALE**--

--THAT YOU MUST **STRIKE** HER DOWN BY **TREACHERY**!

PINK, I HAVE **SUFFERED** YOUR INSOLENCE LONG ENOUGH.

SCHKOW!

THE WOMAN'S LIFE IS **SACROSANCT**. YOURS IS **NOT**!

THOM!

CAN'T TAKE MUCH **MORE** OF THIS-- BUT... I HAVE TO KEEP RONAN'S ATTENTION... **OFF** CAROL...

¿OOOOHHHHH¿

I THOUGHT I'D BEEN THROUGH **HELL** IN MY LIFE... BUT I WAS **WRONG**

I FEEL... **DIRTY** INSIDE-- WORSE THAN I FELT AFTER MODOK TRIED TO **BRAINWASH** ME.*

*MS. MARVEL #7 --ROG.

WHA--?! **MAR-VELL**! RONAN'S **BEATING** HIM TO A PULP!

RONAN! YOU MISERABLE FOOL-- **BEHIND** YOU!

SOMETHING'S GONE **WRONG**! MS. MARVEL ISN'T-- **SQUAWRRRK**!

--UNDER MY CONTROL! RONAN! **RONAN**!

EXCELLENT! I MANEUVERED RONAN INTO **SMASHING** THE COM-PLATE VOLUME CONTROL JUST IN TIME. HE'LL **NEVER** HEAR THE SUPREMOR'S WARNING NOW.

EVEN IF HE **DID**, THE PROBLEM HAS JUST BECOME **ACADEMIC**...

RONAN!!

MS. MARVEL-- **FREE!!**

NO MATTER, MY **UNIVERSAL WEAPON** STOPPED YOU ONCE-- IT WILL DO SO **AGAIN.**

UNNNFFF!

ONLY IF YOU **REACH** IT, ACCUSER!

WHAM!

TOOK **ALL** MY STRENGTH TO FLY WITH THE CHAIR **STRAPPED** TO ME. NOW IT'S UP TO **CAROL.**

KRAKOW!

THE PUNCH HURLS RONAN THE **LENGTH** OF THE STARSHIP, MS. MARVEL **HOT** ON HIS TRAIL EVEN BEFORE HE COMES TO **REST.**

AFTER A WHILE, SHE **RETURNS...**

OKAY, UGLY, I'M GONNA SAY THIS **ONCE,** SO-- FOR YOUR OWN SAKE-- YOU'D BETTER **PAY ATTENTION.**

YOU TRY **ANYTHING** WITH ME AGAIN-- IN PERSON OR THROUGH **SURROGATES**--AND I'LL CATCH THE FIRST STARSHIP TO **KREE-LAR...**

...AND DO TO **YOU** WHAT I JUST DID TO YOUR TIN-PLATED **FLUNKY** HERE.

KZRAKT!

I TRUST WE **UNDERSTAND** EACH OTHER, SUPREMOR. IF WE DON'T, IT'LL BE **YOUR FUNERAL.**

DAWN--IN COLORADO'S *CATHEDRAL CANYON,* IN THE FOOTHILLS OF THE *ROCKY MOUNTAINS...*

THERE HE GOES.

MAC-RONN AND MINERVA WILL *PILOT* RONAN'S STARSHIP TO *KREE-LAR* AND *REPORT* THE SUPREMOR'S RE-AWAKENING TO THE *COUNCIL.* AFTER THAT, IT'S *THEIR* PROBLEM.

I WISH THEM *LUCK.* KNOWING THE SUPREME INTELLIGENCE, THEY'LL *NEED* IT.

ARM *HURTS* LIKE BLAZES-- ALWAYS KNEW THIS SCARF WOULD COME IN *HANDY* SOMEDAY, DIDN'T THINK IT'D BE AS A *SLING,* THOUGH.

CAROL...?

CAROL.

I *HEAR* YOU, MAR-VELL. I'M JUST *NOT SURE* WHAT TO SAY.

ALL MY LIFE, I'VE FOUGHT TO BE MY *OWN* WOMAN. THE LAST THING I WANTED WAS TO BECOME A FEMALE *COPY* OF ANYONE-- ESPECIALLY *YOU.* BUT, FOR BETTER OR WORSE, THAT'S WHAT *HAPPENED.*

I'M NOT *GRIPING,* Y'UNDERSTAND. I...*LIKE* BEING A SUPERHERO, BUT...

MAR-VELL...OUR *POWERS* MAY BE SIMILAR, BUT OUR HEADS *AREN'T.* I'M NOT KREE-- I'M *HUMAN,* AND *PROUD* OF IT.

THAT'S AS IT *SHOULD* BE, CAROL.

I GUESS, I...OH, HELL, GIVE US A *KISS,* FOR OLD TIME'S SAKE.

FRIENDS?

AFTER ALL WE'VE... *BEEN* THROUGH TOGETHER, COULD WE BE ANYTHING *ELSE?*

PAL, I SURE HOPE NOT.

C'MON, THERE'S A *TOWN* IN THAT VALLEY. BEFORE I START BACK FOR *NEW YORK,* I'LL BUY US BOTH *BREAKFAST.*

YOU KNOW, I THINK I'D *LIKE* THAT.

NEXT A NEW COSTUME-- NEW THRILLS-- NEW EXCITEMENT! **A NEW BEGINNING!**

OH, CAROL, THIS TIME YOU'VE OUT-DONE YOURSELF.

'TWAS *NOTHING*, MS. DANVERS. A FRESH-BREWED BATCH OF *UN-STABLE MOLECULES*, A LITTLE DESIGN ASSISTANCE FROM *JANET PYM*--AND *VOILA!*

INSTANT *MAGNI-FICENCE.*

ONE *DRAWBACK*, THOUGH. THIS STUFF IS LITERALLY A *SECOND SKIN*--IF I GAIN EVEN A *GRAM* OF MASS, IT'LL *SHOW.*

SO, WHAT DO I NEED *FOOD* FOR ANYW--OH, *BROTHER!*

BZZZZ

THE *DOORBELL!*

SO HELP ME, IF IT'S AN-OTHER SALESMAN OR *RELIGIOUS NUT--!*

NOPE, IT'S THE NEXT BEST THING--*FRANK GIANELLI.* TO-DAY'S SATURDAY, *PAISAN*--MY *DAY OFF.*

YEAH, WELL I WISH THIS CALL WAS *SOCIAL*, TOO. WE GOT *TROUBLE*, CAROL.

SUCH AS?

SHARON COLE'S *DISAPPEARED.* SHE WAS COVERING THOSE *NEW MEXICO MURDERS* FOR THE "BUGLE".

THEN, A WEEK AGO--*POOF!* SHE *VANISHED.*

OKAY, COME ON IN.

YOU CAN *BRIEF* ME WHILE I HEAT SOME COFFEE.

DAY BECOMES NIGHT, AND IN TRINITY CANYON, AMID NEW MEXICO'S SAN ANDRES MOUNTAINS...

...SHARON COLE IS RUNNING FOR HER LIFE.

NO *SIGN* OF THEM, THANK GOD. MAYBE I'VE GIVEN THEM THE *SLIP.* MAYBE THEY DIDN'T *SEE* ME AT ALL.

CHEST FEELS LIKE SOMEONE'S *STABBED* ME WITH A *WHITE-HOT SPEAR.* SEEMS LIKE I'VE BEEN RUNNING...*FOREVER!*

TUESDAY MORNING, THE *ELEPHANT BUTTE* STATION OF THE *NEW MEXICO STATE POLICE*...

NEW MEXICO STATE POLICE ELEPHANT BUTTE STA.

CAROL HAD BEEN IN AN *IMPORTANT* MEETING WITH JONAH JAMESON WHEN THE *CALL* CAME IN ABOUT SHARON. WITHIN AN HOUR, SHE WAS ABOARD A FLIGHT OUT OF KENNEDY AIRPORT.

JAMESON HAD BEEN IN A FINE *FURY* AT HER SUDDEN EXIT, BUT CAROL COULDN'T CARE *LESS.*

ONE OF HER *FRIENDS* WAS IN TROUBLE--OR WORSE! AND TO CAROL, THAT WAS ALL THAT MATTERED.

...I NEED HELP, I--OH MY *GOD!*

THEY'RE RIGHT BEHIND ME! SOME-ONE--ANYONE--HELP ME! FOR THE LOVE OF-- YEARRRGKH!

IT WAS PURE *LUCK* WE HEARD HER. *FREAK* ATMOSPHERICS.

WE FIGURE HER JEEP WAS GOING OVER A *HUNDRED* WHEN IT CRASHED.

AND YOU'VE NO IDEA WHAT CAUSED IT? OR *ATTACKED* SHARON?!

I'VE DONE SOME *CHECKING,* SERGEANT WHITMORE. TWO *OTHER* PEOPLE VANISHED THAT NIGHT, THE *LATEST* IN A LONG SERIES OF MYSTERIOUS *DISAPPEAR-ANCES.*

EVERYONE KNOWS ABOUT THEM, EVERY-ONE'S *SCARED,* BUT NO ONE WILL *TALK* ABOUT IT. *WHY?*

BECAUSE THEY'VE BEEN *ORDERED* NOT TO.

WHA--?! OH--HELLO, HARRY.

COLONEL BUTLER, TO YOU, MISS DANVERS.

THIS IS A *MILITARY* INVESTI-GATION, AND I'M IN *NO MOOD* TO TOLERATE OUTSIDE *INTER-FERENCE.* ESPECIALLY FROM *YOU.*

IS THAT SO?

WELL, *HEAR THIS,* HARRY BUTLER-- ONE OF MY PEOPLE IS *MISSING* AND I'M GOING TO FIND OUT WHAT *HAP-PENED* TO HER NO MATTER HOW HARD YOU TRY TO *STONEWALL* ME!

I'LL *WARN* YOU ONCE, LITTLE LADY--!

I'M *NOT* LITTLE--AND I'M *NO LADY!*

THAT'S FOR SURE.

GET IN MY *WAY,* DANVERS, AND I'LL *RUN YOU OVER.*

I DON'T TAKE KINDLY TO *THREATS,* MISTER.

I *MEAN IT!* FOR ONCE, *LEAVE* THIS JOB TO MEN WHO CAN *HANDLE* IT!

SOMETIME LATER...

THAT'S SOME *TEMPER* YOU'VE GOT, CAROL.

DON'T I *KNOW* IT. YOU'D THINK BY NOW I'D HAVE LEARNED TO *CONTROL* IT BETTER.

I *DUNNO...* THAT ARMY BOZO HAD HIS *BLACK EYE* COMING.

I SUPPOSE, I HAVE TO ADMIT, IT SURE FELT *GOOD.*

I WANT TO *THANK* YOU FOR HELPING ME, *JIM.*

NO SWEAT, I DON'T LIKE *ANYONE*--EVEN THE ARMY--*MUSCLING* INTO MY CASE.

I *KNEW* SHARON, Y'KNOW. SHE WAS A *NICE* KID.

I WISH WE HAD SOME-THING TO *SHOW* FOR TODAY'S WORK. I'M BEGINNING TO THINK WE'RE CHASING *GHOSTS.*

JIM-- *STOP THE CAR!*

I SAW SOMETHING *FLASH* IN THE MOONLIGHT!

WHAT IN THE--?

IT'S THE *ARMORED COLUMN* BUTLER CALLED UP FROM FORT STARK! *MAIN BATTLE TANKS,* A.P.C.'S--THE WORKS!

THE *WHOLE* COLUMN'S BEEN *WIPED OUT!!*

THIS IS *CRAZY!* EVERYTHING'S BEEN TORN-- *RIPPED*--APART, LIKE THEY WERE *KIDDIE TOYS!*

THE GUNS ARE *HOT.* THE MEN MUST'VE PUT UP ONE *HELLUVA* FIGHT--BUT WHERE ARE THE *BODIES?!* A WHOLE *BATTALION* CAN'T JUST *DISAPPEAR.*

THIS ONE *DID.*

NO *SEVENTH-SENSE* FLASHES--DON'T KNOW WHETHER THAT'S GOOD OR *BAD.*

MY SKIN'S *CRAWLING.* EVERY INSTINCT I HAVE IS *SCREAMING* THAT SOMETHING'S ABOUT TO *HAPPEN*--BUT *WHAT?!*

CAROL.

YIKES!!

SORRY. I DIDN'T MEAN TO *SCARE* YOU.

THAT'S OKAY. JUST *DON'T* DO IT AGAIN, HUH?

OR I MIGHT *"ACCI-DENTALLY"* KNOCK YOU INTO THE MIDDLE OF *NEXT WEEK.*

HEY, JIM--COME HERE! I THINK I'VE *FOUND* SOMETHING!

THWUP!

IT'S A *FOOTPRINT*, WAY LARGER THAN *HUMAN*--MADE BY A THREE-TOED *BIPED*. BUT AS FAR AS I KNOW, THERE *AIN'T* NO SUCH ANIMAL.

WHY ONLY A COUPLE OF TRACKS HERE, BUT *NOWHERE ELSE?*

WAIT A MINUTE! THERE *ARE* OTHER TRACKS--BUT THEY'VE BEEN EXPERTLY *CAMOUFLAGED*.

JIM! WHERE ARE YOU?!

JIM! SERGEANT WHITMORE!?

WHAT *GIVES?!* HE WAS RIGHT *BEHIND* ME A MOMENT AGO.

UH-OH.

NO SIGN OF A *STRUGGLE*, HE MUST HAVE BEEN ZAPPED *INSTANTLY*, WITHOUT EVEN THE SLIGHTEST *SOUND*.

AND I'LL LAY *ANY* ODDS HIS ATTACKER IS STILL *NEARBY*.

I'VE DONE *ALL* I CAN AS CAROL DANVERS.

I THINK IT'S TIME MY *NEW* OUTFIT MADE ITS *OFFICIAL* DEBUT.

HEADS UP, WORLD! NOW TAKING CENTER STAGE...

...IS THE *ALL-NEW, BETTER-THAN-EVER MS. MARVEL!*

DOING THE WORK SHE WAS *BORN* TO DO...

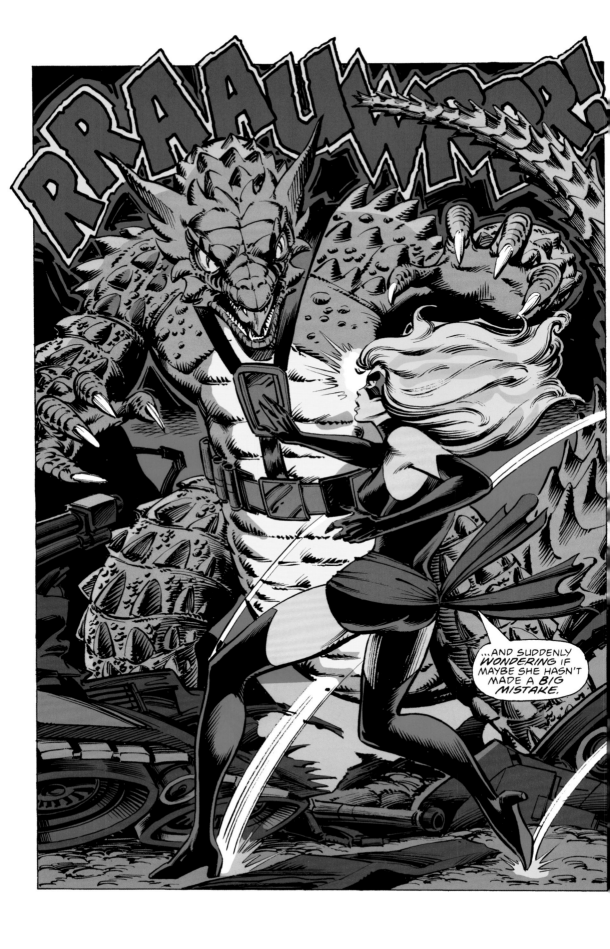

TSSSSS--!!

YOUR SSSTRENGTH FAR **EXCEEDSSS** YOUR PUNY FORM, MAMMAL. THAT ISSS **GOOD**.

I HAVE **LONGED** TO FACE ONE OF YOUR KIND WHO WASSS **WORTHY** OF THE TITLE, **WARRIOR**.

I GAVE HIM MY **BEST SHOT**--THE ONE I USED TO **FLATTEN** RONAN--BUT THAT RE-FUGEE FROM TOHO STUDI-OS ISN'T EVEN **FAZED**.

IS THIS LIZARD SOME MADMAN'S **CREATION**--ACTING UNDER OUTSIDE **CONTROL**? HE SPOKE OF "HIGH ONES".

OR DID HE **EVOLVE**--A WHOLE NEW **RACE**, LIVING SIDE-BY-SIDE WITH MA--?

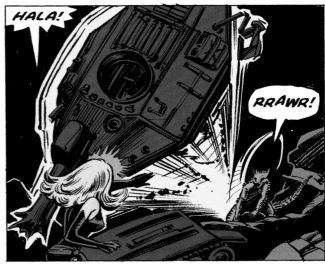

HALA!

RRAWR!

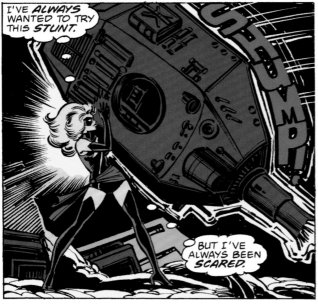

I'VE **ALWAYS** WANTED TO TRY THIS **STUNT**.

BUT I'VE ALWAYS BEEN **SCARED**.

SSS-OMP!

IT ISN'T **EASY** GOING FROM BEING A **NORMAL** WOMAN TO A **SUPER-PERSON**. THE OLD INSTINCTS--THE OLD **FEARS**--DIE HARD

TWANG!

BUT AFTER ALL THESE MONTHS, THE IRRATIONAL FEARS ARE GONE.

YOUR *SSSPEED--* IT *SSSURPASSESSS MY OWN!* TRULY, THISSS WILL BE A *GLORIOUSSS* BATTLE!

THAT'S RIGHT, HORNHEAD, AND IT'LL BE *OVER* BEFORE YOU *KNOW* IT!

PLEASANT DREAMS, GODZILLA.

I'D BETTER TAKE UGLY TO *GAMMA BASE.* THEIR *HULK* HOLDING PENS SHOULD BE ABLE TO *HANDLE* HIM. AND WHEN HE WAKES UP, WE'LL START GETTING SOME *ANSWERS.*

NO, HUMAN! YOU WILL TAKE OUR BROTHER *NOWHERE*. AND IF YOU HAVE CAUSED HIM *LASSSTING HARM*--

EH?!

--YOU WILL *SSSUFFER* FOR IT!!

UNNNGNH!

TAKE *CARE*, COMRADESSS!

KHADAR WASSS A *WARRIOR-PRIME*, YET THE HUMAN *DEFEATED* HIM. SHE ISSS NO *MEAN* FOE.

MORE OF THEM--AND FROM THE *SOUND* OF THINGS, THEY'RE PLAYING THIS A LOT *CAGIER* THAN THEIR BUDDY.

I NEED MORE *INFORMATION*. I'VE GOT TO TRY *TALKING* TO THEM.

I MEAN YOU *NO HARM*. YOUR FRIEND *ATTACKED* ME. I HAD NO CHOICE BUT TO *DEFEND* MYSELF.

THERE'S NO *REASON* FOR US TO *FIGHT*.

THERE ISSS *EVERY* REASON, SSSOFT-SSSKIN.

YOU HAVE *SSSEEN* THE PEOPLE.

AND THE *HIGH ONESSS* HAVE ORDAINED THAT *NONE* OF YOUR KIND MAY *LEARN* OF OUR EXISSSTENCE--

--AND *ESSSCAPE* TO TELL THE TALE.

THAT *TEARS* IT.

WHEN YOUR *BACK'S* TO THE WALL, AS *MIKE ROSSI* USED TO SAY, DO THE *UNEXPECTED.*

CHARGE!!

I'VE ONE BIG *ADVANTAGE.* THOSE BRUISERS CAN'T *FLY.* SO LONG AS I'M IN THE AIR, THEY CAN'T *TOUCH* ME.

WITH ANY LUCK, I CAN *TRACK* THEM TO THEIR LAIR, AND FIND OUT WHAT HAPPENED TO THEIR *VICTIMS.*

MY-- *BACK!!*

SHAKT!

YOU ARE A *FOOL,* MAMMAL, TO THINK YOU CAN ESSSCAPE US THISSS *EASSSILY!*

FLIER CAUGHT ME BY *SURPRISE* --THAT SUCKER-PUNCH OF HIS DARN NEAR *CRIPPLED* ME!

BUT IF THIS REPTILIAN *RED BARON* IS LOOK-ING FOR A *DOGFIGHT--*

--THEN I'LL *GIVE* HIM ONE HE'LL *NEVER* FORGET!

BROTHERSSS! THE MAMMAL SEEKSSS MY LIFE--*HELP ME!*

TAK *PLAYSSS* HISSS ROLE WELL. IN AN-OTHER MOMENT, THE MAMMAL WILL BE *OURSSS.*

--IF I HAVE TO **BEAT** THEM OUT OF YOUR EVER-LOVING **HIDES!**

SKRRRAMMM!

THE NEXT FEW MINUTES ARE SOMEWHAT **PAINFUL** FOR THE GIANT LIZARDS, AS MS. MARVEL TAKES THEIR **BEST SHOTS...**

...AND RETURNS THEM WITH **INTEREST**. SHE'S NEVER CUT LOOSE LIKE THIS BEFORE AND SHE FINDS IT A **HEADY** FEELING, TO HOLD HER **OWN** AND **MORE** A-GAINST CREATURES OVER **TWICE** HER SIZE.

UNFORTUNATELY, HER TRI-UMPH IS **SHORT-LIVED...**

HOLD, WOMAN!

HAH?!

CEASE THIS COMBAT-- **AT ONCE!**

YOU STAND BEFORE THE **HIGH COUNCIL** OF THE PEOPLE. I AM **ARACHT'YR**, THEIR PATRIARCH.

NAME YOURSELF.

I AM CALLED **MS. MARVEL.**

THIS COMBAT WAS **NOT** OF MY MAKING, PATRIARCH. I CAME SEEKING A **LOST** FRIEND WHEN, WITH-OUT **PROVOCATION**, YOUR WARRIORS ATTACKED ME.

NOW, AS THEN, I OFFER **PEACE**. GIVEN A CHOICE, I'D RATHER **TALK** THAN FIGHT.

IF SO, MS. MARVEL, YOU ARE *UNIQUE* AMONG YOUR KIND.

ARACHT'YR, THE *DAWN* APPROACHESSS. AND WE ARE *FAR* FROM HOME.

I AM *AWARE*, HAEMON.

I SENSE *TRUTH* IN YOUR WORDS, WOMAN. I WISH I WERE AL- LOWED TO *TRUST* YOU, BUT WHERE THE *SAFE- TY* OF THE PEOPLE IS CONCERNED, I AM ALLOWED NEITHER TRUST NOR *MERCY*.

HAEMON-- *TAKE HER!*

ASSS YOU *COMMAND*, ARACHT'YR.

AAHRRR!

ENERGY BEAM--SOME KIND OF *TELEPATHIC* ATTACK! MIND...ON *FIRE*, HEAD FEELS ABOUT TO *BURST APART!*

GOT TO *GET AWAY!* BUT...CAN'T FOCUS CONCENTRATION... TO *FLY!* I'M A *SITTING DUCK!*

SHE *CRUMPLES* LIKE A PUPPET WITH ITS STRINGS *CUT*, AND ONCE SHE HITS THE GROUND, SHE DOES NOT *MOVE*.

"ARACHT'YR, ISSS THE MAMMAL FOR *SSSLAYING?*"

"BE *SILENT*, WARRIOR--THOSE DAYS ARE *DONE FOREVER!*"

"LOAD HER ON ARACHT'YR'SSS BEARER--*QUICKLY!* WE HAVE *LITTLE TIME!*"

SHORTLY...

"ARACHT'YR, THE *DAWN* COMESSS--AND, WITH IT, HU-MANSSS IN THEIR UNLIVING *FLIERSSS!*"

"BE *CALM*, TAK. WE ARE ALMOST *HOME.*"

"EVEN NOW, THE GATEWAY OPENS TO *ADMIT* US."

AT THE HEAD OF A BOX CANYON HIDDEN DEEP WITHIN THE SAN ANDRES MOUNTAINS, THE CLIFF FACE SUDDENLY, SI-LENTLY, SPLITS APART.

AS SOON AS THE LAST OF THE LIZ-ARD COLUMN HAS ENTERED, THE GREAT DOORS SWING SHUT AGAIN...

...AND THE CANYON ONCE MORE LOOKS AS IF NO ONE HAS PASSED THIS WAY IN A HUNDRED YEARS.

WITHIN THE MOUNTAIN, THOUGH--AND THE VAST, NATURAL CAVERN COMPLEX THAT EXTENDS FOR MILES IN EVERY DIREC-TION--IT'S ANOTHER STORY.

AND ANOTHER WORLD...ONE WHERE LIZARDS RULE, AND HUMANS ARE THEIR PREY.

NEXT ISSUE **THE DEVIL IN THE DARK!**

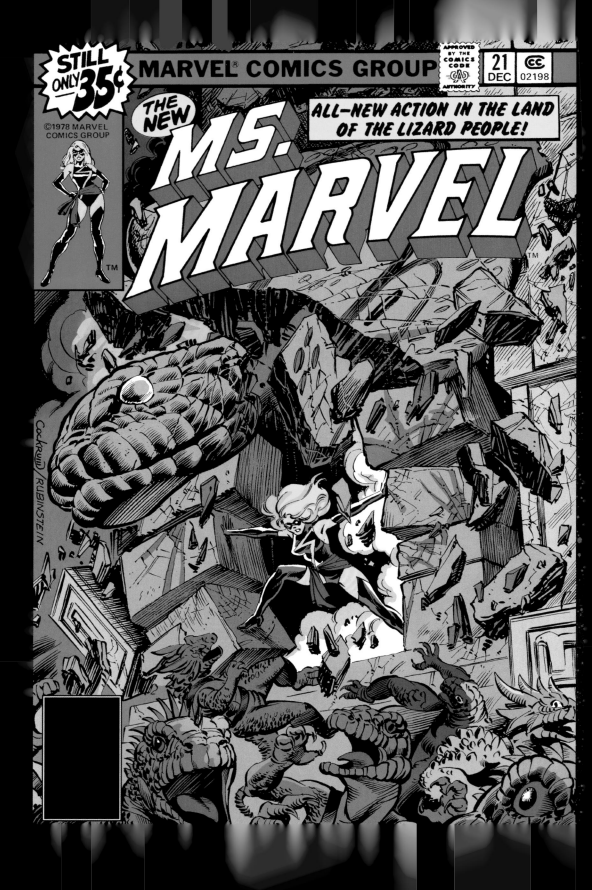

SHE HITS THE ROCK FLOOR *HARD* AND DOES NOT *MOVE*.

AFTER A WHILE, THOUGH, SHE MOANS SOFTLY, LIKE SOMEONE RUNNING A TREADMILL THROUGH A *BAD DREAM*.

IN HER MIND'S-EYE, IT'S THE PREVIOUS DAY.

As *CAROL DANVERS*, SHE'D COME TO NEW MEXICO TO INVESTIGATE THE *DISAPPEARANCE* OF A "WOMAN" MAGAZINE REPORTER, *SHARON COLE*.

SHE SOON *DISCOVERED* THAT THIS WAS MERELY THE *LATEST* IN A LONG LINE OF *MYSTERIOUS* INCIDENTS.

DESPITE BEING *WARNED-OFF* BY THE ARMY, CAROL AND A STATE POLICE *SERGEANT* HAD GONE OUT INTO THE *DESERT*...

...TO SEE IF THEY COULD FIND ANY *LEADS*.

THEY CAME UP WITH *MORE* THAN THEY *BARGAINED* FOR.

IT'S THE *ARMORED COLUMN* FROM FORT STARK! IT'S BEEN *WIPED OUT!*

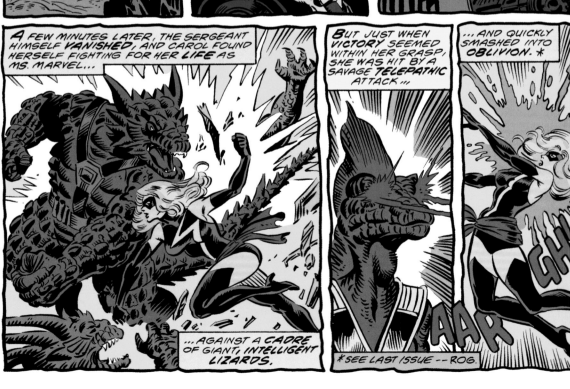

A FEW MINUTES LATER, THE SERGEANT HIMSELF *VANISHED*, AND CAROL FOUND HERSELF FIGHTING FOR HER *LIFE* AS MS. MARVEL...

...AGAINST A *CADRE* OF GIANT, INTELLIGENT LIZARDS.

BUT JUST WHEN *VICTORY* SEEMED WITHIN HER GRASP, SHE WAS HIT BY A SAVAGE *TELEPATHIC* ATTACK...

...AND QUICKLY SMASHED INTO *OBLIVION*. *

* SEE LAST ISSUE — ROG.

:OOOHHH: WHOEVER'S DOING THAT TAP DANCE INSIDE MY SKULL...

...CUT IT OUT, WILLYA?! THE SHOW'S OVER.

MY MIND-- MY ENTIRE NERVOUS SYSTEM-- IS ALL JANGLED UP, LIKE I'D BEEN PLUGGED INTO AN ELECTRIC SOCKET.

HAVEN'T BEEN HIT SO HARD SINCE MODOK'S MIND-RIPPER.* AT LEAST, I'M STILL ALIVE-- THAT'S SOMETHING...

*MS. M #7--ROG.

NOW IF I ONLY KNEW WHERE THE HECK I WAS--!

HEY!!

HER REACTION IS INSTINCTIVE AND INSTANTANEOUS. BEFORE THE MAN QUITE REALIZES WHAT'S HAPPENING, MS. MARVEL HAS TURNED HIS ATTACK AGAINST HIM.

WHAM!

OKAY, PAL, WHAT'S THIS ALL ABOUT-- YOU!!

SERGEANT WHITMORE?!

NO! DON'T HIT ME, PLEASE! DON'T HIT--!

HE'S BABBLING LIKE A CHILD-- HE LOOKS DEEP IN A STATE OF HYSTERICAL PSYCHIC SHOCK.

BY PAMA-- IN THE SHADOWS, A CROWD OF PEOPLE!

YOU CAN ALL COME OUT INTO THE OPEN.

THERE'S NOTHING TO BE AFRAID OF.

WHO *IS* SHE, MIZ COLE?! HOW COME THEM DANG LIZARDS DIDN'T TAKE HER *CLOTHES* LIKE THEY TOOK *OURS*?!

I DON'T KNOW. SHE LOOKS *FAMILIAR*, BUT....

I'M CALLED *MS. MARVEL*.

SOME OF YOU MAY HAVE *HEARD* OF ME. I OCCASIONALLY WORK WITH THE *AVENGERS*.

BUT--AREN'T YOU *SHARON COLE*?!

CAROL DANVERS WILL BE *GLAD* TO HEAR YOU'RE *ALL RIGHT*.

CAROL?! DID THE LIZARDS TAKE *HER*, TOO?! SERGEANT WHITMORE SAID...

STUFF THAT COP, AND MISS *FANCY-PANTS* DANVERS, TOO! YOU SAY YOU'RE AN *AVENGER*, LADY. THEN GET US *OUT* OF HERE!

I ALREADY GAVE YOU *ONE* BLACK EYE, HARRY.

YOU BUCKING FOR A *MATCHED PAIR*?

IT'S NOT THAT *SIMPLE*, MR ---

BUTLER. COLONEL *HARRY BUTLER*, U.S. ARMY. AND WHY *ISN'T* IT?! YOU'VE GOT THE POWER--*USE IT!*

ONLY WHEN I *KNOW* WHAT I'M *UP AGAINST*, COLONEL.

FIRST THINGS FIRST-- HOW DID *YOU* GET HERE?

THE *HARD* WAY, BABE.

"I COMMAND-- COMMANDED-- AN *ARMORED RANGER* OUTFIT, THE BEST IN THE ARMY. WE WERE *SCOURING* THE DESERT EAST OF *ELEPHANT BUTTE*.

"THERE'D BEEN A LOT OF *CRAZY* STORIES COMING OUT OF THE *SAN ANDRES MOUNTAINS* LATELY, TOO MANY FOR THE BRASS TO *IGNORE*--

"--ESPECIALLY THAT *CLOSE* TO *ALMAGORDO* AND THE *WHITE SANDS MISSILE RANGE*. MY UNIT WAS SENT TO *CHECK* THINGS OUT.

"WE WERE DEEP IN THE BADLANDS WHEN WE GOT HIT. ONE SECOND, EVERYTHING WAS FINE..."

"...THE NEXT, THOSE BLASTED LIZARDS WERE ALL AROUND US.

"BY THE TIME WE'D RECOVERED FROM THE SHOCK THEY WERE TEARING US TO PIECES.

"EVEN SO, MY MEN PUT UP A HELLUVA FIGHT.

"BUT NOTHING LESS THAN HEAVY MACHINE GUN OR CANNON FIRE EVEN SLOWED THEM DOWN, MUCH LESS KILLED THEM.

"IN MINUTES, THEY TURNED MY TANK SQUADRON INTO SO MUCH SCRAP METAL. BUT, AS THEY DID IT, THEY SEEMED TO TAKE SPECIAL CARE NOT TO HURT ANY OF MY MEN."

WHAT HAPPENED TO THEM?

THEY'RE OVER THE NEXT RISE FROM THE BATTLE SITE, FAST ASLEEP ON THE GROUND. THAT BASILISK, HAEMON, ZAPPED THEM ALL WITH HIS EYE BEAMS.

AND ONLY YOU WERE TAKEN PRISONER.

YEAH. HAZARDS OF COMMAND, I --OH, NO!!

YOU!!

COSSSTUMED ONE! THE HIGH ONESSS HAVE SSSUMMONED YOU!

MS. MARVEL--PEOPLE --SCATTER! GET IN THE SHADOWS! HIDE IN THE ROCKS!

EVERYONE'S PANICKING! THE LIZARDS ARE DELIBERATELY TRYING TO SCARE US--AND THEY'RE ENJOYING IT!

RRAWR

SSSEE, B'OK? IT ISSS AS I TOLD YOU.

AYE, M'DHAR. THIS FEMALE HAS THE HEART OF A WARRIOR.

THEY'RE LAUGHING. THIS WAS SOME SORT OF TEST, AND I GUESS I PASSED.

THESE CLOWNS NEED A LESSON IN MANNERS-- AND I'M JUST THE PERSON TO TEACH 'EM-- BUT I'VE GOT TO KEEP A LID ON MY TEMPER.

THERE'S TOO MUCH AT STAKE.

CAREFUL, MY BROTHERSSS. THE MAMMAL IS SSMALL BUT DEADLY.

SUDDENLY, THE DARK CORRIDOR GIVES WAY TO WHAT SEEMS TO BE BLINDING SUNLIGHT...

...AND MS. MARVEL GASPS IN ASTONISHMENT-- AND NOT A LITTLE AWE-- AS SHE BEHOLDS THE SPRAWLING UNDERGROUND CITY OF THE "PEOPLE"

THIS IS INCREDIBLE. THE MAIN CAVERN MUST BE MORE THAN A MILE ACROSS, AND HIGHER THAN THE SEARS TOWER-- YET THIS CITY FILLS IT.

COME, MAMMAL. THE HIGH ONESSS AWAIT.

SOON... IDENTIFY YOURSELF, MAMMAL.

I AM CALLED MS. MARVEL. WHO ARE YOU... BEINGS? AND WHY HAVE YOU SUMMONED ME HERE?!

WELCOME, MS. MARVEL.

WE ARE THE HIGH COUNCIL OF THE PEOPLE. I AM ARACHT'YR, THEIR ELECTED PATRIARCH.

YOU ARE HERE BECAUSE YOU POSE US A CONSIDERABLE PROBLEM.

YOU ARE THE MOST POWERFUL HUMAN-MAMMAL WE HAVE YET ENCOUNTERED -- YOUR STRENGTH RIVALS THAT OF OUR WARRIORS-PRIME. WE MUST DETERMINE WHAT TO DO WITH YOU.

YOU MAKE IT SOUND LIKE I'M ON TRIAL.

YOU ARE.

I TOLD YOU WHEN WE FIRST MET, ARACHT'YR-- I CAME IN PEACE, SEEKING A LOST FRIEND. A FRIEND I NOW KNOW YOU CAPTURED!

YOUR WARRIORS STRUCK THE FIRST BLOW. I MERELY DEFENDED MYSELF.

REGRETTABLY, THAT DOES NOT MATTER. NOW, AS THEN, THE SAFETY OF THE "PEOPLE" IS MY PRIMARY CONCERN. MANY ON THE COUNCIL SEE YOU AS A DEADLY THREAT...

...ONE THAT MUST BE QUICKLY DEALT WITH.

YOU'LL FIND THAT EASIER *SAID* THAN DON--

--UNNNGNH!

SMEK

SSSILENCE, SSSOFT-SKIN

FAELAR-- *NO!!* I SAID THE WOMAN WAS *NOT* TO BE *TOUCHED!*

WITH *RESSSPECT,* ARACHT'YR, I HAVE HEARD ENOUGH OF HER *INSSSOLENCE.* WE NEED NOT *TALK* WITH THE MAMMALS --

--WE NEED ONLY *SSSMASH* THEM!

SMASH?

BUSTER, YOU DON'T KNOW THE *MEANING* OF THE WORD!

WHAMMO!

THE SSSOFT-SKIN-- SHE *ESCAPESSS!*

TAKE HER, MY BROTHERSSS! ALIVE OR *DEAD*-- --THE MAMMAL MUST BE *SSSTOPPED.*

THE LIZARD WARRIORS DO THEIR BEST...

...BUT THEY'RE OUT-MATCHED FROM THE BEGINNING, BY A FOE WHO HAS NO INTENTION OF LOSING THIS FIGHT...

...EVEN THOUGH SHE *KNOWS* IT'S A FIGHT THAT *NEVER* SHOULD HAVE STARTED IN THE FIRST PLACE.

OF ALL THE BONEHEAD--! I *LOST* MY BLASTED TEMPER! I'M SUPPOSED TO BE A *BIG* GIRL, A RATIONAL, *MATURE* ADULT. I'M SUPPOSED TO *THINK* BEFORE I REACT!

BTHAM!

FROM HERE ON, WHAT-EVER HAPPENS IS *MY FAULT* --HALA!

MY ENTRANCE *COLLAPSED* THE WALL-- NOW THE WHOLE STRUCTURE'S *CAVING IN!*

HAVE TO USE THIS BEAM AS A *BRACE*--LORD, IT'S HEAVY--KEEP THE *ROOF* UP FOR JUST A FEW *SECONDS*...

GET *OUT* OF HERE, WOMAN! I CAN'T *HOLD* THIS MESS FOR *LONG!*

YOU WILL NOT *HAVE* TO, MS. MARVEL.

HAEMON!

HE'S *TEARING* AT MY MIND LIKE THE LAST TIME! I'M *LOSING* MY BALANCE --FALLING!

I AM TRULY *SSSORRY,* LITTLE ONE. YOU *SSSAVED* THE LIVESSS OF MY *WIFE* AND MY *CHILD,* YET MY DUTY DEMANDS THAT I *TAKE* YOURSSS.

MAY GOD *FORGIVE* ME.

CRUMP

HAEMON'S WON A *PYRRHIC VICTORY*, HOWEVER-- FOR, AS MS. MARVEL FALLS, *SHOCK-WAVES* TRIPHAMMER THROUGH THE VAST *STADIUM...*

SKTHO...DOOM!

...UNTIL, FINALLY, THE *HEART* OF THE COUNCIL CHAMBER, THE GREAT, VAULTING *COBRA HEAD,* COMES CRASHING DOWN!

FOR A TIME, THE LIZARDS ARE TOO *STUNNED* TO MOVE OR *SPEAK.*

THE STATUE HAD BEEN THE *CENTER-PIECE* OF THEIR CITY, A *TESTAMENT* TO THEIR STRUGGLE UP FROM MIND-LESS SAVAGERY TOWARDS CIVILIZATION.

NOW, IN THE TWINKLING OF AN EYE, IT IS *NO MORE.*

ARACHT'YR, I...

DO NOT *BLAME* YOURSELF, HAEMON. THE DAMAGE WAS DONE WHEN A WARRIOR *HURLED* MS. MARVEL THROUGH THE *MAIN WALL.*

A *STATUE* MAY BE *DESTROYED,* MY FRIEND, BUT THE IDEALS AND *DREAMS* WILL *ENDURE.*

ONE *CON-SSSOLATION* IS THE DEATH OF THE MAMMAL. SHE COULD NOT HAVE *SSSUR-VIVED* THIS CRASH.

STILL... I WISH THIS *HADN'T* HAPPENED. OF ALL THE HUMAN-MAMMALS I HAVE *MET...*

...MS. MARVEL *ALONE* I FELT I COULD *TRUST.*

ARACHT'YR LEAVES HAEMON IN CHARGE OF THE CLEAN-UP AS HE HEADS HOME, HIS PACE SLOW, HIS HEART SUDDENLY HEAVY.

THE PEOPLE HAVE BEEN LUCKY FOR SO LONG, AS THEY EVOLVED INTO A VIABLE CULTURE LITERALLY UNDER MANKIND'S COLLECTIVE NOSE. BUT NOW, ARACHT'YR FEARS, THEIR LUCK MAY HAVE RUN OUT.

MY *HUSSSBAND,* WELCOME HOME!

CHILDREN, GIVE YOUR FATHER A *HUG.*

JUST WHAT I *NEEDED,* MIRIELLE.

AND HOW DID YOU YOUNG ONES DO ON YOUR *EXAMINATIONS?*

THEY DID WELL. MY LOVE, YOU LOOK SO *TIRED.*

I *AM,* A BIT.

WHAT'S FOR DINNER --EH?

MY WIFE, *TAKE* THE CHILDREN TO HAEMON'S. *QUICKLY!*

THUD

BUT *WHY--?!*

DO NOT ARGUE--*GO!*

MIRIELLE IS NO *FOOL*. ONCE THE CHILDREN ARE *SAFE*, SHE'LL SUMMON WARRIORS. I PRAY I'M STILL *ALIVE* TO GREET THEM.

AS I *SUSPECTED*, MY SECURITY GUARDS HAVE BEEN KNOCKED *UNCONSCIOUS*.

POOR HAEMON-- HE WAS SO *SURE* MS. MARVEL HAD *PERISHED*.

I DIE SOMEWHAT *HARDER* THAN MOST, PATRIARCH.

AND NOW, IS IT *MY* TURN TO *DIE?*

I TOLD YOU BEFORE, I CAME TO *TALK*. I'M HOPING WE CAN FIND A WAY TO *RESOLVE* OUR DIFFERENCES WITHOUT *VIOLENCE*.

AN *ADMIRABLE* DREAM-- BUT GIVEN THE *HISTORY* OF YOUR RACE, I HAVE *LITTLE* HOPE OF SUCCESS.

YOU *SLAUGHTER* YOUR OWN KIND WITHOUT A *SECOND* THOUGHT. WHY SHOULD I EXPECT YOU TO TREAT MY PEOPLE ANY *DIFFERENTLY?*

ONE-ON-ONE, WE ARE *MORE* THAN A MATCH FOR YOU. BUT AGAINST YOUR *TECHNOLOGY*, WE HAVEN'T A *CHANCE*.

BY THE FIRST EGG, WOMAN, WE WERE *SPAWNED* OUT OF YOUR DESIRE TO *KILL* ONE ANOTHER MORE *EFFICIENTLY*--

"-- BY YOUR FIRST *NUCLEAR BOMB TEST.*"

"*SOMEHOW*, THE RADIATION FROM THE TEST *INTER- ACTED* WITH THE UNIQUE MINERAL STRUCTION OF THIS MESA..."

"...ACCELERATING THE *EVOLUTIONARY PROGRESS* OF THE REPTILES LIVING HERE TO AN *AWESOME* DEGREE.

"IN A FEW GENERATIONS, WE WALKED *ERECT*. WITHIN A DECADE, WE HAD A *TRIBAL* CULTURE AND THE BEGINNINGS OF A *WRITTEN LANGUAGE.*

"AT FIRST, NOT *KNOW-ING* ANY BETTER, WE *HUNTED* YOUR KIND, AS WE WOULD ANY *OTHER* PREY. WE SOON LEARNED THE *ERROR* OF THOSE WAYS.

"ALL WE *WANT* IS TO BE ALLOWED TO LIVE OUR LIVES IN *PEACE.* IF WE ARE DISCOVERED, THAT CAN *NEVER* BE."

EITHER YOUR MILITARY WILL *DESTROY* US, OR YOUR *CULTURE* WILL OVERWHELM US. EITHER WAY, WE *LOSE.*

OH? AND *HOW* ARE YOU GOING TO *STOP* ME?

THERE IS A *WAY.*

FAREWELL, MS. MARVEL. GOD GRANT YOU A *QUICK* AND PAINLESS *END.*

WE SURVIVE BECAUSE OUR EXIST-ENCE IS A *SECRET.* I AM SORRY, BUT I CANNOT LET YOU OR YOUR FRIENDS *FREE.*

A FEW, FAST-PACED MINUTES LATER...

HOLY--!

KROMM

OH--!!

MS. MARVEL!

ALL RIGHT, PEOPLE, TIME TO *GO!* I'VE FOUND A WAY *OUT* AND CREATED ENOUGH DIVERSIONS TO KEEP THE LIZARDS *OCCUPIED.*

WE...WE *CAN'T*--! WHEN WE WERE FIRST *CAPTURED,* TWO MEN TRIED TO *ESCAPE.*

WE HEARD SOMETHING *HUGE* SLITHERING THROUGH THE TUNNEL AFTER THEM-- THEN TERRIBLE *SCREAMS!*

THE PROFESSOR'S *RIGHT.* THE LIZARDS CALL THE THING THEIR *GUARDIAN.*

IF IT EXISTS, I'LL *DEAL* WITH IT.

MEANTIME, YOU ALL MIGHT PRAY THAT *I* GET BACK HERE BEFORE THE *LIZARDS.*

I DIDN'T MEAN TO *SNAP* AT THEM. THEY'RE *ORDINARY* PEOPLE IN A *FAR* FROM ORDINARY SITUATION. THEY HAVE A RIGHT TO BE *SCARED.*

IT'S PARTLY MY OWN *FRUSTRATION.* I WANT TO SAVE ARACHT'YR'S PEOPLE, TOO-- BUT I DON'T KNOW *HOW!*

I WAS *SNAKE-BIT* ONCE IN AIR FORCE DESERT TRAINING. IT WAS A *JOY* COMPARED TO THIS. CAN'T KEEP MY *BALANCE*.

VENOM'S A *NEURO-TOXIN*... IT'S HARD TO THINK STRAIGHT...C-CAN BARELY *SEE*.

PAMA! THE SNAKE'S...GOT ME *PINNED*! DON'T UNDERSTAND-- WHY ISN'T HE TRYING TO *FINISH* ME OFF?!

WHY *BOTHER?* MY HEART'S BEATING A *MILE* A MINUTE, COBRA VENOM *RACING* THROUGH MY SYSTEM.

A CRITTER THIS *SIZE*-- A COUPLE OF *DROPS* WOULD PROB-ABLY KILL AN *ARMY*.

EVERY *CELL* IN MY BODY FEELS LIKE IT'S BEEN DIPPED IN *ACID*.

DON'T KNOW IF MY HALF-KREE METAB-OLISM....

...CAN *STAND* A SECOND BITE.

AND I DON'T INTEND TO *FIND OUT!*

THE *BATTLE RAGES* THROUGH THE *ENDLESS TUNNELS*...

...AND FROM THERE, INTO THE *HEART* OF THE *CITY* ITSELF.

THIS IS NO DUMB *BEAST* I'M FIGHTING, IN HIS OWN WAY, THE COBRA'S AS *INTELLIGENT* AS THE LIZARDS.

HE SEES ME AS AN *ENEMY* OF HIS PEOPLE. SO HE'S TRYING TO STOP ME *ANY* WAY HE CAN.

I'VE *LURED* HIM HIGH ABOVE THE CAVE FLOOR. HE'S *EXTENDED* ABOUT AS FAR AS HE CAN *GO*.

NOW, BEFORE HE CAN PULL BACK--!

TAGGED HIM-- OH, *NO.!!*

SHE'D BEEN SO *RAVAGED* BY THE VENOM THAT SHE HADN'T SEEN THE *STALACTITE* UNTIL IT WAS TOO LATE.

AND A *BLOW* INTENDED MERELY TO *STUN*, HAD INSTEAD TAKEN A *LIFE*.

I DIDN'T *WANT* THIS-- BUT, PERHAPS, I CAN TURN THIS *TRAGEDY* TO OUR MUTUAL *ADVANTAGE*.

MICKEY ROSSI ALWAYS SAID I COULD RUN A *BLUFF* BETTER THAN ANYONE HE KNEW.

HERE'S MY CHANCE TO *PROVE* IT. I CAN BARELY *STAND*, BUT I'VE GOT TO MAKE THE LIZARDS BELIEVE I'M AS *STRONG* AS EVER.

ARACHT'YR!

YOU SENT YOUR *GUARDIAN* AFTER ME, AND NOW HE'S *DEAD*. AND I'M IN NO MOOD TO BE PATIENT OR *REASON-ABLE--!*

I CAN LEAVE, OR *LEVEL* YOUR CITY, AND YOU COULDN'T *STOP* ME.

BUT I OFFER YOU A *DEAL.* RELEASE YOUR CAPTIVES AND PROMISE *NEVER* TO TAKE ANY OTHERS, AND I'LL KEEP YOUR EXISTENCE A *SECRET.*

AND IF I *REFUSE?*

DON'T.

I TRUST *YOU,* MS. MARVEL, BUT WHAT'S TO *PREVENT* THE OTHERS FROM *TALKING?*

HAVE HAEMON TELEPATHICALLY *SCRAMBLE* THEIR MEMORIES, TO MAKE THIS SEEM LIKE NO MORE THAN A *DREAM.*

I DO NOT WHOLLY *LIKE* YOUR PLAN, MS. MARVEL...

...BUT FOR THE *GOOD* OF ALL, I WILL *ACCEPT.*

EPILOGUE:

HOME, SWEET *HOME!* BE IT EVER SO *HUMBLE"...!*

THANK HEAVEN, MY *IDEA WORKED!* EVERYONE'S HOME SAFE, ALBEIT A LITTLE *CONFUSED.*

CAROL DANVERS

WHAT'S *THAT?*

A BABY *IGUANA,* AND A NOTE: *"SOMETHING* TO *REMEMBER* US BY. WE HAVE PLACED OUR *FUTURE* IN YOUR HANDS. DO *NOT FAIL US."*

FROM *ARACHT'YR,* AND ADDRESSED TO... *CAROL DANVERS!* BUT HOW COULD HE HAVE *KNOWN?!*

TELL ME, *LITTLE ONE,* DID I DO THE *RIGHT* THING...

...OR DID I MAKE THE *BIGGEST MISTAKE* OF MY LIFE?

NEXT: DEATH-BIRD RETURNS!

REACHING FOR THE STARS!

HOW MS. MARVEL'S POWERS WENT SUPERNOVA!

NEW AVENGER

Her debut series may have been cancelled in 1979, but Marvel wasn't giving up on Carol Danvers yet. The publisher's editor-in-chief and then-*Avengers* writer, **Jim Shooter** had already featured Ms. Marvel as a guest-star in the title, and in *Avengers #183* he made her an official member of the team, staying with Earth's Mightiest Heroes until issue #200.

With 1981's *Avengers Annual #10*, Ms. Marvel was reunited with her original series writer **Chris Claremont**, who had big plans for Carol. Suffering amnesia due to a run-in with the power-absorbing mutant Rogue, Carol was taken in by the X-Men's leader Professor Xavier who hoped to use his psychic powers to aid Carol's recovery. It was during this time with the X-Men that Carol underwent a startling transformation. As Claremont explained, "When I wrote the annual, I had the great good fortune of working with **Michael Golden** who turned it into one of the best visual presentations it's ever been my pleasure to work with. But that in turn set in motion a sequence of events which led to me teaming with **Dave Cockrum** again and Dave coming up with one of the more brilliant designs of his Marvel career, which is Binary."

Travelling into space with the X-Men, Carol and the other members of the mutant team found themselves captured by the Brood. The parasitic aliens were fascinated by Carol's genetic structure and performed a barrage of experiments. Somehow, they boosted her powers and abilities to an unprecedented level, transforming her into the energy-wielding Binary.

But upon her return to Earth, Carol made a shocking discovery which saw her part ways with the X-Men. Similarly traumatised by absorbing Carol's memories and powers, Rogue had turned up at the X-Men's door seeking help. Ever compassionate to mutant needs and hoping to rehabilitate her, the X-Men allowed Rogue to join the team. This was the last straw for Carol who left Earth to forge a new life among the stars.

GOING ROGUE

For Claremont, this rebirth of Carol was the end result of where he had always wanted to take the character. "She was someone who had a really cool set of powers," said Claremont. "I mean just the first moment in the *X-Men* that **Walt Simonson** pencilled where she walks into the door of the mansion – and the next thing she's flying out the roof. One punch and Rogue doesn't stop until she's 200,000 miles out – some hit! Then she goes roaring back and Carol does it again and it's like, 'Why are you hitting me? I don't know you!' and then Carol turns off the power and, 'Oh, it's you – sorry about that!' You know, actions have consequences and for me the consequence there was finally Carol had a chance as a free and unique spirit to forge her own destiny."

HUNT-MASTER T'CRILEE REPORTING CONTACT WITH ALIEN VESSEL-- IMPERIAL SHI'AR YACHT *Z'REEE SHAR*.

VELOCITY: POINT FOUR LIGHT AND INCREASING. COURSE: OUT OF THIS SYSTEM, AT MAXIMUM ACCELERATION.

BIO-SCANS INDICATE MULTIPLE LIFEFORMS ABOARD, ALSO ALIEN, PROBABLY THE SHI'AR EMPRESS, *LILANDRA*, AND THE TERRANS CAPTURED WITH HER, THE *X-MEN*.

WE HAVE FIRED WARNING SHOTS, BUT THE TARGET HAS NOT RESPONDED.

TACTICAL PROJECTION IS THAT THE TARGET WILL SHIFT INTO WARP AS SOON AS IT IS ABLE. MY CADRE LACKS FASTER-THAN-LIGHT CAPABILITY.

REQUEST INSTRUCTIONS.

T'CRILEE, HEED THE WORDS OF YOUR *GREAT MOTHER*. THE X-MEN AND LILANDRA HAVE INDEED ESCAPED-- WRECKING THE INNER HIVE AND NEARLY SLAYING ME IN THE PROCESS.

THEIR STARSHIP IS TO BE DISABLED, AND ALL ABOARD TAKEN ALIVE AND UNHARMED -- WITH ONE EXCEPTION.

THE X-MAN, *WOLVERINE*, MAY BE SLAIN. HE AND HIS COMPANIONS ARE HOST-FORMS FOR MY PROGENY, BUT SOMEHOW HE MANAGED TO DESTROY THE EGG IMPLANTED WITHIN HIM. NO MORE OF MY CHILDREN ARE TO DIE, IS THAT CLEAR?!

ANY SACRIFICE TO THAT END IS ACCEPTABLE. SHOULD YOU FAIL, HUNT-MASTER, BE CERTAIN YOU YOURSELF ARE AMONG THE SLAIN.

AFTER MAKING CERTAIN SHE HAS THE NECESSARY EQUIPMENT AND THAT IT'S FUNCTIONING PROPERLY...

...KITTY PHASES THROUGH THE PRIMARY HULL.

WOW!

"STAR WARS" WAS NEVER LIKE THIS!

THE BUSTED MODULE IS AFT, BENEATH THE SOLAR FINS.

I WANT TO RUN, BUT I CAN'T. I'M NOT USING A SAFETY LINE. ONE MISSTEP'LL THROW ME OFF INTO SPACE...

...AND THE OTHERS WON'T BE ABLE TO STOP AND COME BACK FOR ME.

AT THAT MOMENT, IN WEAPONS CONTROL...

WHAT THE--?!?

MY VISION SUDDENLY WENT BLURRY-- I SAW COLORS, IMAGES I NEVER DREAMED POSSIBLE.

BUT EVERYTHING'S NORMAL NOW. PROBABLY STRESS-- A DELAYED REACTION TO THE TREATMENT I RECEIVED FROM THE BROOD.

ON THE YACHT'S HULL-- AN X-MAN-- THE YOUNGLING!

USE STUN AND 'PRESSOR BEAMS ON HER! TRY TO KNOCK HER LOOSE. ONCE SHE'S IN FREE SPACE, WE CAN EASILY TAKE HER PRISONER.

SPAWN OF THE BLOODMOON-- MY BOLTS HAVE NO EFFECT!

÷WHEW!÷

I KNOW I'VE BEEN THROUGH MOMENTS LIKE THIS BEFORE...

...BUT THEY DON'T GET ANY EASIER. I CAN'T HELP WONDERING WHAT'LL HAPPEN THE ONE TIME MY POWER DOESN'T WORK.

WHY'D I OPEN MY BIG MOUTH ANYWAY?! WHAT AM I DOING HERE?! I'M JUST A KID.

NO. NOT ANYMORE, I'M AN X-MAN. I EARNED MY PLACE ON THE TEAM-- AND HERE'S WHERE I PROVE IT!

THE SAME, IN A WAY, HOLDS TRUE FOR CAROL.

YEARS AGO, A FREAK ACCIDENT COMBINED THE BEST GENETIC ELEMENTS OF HUMAN AND THE ANCIENT, STAR-FARING **KREE** TO TRANSFORM HER INTO MS. MARVEL.

AND WHILE SHE LATER LOST HER SUPER-POWERS TO THE MUTANT ROGUE, THOSE HYBRID GENES REMAINED. NOW, THANKS TO THE BROOD'S MEDDLING, THEIR UNTAPPED POTENTIAL IS BEING REALIZED, WITH A VENGEANCE.

SHE CRIES OUT--IN WONDER MORE THAN FEAR, FOR THE PROCESS SEEMS SURPRISINGLY NATURAL...

...RATHER LIKE A BUTTERFLY EMERGING FROM ITS CHRYSALIS.

A BLINDING LIGHT FLARES WITHIN HER SOUL, A THING APART FROM HER THAT INSTANTLY BECOMES A PART OF HER TO FORM A UNION THAT WILL LAST 'TIL DEATH.

THE LIGHT IS POWER...

...AND CAROL USES IT, WITHOUT HESITATION.

EVERYTHING'S FIXED! THROW THE SWITCH, LILANDRA!

THROW US INTO WARP!

BLESS YOU, CHILD! WE'RE ON OUR WAY!

KITTY, ARE YOU THERE?!

KITTY!!!

PROFESSOR XAVIER'S SCHOOL FOR GIFTED YOUNGSTERS -- SALEM CENTER, NEW YORK.

THE TITLE IS SOMETHING OF A MISNOMER THESE DAYS. THOUGH THE MANSION HAS BEEN REBUILT-- BETTER THAN BEFORE, COURTESY OF CONSTRUCTION ROBOTS PROVIDED BY LILANDRA--

-- THE SCHOOL IS, IN TRUTH, NO MORE.

AS A YOUNG MAN, CHARLES XAVIER HAD A DREAM, OF AN EARTH WHERE HUMANITY AND MUTANTKIND LIVED TOGETHER IN PEACE. TO FULFILL THAT DREAM--

-- AND TO PROTECT THE WORLD FROM THE DEPREDATIONS OF EVIL MUTANTS-- HE FORMED THIS SCHOOL, WHOSE STUDENTS BECAME THE UNCANNY *X-MEN*. UNSUNG HEROES, FEARED, OFTEN HATED, BY THE VERY PEOPLE THEY WERE SWORN TO SAVE.

THEY BECAME HIS SURROGATE CHILDREN-- WHOM HE LOVED WITH ALL HIS HEART.

AND, SINCE THEIR ABDUCTION, HIS NIGHTS HAVE BECOME HAUNTED, HIS HANDS, HE BELIEVES, COVERED WITH BLOOD.

THE DREAM MAY STILL BE GOOD...

...BUT THIS DREAMER IS DONE.

YOU CALL ME, PROFESSOR?

DINNER'S READY, ILLYANA.

GREAT! I'M STARVED!

THE GIRL IS *ILLYANA RASPUTIN,* COLOSSUS' SISTER.

I'VE BEEN EXPLORING THE HOUSE. IT'S ALMOST EXACTLY AS I REMEMBER IT...

...THOUGH IT'S A BIT SPOOKY WITH JUST THE TWO OF US HERE.

MOIRA WILL BE BACK ON MONDAY.

THAT'S WONDERFUL! I LIKE DR. MacTAGGERT A LOT.

I'M SURE SHE'LL BE PLEASED TO HEAR THAT.

I LIKE YOU, TOO, PROFESSOR. HONEST.

PROFESSOR, SOMETIMES I HEAR YOUR VOICE PERFECTLY CLEARLY, BUT YOU'RE NOWHERE AROUND.

AND I DON'T ACTUALLY HEAR ANYTHING--THAT IS, WITH MY EARS--THE WORDS SEEM TO POP INTO MY HEAD. HOW IS THAT?

AND HOW COME, BEFORE I RETURNED HERE WITH YOU AND DR. MacTAGGERT, I COULD ONLY SPEAK RUSSIAN? I REMEMBER YOU TOUCHING MY FOREHEAD ONE NIGHT AS I FELL ASLEEP AND THE NEXT MORNING, WHEN I WOKE UP, I SPOKE PERFECT ENGLISH!

I TAUGHT YOU, WHILE YOU SLEPT.

I FIGURED THAT-- BUT HOW?!

WITH MY THOUGHTS.

OH!

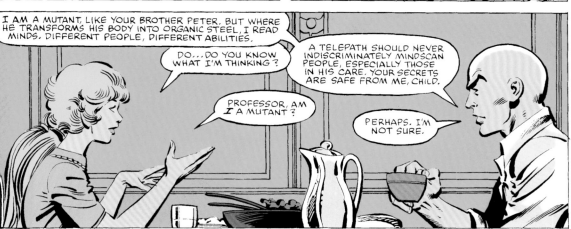

I AM A MUTANT, LIKE YOUR BROTHER PETER. BUT WHERE HE TRANSFORMS HIS BODY INTO ORGANIC STEEL, I READ MINDS. DIFFERENT PEOPLE, DIFFERENT ABILITIES.

DO...DO YOU KNOW WHAT I'M THINKING?

A TELEPATH SHOULD NEVER INDISCRIMINATELY MINDSCAN PEOPLE, ESPECIALLY THOSE IN HIS CARE. YOUR SECRETS ARE SAFE FROM ME, CHILD.

PROFESSOR, AM I A MUTANT?

PERHAPS. I'M NOT SURE.

I CAN DO NEAT THINGS, TOO, JUST LIKE PIOTR!

SUCH AS WHAT?

OH... THINGS.

ILLYANA'S THOUGHTS ARE PROTECTED BY AN EXTRA-ORDINARILY POWERFUL AND SOPHISTICATED PSIONIC SHIELD.

IT COULD BE NATURAL--BUT I DOUBT IT. ACCORDING TO MOIRA, SHE WAS ABDUCTED BY A DEMON-LORD NAMED BELASCO, AND HELD FOR SEVEN YEARS IN HIS MYSTIC DOMAIN--THOUGH ONLY MOMENTS PASSED HERE ON EARTH.*

WHAT SHE EXPERIENCED THERE-- FOR GOOD OR ILL--NO ONE KNOWS.

I OUGHT TO INVESTI-GATE-- FIND A WAY TO PIERCE THAT BARRIER--BUT...I NO LONGER CARE ENOUGH TO MAKE THE ATTEMPT. LET MOIRA DEAL WITH HER. ALL I WANT...

...IS TO BE LEFT ALONE.

*X-MEN #160--L.

LATER, AFTER THE OTHERS HAVE BEEN REVIVED...

IS THE CHANGE PERMANENT, CAROL?

I HOPE SO.

SHE'S BEAUTIFUL. WHEN I FIRST SAW HER, I THOUGHT SHE WAS AN ANGEL.

HUSH, *KÄTZCHEN.* SAVE YOUR STRENGTH AND LET ME COMPLETE MY EXAMINATION.

FUNNY, ISN'T IT--NOT LONG AGO, I WAS TAKING CARE OF YOU.

UH-HUH.

KURT... FUZZY-ELF... I FEEL SO COLD.

WE ALL DO.

BUT WHY AREN'T WE MOVING?

YOUR REPAIR SAVED US--BUT IT WAS ONLY A STOP-GAP. THE WARP-DRIVE IS NOW TOTALLY *INERT.* WITH IT, WE'VE LOST MAIN AND AUXILIARY POWER--THAT MEANS NO LIFE SUPPORT.

UNLESS WE REGENERATE THE MATTER-ANTI-MATTER CORES, WE'LL FREEZE, OR SUFFOCATE. SOON.

HOW DO WE DO THAT?

BY SATURATING THE CELLS WITH ENERGY...

MY LIGHTNING? CYCLOPS' OPTIC BLASTS...?

NOWHERE NEAR ENOUGH, ORORO, TO DO IT RIGHT...

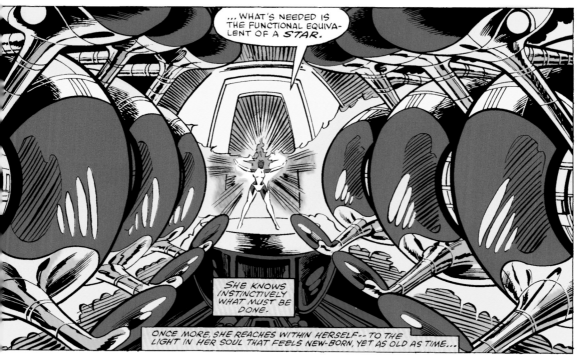

...WHAT'S NEEDED IS THE FUNCTIONAL EQUIVA-LENT OF A *STAR.*

SHE KNOWS INSTINCTIVELY WHAT MUST BE DONE.

ONCE MORE, SHE REACHES WITHIN HERSELF-- TO THE LIGHT IN HER SOUL THAT FEELS NEW-BORN, YET AS OLD AS TIME...

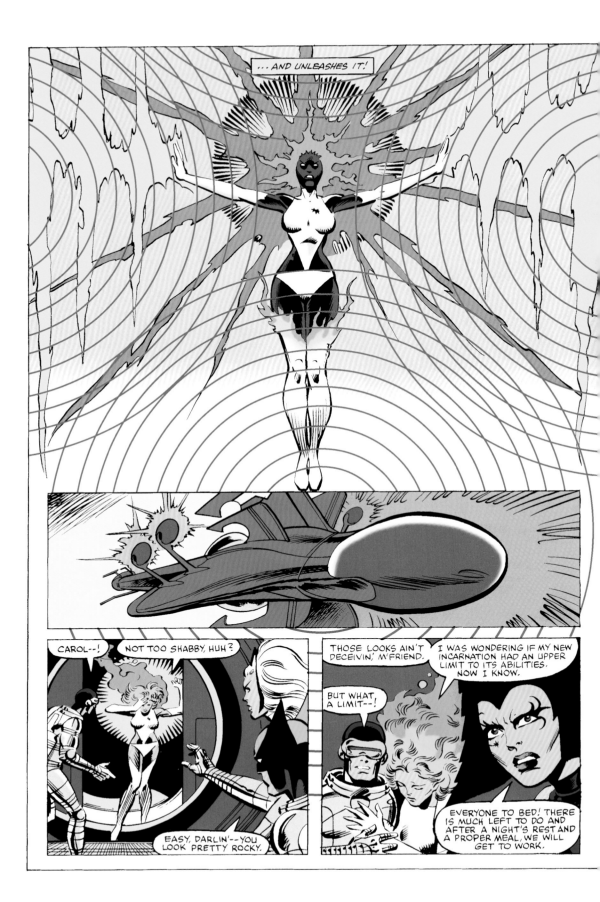

AND SO...

MY OLD FRIEND, *CAPTAIN MARVEL* WAS GIFTED WITH *COSMIC AWARENESS*-- AN ABILITY TO BECOME ONE WITH THE UNIVERSE. I THINK I'VE GONE BEYOND THAT.

HIS WAS A SPIRITUAL MERGER, MINE IS PHYSICAL, SOMEHOW, WHEN I USE MY POWER, I TAP INTO A WHITE HOLE-- MY ENERGY SOURCE IS THE PRIMAL FABRIC OF A UNIVERSE!

LIKE A STAR, I CAN GENERATE HEAT, LIGHT-- RADIATION ACROSS THE SPECTRUM-- GRAVITY. AND MY PERCEPTIONS --COLOSSUS, YOU CAN'T IMAGINE WHAT I SEE, HOW WONDROUS IT IS.

YOU SOUND VERY HAPPY.

DON'T I THOUGH!

SUCH ABILITIES WOULD BE INVALUABLE TO THE X-MEN.

YOU INVITING ME TO JOIN, *TOVARISCH*?

YOU ARE NOW A MUTANT, AND YOU HAVE ALWAYS BEEN A FRIEND.

BEST OFFER I'VE HAD ALL DAY, BIG FELLA.

BUT IT'D MEAN LIVING AND WORKING ON EARTH.

WHAT IS WRONG WITH THAT?

NOTHING. EVERYTHING.

WHEN I WAS A TEENAGER, I HITCHHIKED TO CAPE CANAVERAL TO WATCH AN APOLLO LAUNCH. MY DAD WHALED THE TAR OUTTA ME, BUT IT WAS WORTH IT. I WANTED SO BADLY TO BE AN ASTRONAUT-- TO EXPLORE SPACE, DISCOVER NEW WORLDS, ALIEN CIVILIZATIONS.

AS MS. MARVEL, I ALMOST MADE IT.

NOW, SUDDENLY, MY DREAM'S COME TRUE-- BEYOND MY WILDEST EXPECTATIONS!

BUT THERE'S A PRICE. RETURNING WITH YOU MEANS REJECTING MY HEART'S DESIRE-- BUT FULFILLING THAT DESIRE MEANS LEAVING EVERYONE, EVERYTHING I LOVE.

EARTH WAS *CAROL DANVERS'* HOME, COLOSSUS, BUT I FEAR IT HAS NO PLACE FOR--

--*BINARY.*

STOP FIDGETING. I'M NEARLY FINISHED.

DEEP BREATH. AGAIN, COUGH.

≠KOFF!≠

WHAT'S THE VERDICT, DOC? WILL I LIVE?

UMMM...

GREAT ANSWER. ARE YOU SURE YOU KNOW WHAT YOU'RE DOING?

LET'S HOPE SO, FOR YOUR SAKE.

YOU'RE BETTER, BUT NOT YET BEST.

I FEEL FINE, KURT.

EXCEPT I FEEL ROTTEN GOOFING OFF IN BED WHILE THE REST OF YOU ARE WORKING SO HARD.

HOW NOBLE. YOU'RE ENTITLED TO GOOF OFF, KIDDO. YOU'RE SICK.

STAY IN BED, TRY TO SLEEP, DRINK MORE HOT LEMON-HONEY TEA AND CHICKEN BROTH. I'LL CHECK ON YOU IN A FEW HOURS. VERSTEHEN? SEHR GUT. AUF WEIDERSEHEN, KATZCHEN.

WITH THAT, NIGHTCRAWLER TELEPORTS TO THE COMMAND DECK, HIS SMILE TURNING INTO A TROUBLED FROWN.

CYCLOPS, WHAT'S THE STATUS OF THE COMPUTERS-- SPECIFICALLY THE MEDISCAN SYSTEMS?

THE WHOLE NETWORK HAS TO BE PURGED AND RECYCLED, KURT. NOTHING'LL BE ON-LINE ANY SOON. WHY? PROBLEMS?

PERHAPS. I'VE JUST EXAMINED KITTY. SHE'S FULLY RECOVERED.

THAT'S A PROBLEM?

BARELY A DAY AGO, SHE WAS DYING.

THE SHRAPNEL TORE A NASTY HOLE IN HER SIDE, INTRODUCING RADIOACTIVE ELEMENTS INTO HER BLOODSTREAM. FROM THAT, AND THE WARP TRANSITION, SHE ABSORBED ENOUGH HARD RADIATION TO KILL A SCORE OF PEOPLE. SHE SHOULDN'T HAVE SURVIVED THE NIGHT, YET AT THIS MOMENT SHE'S IN PERFECT HEALTH.

NOTHING I DID HEALED HER, BUT I'D VERY MUCH LIKE TO LEARN WHAT DID...

SOME QUESTIONS ARE BETTER LEFT UNANSWERED, ELF.

WHAT THE BLAZES IS THAT SUPPOSED TO MEAN?

THE KID'S FINE-- WHAT MORE D'YOU WANT?

THE REASON WHY MEIN FREUND.

YOU'VE BEEN LURKING ABOUT LIKE A BLASTED SPECTRE EVER SINCE WE ESCAPED FROM THE BROOD. MAYBE IT'S TIME YOU EXPLAINED YOURSELF.

WHY DIDN'T YOU HELP ME NAIL THEIR QUEEN WHEN WE HAD THE CHANCE, CYKE?! THAT WOULD HAVE DONE SOME REAL DAMAGE-- POSSIBLY CRIPPLED THEIR ENTIRE RACE!

I TOLD YOU, WOLVERINE: X-MEN DON'T KILL.

SNIKT

WANNA BET?

SORRY, I ... DIDN'T MEAN T' DO THAT. I GUESS ALL THAT'S HAPPENED HAS DRIVEN ME KIND'A BUGGY.

YOU'RE RIGHT, WHAT'S THERE TO GET UPSET ABOUT? WE ESCAPED, WITH OUR SKINS INTACT. EV'RYTHIN'S HUNKY-FLAMIN'-DORY.

MEIN GOTT.

WE ARE, FRIENDS, HE AND I, SCOTT. PERHAPS HE WILL TALK TO ME.

STAY WITH LILANDRA, KURT. GIVE HER A HAND.

THERE'S A PATTERN FORMING-- KITTY'S ONE PIECE, LOGAN'S ANOTHER-- AND I MEAN TO FIND OUT WHAT IT IS.

THE SHUTTLE BAY... THIS IS THE ONLY SPACE LARGE ENOUGH FOR ME TO CREATE ANY TRUE WEATHER. HERE, AT LAST, I CAN FLY.

WHEN I TRIED TO ATTUNE MY SPIRIT TO THAT OF THE BROOD'S WORLD--THE BETTER TO UTILIZE MY POWERS THERE--AND FAILED, I BELIEVED IT WAS BECAUSE THE BROOD HAD SO TOTALLY CORRUPTED THE PLANET'S LIFE-FORCE.

BUT I FEAR THE FAULT WAS MINE.

I AM LOSING TOUCH WITH *MY* ESSENTIAL SELF.

SOME ELEMENT IS DISRUPTING THE CRITICAL HARMONY OF MIND, BODY AND SOUL. I MUST FIND IT...

...AND PUT THINGS RIGHT...

...BEFORE IT IS TOO LATE.

A WIND LIFTS HER GENTLY FROM THE DECK...

...BUT THEN, WITHOUT WARNING...

AAHHHRRR!!

STORM!

ORORO!!

LEAVE ME BE, SCOTT, I BEG YOU. I AM UNINJURED AND I WOULD REALLY RATHER BE LEFT ALONE.

NO DICE, THAT'S MY RIFF.

SOMETHING'S TEARING US APART, ORORO. IF WE DENY ITS EXISTENCE, IF WE TURN AWAY FROM THOSE WHO WANT TO HELP US, WE'RE AS GOOD AS DEAD.

I FEAR I AM BEYOND YOUR HELP. I AM CONSECRATED TO LIFE, MY MUTANT POWERS--AND MORE IMPORTANTLY, MY VERY SOUL--ARE BOUND TO THE PRIMAL FORCE OF A LIVING WORLD, OUR EARTH.

REMOVED FROM THAT ENVIRONMENT, MY ABILITIES--IN AND OF THEMSELVES --REMAIN UNIMPAIRED. I AM AS STRONG, IN PURELY PHYSICAL TERMS, AS I EVER WAS.

BUT MY SOUL IS STRICKEN, MY SPIRIT IS WASTING AWAY, AND THE LONGER I AM SEPARATED FROM MY HOME, THE MORE I WILL LOSE.

HOW WILL I EVER REGAIN THOSE MISSING, RAVAGED PIECES OF MYSELF, SCOTT? AND WHEN THERE'S NOTHING LEFT, WHAT WILL BECOME OF ME?! CAN A BODY LIVE WITHOUT ITS SOUL?!

BEING ABOARD THIS VESSEL ONLY MAKES MATTERS WORSE. LOOK ABOUT YOU-- NOTHING BUT STEEL. COLD METAL, UNLIVING PLASTICS, SYNTHETICS.

I HATE IT!

I NEED LIFE TO SUSTAIN ME. THERE IS NONE HERE, NOT EVEN THE JOY AND LOVE I FELT FOR THE X-MEN.

I DON'T UNDER- STAND. WE HAVEN'T CHANGED. WE STILL FEEL THE SAME.

BUT I AM CHANGING--I HAVE BEEN EVER SINCE OUR ESCAPE--DEEP DOWN IN THE CORE OF MY BEING! AND I KNOW NEITHER THE CAUSE NOR THE FINAL EFFECT.

OHHH--!?!

THAT DOES IT, I'M CALLING NIGHTCRAWLER. YOU'RE SICK, ORORO, YOU SHOULD BE IN BED.

IS THIS NOT IRONIC? KITTY MIRACULOUSLY RECOVERS FROM SEEM- INGLY MORTAL WOUNDS WHILE I--WHO'VE NEVER BEEN ILL A DAY IN MY LIFE-- FALL PREY TO SOME MYSTERIOUS MALADY.

IT IS AS IF I HAVE BECOME A STRANGER TO MYSELF, INHABITING A BODY NO LONGER...

...MY OWN-- BRIGHT LADY, COULD THAT BE THE ANSWER?!

IT IS SO OBVIOUS, SO UNTHINKABLE, I NEVER CONSIDERED IT.

SCOTT, I SENSE... LIFE WITHIN ME!

A...CHILD!

BUT HOW CAN THIS BE?!

I MUST PROBE DEEPER-- WHERE DO YOU COME FROM, MY LITTLE ONE? WHO--?

NO.

OH, NO!

GODDESS!

WITH THAT CRY COMES A HURRI-CANE GUST OF WIND THAT SWEEPS CYCLOPS THE LENGTH OF THE BAY...

...AND OUT THE HATCH.

SLAM!

ORORO?!?

STORM!?!

SHE WENT BERSERK, TOOK A SCOUTSHIP, BLASTED OFF. BUT WHY LEAVE HER COSTUME BEHIND?

CAROL, BRING HER BACK. WE HAVE NO OPERATIONAL SENSORS. ONCE SHE'S OUT OF SIGHT IN THIS CLOUD, WE'LL NEVER FIND HER.

YOU EVER FIGURE THAT MIGHT BE WHAT SHE WANTS.

SHE'S IRRATIONAL.

WITH GOOD REASON, BUB.

LIKE WHAT?! I'M IN NO MOOD FOR GAMES, PAL. YOUR EXPLANATION'S LONG OVERDUE!

YEAH, I GUESS IT IS.

I SHOULD'A TOLD YOU ON SLEAZEWORLD, OR AFTER WE CUT LOOSE INTO SPACE.

I TRIED A FEW TIMES -- BUT I COULDN'T. IT HURT TOO MUCH.

I THOUGHT O' KILLIN' YOU -- COULDN'T DO THAT, EITHER. I FIGURED THERE WAS HOPE, THERE'S ALWAYS HOPE, WE'D SOMEHOW GET LUCKY, RUN INTO A MIRACLE.

WHO KNOWS, I COULD BE RIGHT.

BUT I WOULDN'T COUNT ON IT.

WHEN THE SLEAZOIDS CAP- TURED US, WE WERE TAKEN BEFORE THEIR QUEEN -- THEY CALL HER THE "GREAT MOTHER" -- AN' SHE IM- PLANTED AN EGG IN EACH OF US.

EACH EGG CONTAINS AN EMBRYONIC QUEEN. IT BONDED ITSELF TO OUR NERVOUS SYSTEMS, SO IT CAN'T BE SURGICALLY RE- MOVED. WHEN IT HATCHES, A PHYSICAL METAMORPHOSIS OCCURS.

THE HOST-BODY IS RESHAPED INTO THE BIRTH-FORM OF THE YOUNG SLEAZOID. IN THE PROCESS, IT ABSORBS THE GENETIC POTENTIAL AND ABILITIES OF THE HOST, TO PASS ON TO ITS PROGENY.

IN MY CASE, THEY RECKONED WITHOUT MY MUTANT POWER-- THE HEALIN' FACTOR. MY BODY TREATED THE EGG AS AN INVADIN' DISEASE ORGANISM AN' WENT AFTER IT WHOLE HOG. THAT FIGHT FLAMIN' NEAR KILLED ME.

THAT WAS PARTLY WHY I COULDN'T TELL YOU THE TRUTH-- I FELT GUILTY, A LITTLE ASHAMED, BECAUSE I WAS FREE. I WOULD LIVE...

...AN' YOU WOULDN'T.

THE EMBRYO QUEENS POSSESS A DEGREE OF AWARE- NESS. THEY KNOW WHEN THEY'RE THREATENED AN' THEY'LL TAKE ANY STEPS TO ENSURE THEIR SURVIVAL. IN KITTY'S CASE, THAT MEANT CURIN' HER-- A DEAD HOST IS OF NO USE TO 'EM.

BUT THEY CAN JUST AS EASILY BE NASTY.

"NASTY," LOGAN?! THEY DON'T KNOW THE MEANING OF THE WORD!

BUT BY ALL I HOLD HOLY--

--THEY'RE GOING TO *LEARN!*

ORORO'S CRY WAS ONE OF GRIEF AND DESPAIR. CAROL'S, EQUALLY MAD, IS OF RAGE.

AND THEN, LIKE STORM, SHE IS GONE.

UNLIKE STORM, HOWEVER, SHE NEGLECTS TO OPEN THE HATCH.

EXPLOSIVE DECOMPRESSION!

WE'RE BEING SUCKED OUT INTO SPACE!!

NEXT ISSUE: TRANSFIGURATIONS!

THWUSHHHHHHHHH

THREE SECONDS IN A MUSEUM AND YOU'RE SOUND ASLEEP.

WHY AM I NOT SURPRISED?

KCK

KCK

NEXT TIME I'LL SKIP THE PUNCHING AND JUST READ YOU A BOOK.

...AND WHAT CAN YOU TELL US ABOUT YOUR NEW ALLY?

WHAT NEW--? OH.

WHAT...?

YOU KNOW WHAT.

I WAS A LUCKY KID BECAUSE I HAD TWO HEROES--MY DAD AND A PILOT NAMED HELEN COBB.

HELEN HELD FIFTEEN SPEED RECORDS WHEN SHE RETIRED.

FIFTEEN.

I'M NOT PRONE TO ENVY. BUT THOSE RECORDS...

I ENVY THOSE RECORDS.

I CAN FLY. FAST.

REAL FAST.

BUT THESE "ABILITIES" COME AT A COST. FOR ONE THING, I'LL NEVER BE ALLOWED TO HOLD A RECORD LIKE HELEN'S.

I CAN'T EVEN COMPETE. WOULDN'T BE A FAIR FIGHT.

I LOST MY SHOT WHEN I WAS CAUGHT IN THE BLAST OF THAT ALIEN PSYCHE-MAGNETRON DEVICE.

THE PARTICLE BOMBARDMENT GRAFTED THE GENETIC STRUCTURE OF THE KREE WARRIOR MAR-VELL ONTO MY OWN DNA.

IT'S A HELL OF A REWARD...BUT IT ERASED WHAT I LOVED MOST...

...THE RISK.

ONE MINUTE, FIFTY-EIGHT SECONDS FROM BROADWAY TO THE END OF OUR ATMOSPHERE, A NEW PERSONAL BEST.

LUCKY ME.

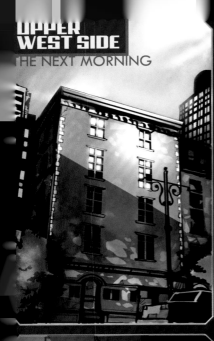

COFFEE, COFFEE...WHO HIDES THEIR COFFEE...?

MORNING PERSON

MAKE WORK

WELL, HELLO, BEAUTIFUL.

CUT THE CRAP, DANVERS.

I LOOK ABOUT AS GOOD AS I FEEL, AND I FEEL LIKE DEATH'S AUNT FANNY.

THEN WHAT ARE YOU DOING OUT OF BED, BURKE?

YOU COME HALF-WAY ACROSS TOWN TO PLAY *NURSEMAID* TO A 60-YEAR-OLD INVALID, LEAST I CAN DO IS PUT ON COFFEE.

COFFEE'S MADE.

YOU USE THE MACHINE? S'GONNA TASTE LIKE *CRAP*. HEATING ELEMENT IS SHOT. YOU GOTTA BOIL A POT ON THE STOVE AND--

TASTE.

DID YOU HAVE THIS DELIVERED?

I THINK *WARM THOUGHTS*.

DAMN CHEMO.

90 DEGREES OUT AND I'M *FREEZING MY BALLS OFF*.

YOU DON'T HAVE BALLS, TRACY.

YOU DON'T KNOW THAT.

MY PRESENCE IN THE APARTMENT SHOULD RAISE THE TEMPERATURE 2-3 DEGREES, FOR WHATEVER THAT'S WORTH.

AND I THINK I'VE GOT THE COFFEE MAKER PROBLEM FIXED.

SZZT

REALLY? I DON'T REMEMBER FEELING A DIFFERENCE AT THE MAGAZINE WHEN YOU WORKED FOR ME.

YOU WORKED FOR ME.

KEEP TELLING YOURSELF THAT.

I MADE SOME CALLS AFTER YOU WENT TO BED. THE LANDLORD'S SENDING A GUY OVER TO LOOK AT THE THERMOSTAT LATER TODAY.

I HAVEN'T EVEN BEEN ABLE TO GET THAT TIGHT BASTARD TO ANSWER THE PHONE!

I RESORTED TO THREATS.

I STARTED WITH THREATS.

I MUST BE MORE INTIMIDATING THAN YOU.

LIKE HELL.

DO YOU NOT EAT? THERE'S NOTHING IN HERE. MAKE ME A LIST AND I'LL RUN OUT--

CAROL... HAVE YOU SEEN THE PAPER?

OH. YEAH. THAT--

NO, NOT THAT--

DAILY BUGLE
NEW YORK'S FINEST DAILY NEWSPAPER

SINCE 1897
FINAL
$1.00 (in NYC)
$1.50 (outside city)

New Captain Marvel! And He's a She!

Iconic Pilot Dies in Fire at Historic Aviation Club

at Historic Aviation Club

HELEN COBB, PILOT
POWDER PUFF DERBY WINNER, 1958.
FROM BUGLE FILE PHOTO.

THAT.

Of higher, further, faster...more. Always more.

I WAS JUST ADMIRING YOUR TROPHIES.

THAT'S WHAT THEY'RE THERE FOR. GOT 15 RECORDS TOTAL.

We came into the world spittin' mad, running full bore...

To or from what, I ain't never been able to tell.

CAROL HERE'S IN AIR FORCE PILOT-TRAINING.

CAPTIVE AUDIENCE! HERE'S YOUR CHANCE. TELL HER WHAT YOU TOLD ME ABOUT YOUR ASTRONAUT DAYS--

YOU WERE IN THE *MERCURY 13* PROGRAM?

TESTED AT THE SAME TIME AS *JOHN GLENN.* YOU CAN LOOK THAT UP.

NOW THOSE GALS--THOSE WERE SOME PILOT OUTSCORED THE SEVEN BOYS ON JU ABOUT EVERY TES WE TOOK.

WE'D'VE WIPED THE FLOOR WITH WHAT PASSES FOR A *NINETY-NINER* TODAY.

NO OFFENSE.

HEH. NONE TAKEN.

SALUT, THEN! I COMMEND YOU ON YOUR GOOD TASTE IN HEROES, KID.

Over the years, I've come to think of these particular traits as the shared attributes of a chosen people...

MS. COBB...

IF YOU DON'T HAVE PLANS FOR THE MORNING, WHY DON'T YOU FLY WITH ME? YOU COULD TEACH ME A THING OR TWO...

AND I COULD SHOW YOU WHAT A YOUNG PILOT CAN DO.

...the Lord put us here to punch holes in the sky.

GOT UNDER YOUR SKIN, DIDN'T I? YOU ARE *ON,* KITTEN. WE WILL DUEL AT SUNRISE!

...And we will be the stars we were always meant to be.

KELLY SUE DeCONNIC
WRITE

DEXTER SO
ARTIS

ED McGUINNESS, DEXTER VINES & JAVIER RODRIGUE
COVE

VC'S JOE CARAMAGN
LETTERE

ELLIE PYLE
ASSISTANT EDITOR

SANA AMANAT
ASSOCIATE EDITOR

STEPHEN WACKER
PRETTIEST

JOE QUESAD
CHIEF CREATIVE OFFICE

CAPTAIN MARVEL COSTUME DESIGNED BY JAMIE McKELVI

Binary lives again! From *Ms. Marvel Vol. 2 #37*. Art by **Phil Jiminez.**

Secret agent Carol Danvers, working undercover in *Ms. Marvel Vol. 2 #33*. Art by **David Yardin.**

An homage to the cover of *Ms. Marvel #1*, from *Captain Marvel #10*. Art by **David Lopez.**

The cosmic majesty of Captain Marvel from *Infinity Countdown #1*. Art by **Adi Granov**.

PREVIOUSLY...

WHEN AN ALIEN REFUGEE NAMED TIC CAME TO EARTH REQUESTING HELP FROM THE AVENGERS TO PREVENT AN INTERPLANETARY TURF WAR, CAPTAIN MARVEL GOT INVOLVED AND PROMISED TO NOT ONLY BRING THE YOUNG GIRL HOME, BUT ALSO TO BRING PEACE TO HER PLANET.

NOW, THE CRISIS IS AVERTED, BUT TIC HAS REFUSED TO LEAVE CAPTAIN MARVEL'S SIDE. SHE STOWED AWAY ABOARD CAROL'S SHIP, AND HAS ONLY MADE THINGS MORE COMPLICATED NOW THAT EARTH'S MIGHTIEST HERO NEEDS TO RENDEZVOUS WITH THE GUARDIANS OF THE GALAXY, WITH WHOM SHE ENTRUSTED HER SHIP AND PET CAT, CHEWIE.

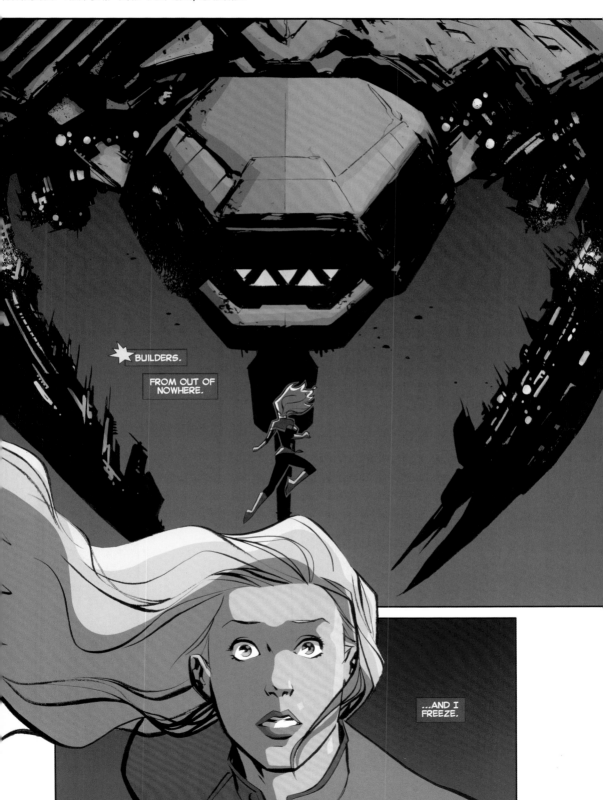

NO...
NO.

HE CAN'T BE GONE. HE CAN'T BE.

CAROL, WE'RE SITTING DUCKS!

DAMMIT, DO SOMETHING!

CAPTAIN MARVEL WILL SAVE US, CHEWIE.

COME ON, COME ON, COME ON, COME ON, MOVE FASTER!

THERE ISN'T TIME TO GRIEVE. HEAD IN THE GAME, CAROL.

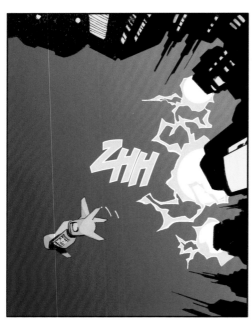

ZHH

IT'S GONNA HIT US!

NOOOOO!

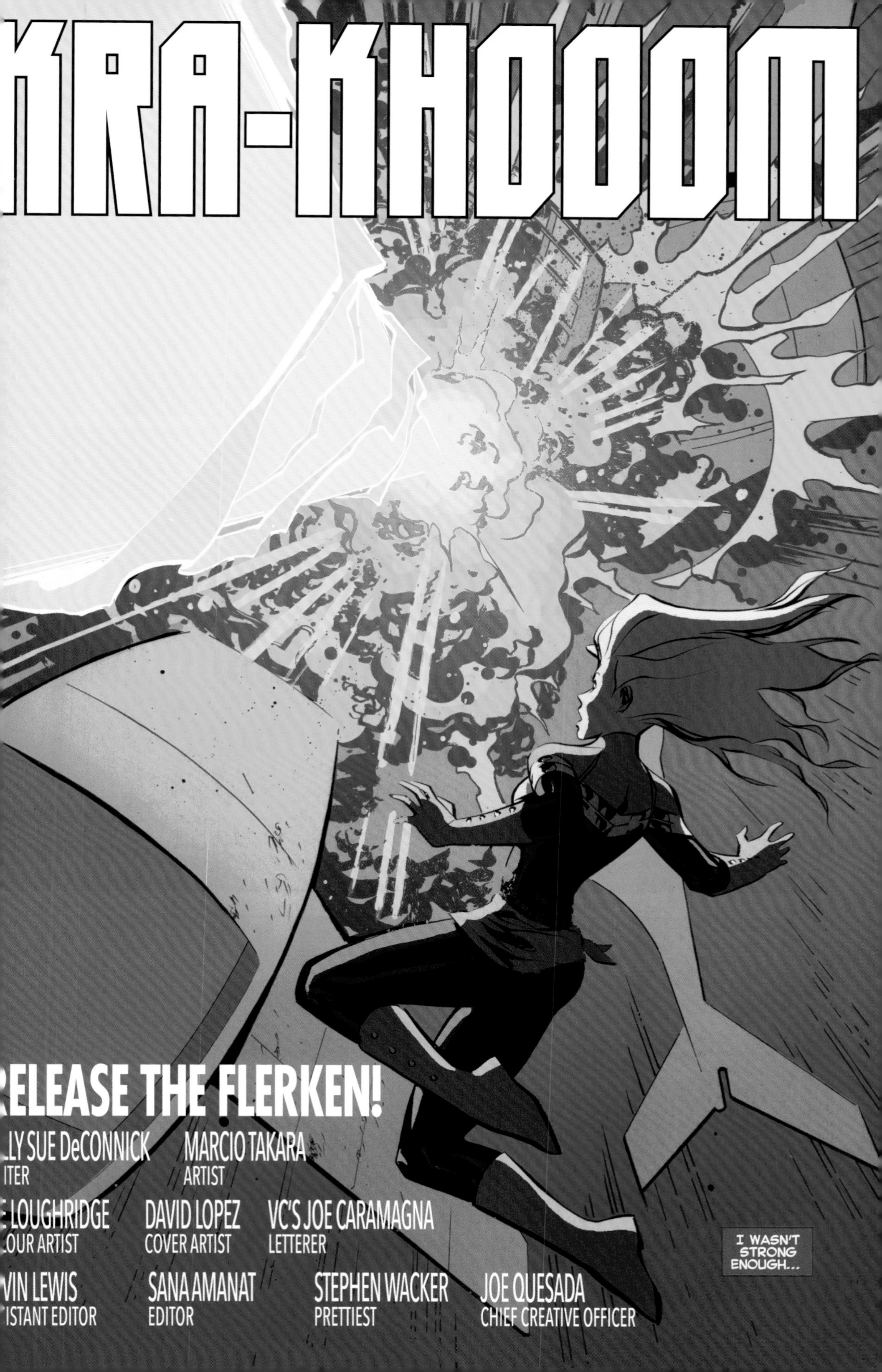

KRA-KHOOOM

RELEASE THE FLERKEN!

LY SUE DeCONNICK
ITER

MARCIO TAKARA
ARTIST

LOUGHRIDGE
OUR ARTIST

DAVID LOPEZ
COVER ARTIST

VC'S JOE CARAMAGNA
LETTERER

VIN LEWIS
ISTANT EDITOR

SANA AMANAT
EDITOR

STEPHEN WACKER
PRETTIEST

JOE QUESADA
CHIEF CREATIVE OFFICER

I WASN'T STRONG ENOUGH...

HOW IS THAT RELEVANT?!

I COULD BE YOUR SECOND!

I ALREADY HAVE SPIDER-WOMAN AND THAT'S ALL THE DRAMA I CAN HANDLE, THANK YOU.

I MET HER ONCE.

ON THE RING WORLD. YOU TOLD ME.

SPURT

TIC, WHAT HAPPENED TO "TORFA IS MY HOME!"?

NOTHING! "HOME" ISN'T THE PLACE YOU *NEVER LEAVE*, CAPTAIN. IT'S THE PLACE YOU *ALWAYS RETURN* TO.

...

HOW OLD ARE YOU?

...OLDER THAN YOU THINK.

BIP BIP BIP

HARRISON! IT'S BEEN TOO LONG, MY FRIEND. PREP FOR DOCKING.

HARRISON'S OFF-LINE.

WHAT KIND OF A NAME IS THAT, ANYWAY? IT'S NOT EVEN AN ACRONYM.

WHO THE--?!

ROCKET! QUILL LEFT YOU ALONE WITH MY *SHIP* AND MY *CAT*?! YOU, WHO TRIED TO *MURDER*--

YOUR *FLERKEN*. AND YES. I GAVE MY WORD I WOULDN'T HURT IT. UNLIKE *SOMEBODY* I KNOW, *STAR-LORD* TRUSTS ME.

SEE? SHE'S FINE.

GRRRRR

WHAT ARE YOU DOING HERE? I THOUGHT THE WHOLE POINT WAS TO TAKE YOU HOME.

THE CAPTAIN AND I SAVED MY PEOPLE. NOW I HAVE SIGNED ON TO BE HER SECOND.

REALLY? CONGRATS.

THAT IS NOT EXACTLY HOW IT WENT DOWN AND *NO*, YOU HAVE NOT!

I'M HERE, CHEWIE. WHAT DID THAT HORRIBLE, UGLY WEASEL DO TO MY BABY GIRL?

RRRRRR

HEY, I *HEARD* THAT!

GOOD. YOU HAVE *FIVE* SECONDS TO *APOLOGIZE* BEFORE TIC AND I DINE ON *GRILLED WEASEL SHISH KABAB.*

ONE...

I DON'T TAKE *THREATS* WELL, LADY. LOOK, I AM DOING YOU A *FAVOR.*

MRRR...?

TWO...

I'VE BEEN ASKING AROUND. DO YOU KNOW WHAT A LIVING FEMALE FLERKEN IS *WORTH* ON THE OPEN MARKET?

MRAO...!

THREE!

IN ADDITION TO BEING *VICIOUS KILLERS,* THEY'RE ALSO *LIVING GATEWAYS* TO *POCKET DIMENSIONS.*

LOOK, I GOTTA GUY WHO'LL GIVE YOU *FIFTY THOUSAND--*

HISSSSEEE!

FOUR!

BOOTING UP HARRISON!

THAT'S NOT GOING TO BE HELPFUL.

I GET THE WHOLE PILOT-BY-THE-FORCE THING, BUT A) *TOOLS!*-- AND B)--

NO! IT'S NOT GOING TO BE HELPFUL BECAUSE I WAS--

DAMAGE REPORT GENERATING. THRUSTERS ARE OFF-LINE, SOMETHING IS TRYING TO ACCESS LIFE SUPPORT!

ACCESS IT HOW?

PHYSICALLY! INTRUDERS JUST PENETRATED THE HULL AND ESTABLISHED HARD CONNECTION TO OUR CONTROLS.

BECAUSE I WAS *DOING SOMETHING* WITH HARRISON AND I WASN'T DONE YET!

BOOT HIM UP ANYWAY!

CHEWIE, I NEED YOU TO NOT BE UNDER-FOOT RIGHT NOW.

ALL RIGHT, I'M GOING *OUT THERE* TO SEE IF I CAN GET A GOOD LOOK AT WHAT WE HIT!

MRF

DAMMIT! SCRATCH THAT! HATCH IS JAMMED.

OH, CRAP.

HARRISON, WHAT AM I LOOKING AT? WHAT'S GOT A HOLD OF US?

MROWWWWWWWWWWW

ROCKET, DID MY SHIP'S COMPUTER JUST *MEOW* AT ME?

YES. AND THERE IS A *PERFECTLY* LOGICAL EXPLANATION.

IT'S NOT POISON. IT'S LIKE A DYE YOU DRINK BEFORE THE DOC TAKES A PICTURE OF YOUR GUTS.

THEY'RE USING IT TO MAP THE INSIDE OF THE SHIP!

WHY? WHAT ARE THEY LOOKING FOR?

ARE THEY PIRATES, MAYBE? THIS SEEMS A LITTLE ADVANCED FOR THE HAFF.

THURNK

...THE FLERKEN!

I SAY WE GIVE IT TO THEM!

OH HELL NO! I'M NOT GIVING ANYONE MY CAT!

MRAOOOO

LOOK, CLEARLY WORD GOT AROUND--

AND HOW DO YOU THINK THAT HAPPENED *EXACTLY?!*

MRAOOOOOO

IT DOESN'T MATTER!

THURNK

IF WE DON'T HAND THAT THING OVER, WHATEVER IS ON THE OTHER SIDE OF THAT DENT IS GONNA COME THROUGH AND *TAKE IT!*

SO LET THEM COME!

WHAT'S THE MATTER, WEASEL? YOU *SCARED?*

THURNK

I'M NOT A *WEASEL* AND I'M NOT *SCARED!*

BUT I'M NOT RISKING MY *LIFE* FOR A *FLERKEN!*

SHE CAN HEAR YOU! YOU'RE UPSETTING HER!

REALLY? BECAUSE I'D RISK *MY LIFE* FOR *ANY* MEMBER OF MY CREW.

RAOOOOOO

CAPTAIN MARVEL (2014) #8
COVER ARTWORK

WHERE WERE WE?

SPACE.

OH, RIGHT.

I WAS EN ROUTE FROM TORFA IN A BORROWED SHUTTLE WITH TIC, A NOWLANIAN STOWAWAY, WHEN WE RENDEZVOUSED WITH *MY SHIP*-- HARRISON--WHICH WAS BEING WORKED ON BY A TALKING RACCOON FROM THE *GUARDIANS OF THE GALAXY* NAMED "ROCKET"...

ROCKET, CONVINCED MY CAT, *CHEWIE*, WAS A MEMBER OF A RARE AND DANGEROUS ALIEN SPECIES CALLED THE *FLERKEN* PUT THE WORD OUT INTERGALACTICALLY THAT HE HAD A *FLERKEN* IN HIS CUSTODY...

WHICH RESULTED IN OUR BEING CAPTURED BY *WHATEVER THIS THING IS* BECAUSE IT WANTS MY CAT...

WHO, IT TURNS OUT ACTUALLY *IS* A *FLERKEN* AND HAS L AN IMPOSSIBLE NUME OF *EGGS* IN THE CARGO STOW WHER SHE IS HIDING WITH TIC NOW.

GOT THAT OH, AND--

THE *RACCOON* REPROGRAMMED MY SHIP'S COMPUTER, SO NOW IT SPEAKS CAT.

RRNK RRNK MROW! MROW-ROW-ROW! RRNK RRNK

OR *FLERKEN*, I GUESS.

FLERKEN CAT.

PINCH ME.

OW! PINCH, NOT PUNCH!

BAP

WHATEVER. YOU'RE NOT *DREAMING.*

IT'S OVER. HOSTILE VESSEL HAS GOT FULL CONTROL OF HARRISON. I CAN'T OVERRIDE.

ATTENTION VESSEL! RECON VAPORS CONFIRM THE PRESENCE OF THE UNIVERSE'S *LAST KNOWN* LIVING FLERKEN.

PREPARE FOR *BOARDING* AND CUSTODY TRANSFER IN TEN...

LIKE *HELL.*

THE
LAST...?

THEY
DON'T KNOW
ABOUT THE
EGGS.

TIC!

I KIND
OF HAVE MY
HANDS FULL,
CAPTAIN.

TOO
BAD!

GRAB AS
MANY EGGS AS
YOU CAN! WE'RE
PUTTING THEM, YOU,
CHEWIE AND ROCKET
ON THE
SHUTTLE!

...NINE...

MROW?

THE PASSAGE
CHAMBER IS
SEALED FOR
DECOMPRESSION.

SO
UNSEAL
IT!

I'M
TRYING!

...EIGHT...

THEY'RE HATCHING!
I DON'T THINK THIS
IS A GOOD TIME TO
MOVE THEM!

I
DON'T
CARE!

GO!
GO!
GO!

...SEVEN...

SORRY,
KITTIES!

...SIX...

CAN WE STOP CALLING THEM *KITTENS* NOW? THEY'RE *FLERKEN*.

WILL YOU MOVE, PLEASE? WE CAN FIGHT ABOUT WHAT TO CALL THEM LATER!

ONCE YOU'VE GOT SHUTTLE CONTROL, GET THE THE HELL OUT OF HERE. DON'T COME BACK UNTIL YOU GET MY SIGNAL.

AND ONE MORE THING--

YOU HURT MY CAT--

YOU MEAN YOUR *FLERKEN*--

YOU HURT MY *FLERKEN*-- *ANY* OF MY FLERKEN AND SO HELP ME--

...FIVE...

RRRRRr

CHEWIE, NO!

HSSSSSSS

GRAB HER!

...FOUR...

HSSSSSS

AHHHHHH!

LOOK, I KNOW YOU'RE STILL SORE 'CUZ I TRIED TO *KILL YOU* AND ALL.

...TWO...

I GET THAT, OKAY?! BUT YOU'RE JUST GOING TO HAVE TO TAKE MY WORD THAT I FEEL A CERTAIN *KINSHIP* WITH ANYTHING THAT'S THE *LAST OF ITS KIND.*

EVEN *MURDEROUS VERMIN!*

...ONE...

THOOM

MRPH?

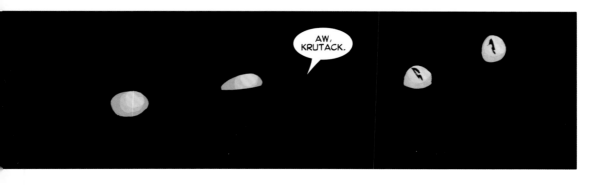

AW, KRUTACK.

IT'S GENERATING ITS THRUST BURNING SOME KIND OF ORGANIC MATTER AT THE BUTT END.

THE MORE IT BURNS, THE FASTER IT MOVES. SO...

LET'S TURN UP THE HEAT AND SEE IF WE CAN SEND THIS THING BACK TO WHATEVER *HELLHOLE* IT CAME FROM.

TSSST

FWSHHHH

JUST LIKE NEW, EH? MIRACULOUS WHAT THEY CAN DO IN A FEW WEEKS.

"JUST LIKE NEW" MIGHT BE A STRETCH. BUT ROCKET DID WORK SOME MAGIC. BOTH SHIPS ARE AIRTIGHT AND UP TO CODE...

ANY MORE LUCK WITH THE TRANSLATOR ALGORITHM, DOCTOR MOHAN?

WELLLL, NOT REALLY. WE STILL CAN'T PARSE FLERKEN, BUT WE HAVE LEARNED A LITTLE MORE SINCE I WROTE YOU.

FOR ONE THING, WE THINK CHEWIE HAS BEEN GESTATING HER EGGS THE ENTIRE TIME SHE'S BEEN WITH YOU.

THAT WOULD CERTAINLY EXPLAIN HER TEMPERAMENT.

BUT I TOOK HER TO MEDICAL EXAMS. HOW WAS THAT NEVER TURNED UP?

IF WE EVER FIGURE OUT HOW TO TALK TO HER, WE'LL ASK. UNTIL THEN, WE THINK IT HAS TO DO WITH HER POCKET DIMENSIONS.

LIKE HAMSTER CHEEKS, ALMOST. CHEWIE HAS PHYSICAL ACCESS TO BUBBLES OF SPACE AND TIME THAT EXIST IN OTHER WORLDS.

SHE CAN HIDE THINGS LARGER THAN SHE WOULD APPEAR TO BE INSIDE THOSE POCKETS--EGGS, FOR INSTANCE--

--TENTACLES.

--YES! AND WE THINK THAT SHE CAN USE THEM FOR TRANSPORT, THOUGH WE'RE NOT SURE HOW.

ARE YOU READY?

READY AS I'LL EVER BE.

BLEE-DOOP

POP

HI. WE FIGURED OUT HOW THE TRANSPORT THING WORKS. IT'S...GROSS.

LET'S NEVER DO IT AGAIN.

TIC, NO! I TOLD YOU--

YEAH, YOU DID. AND YOU WERE *WRONG.*

LISTEN, YOU THINK YOU KNOW EVERYTHING ABOUT ME, BUT YOU DON'T. I'M NOT WHAT YOU THINK I AM.

AND WE GET THAT YOU'RE SCARED OF SOMETHING HAPPENING TO CHEWIE, BUT THAT'S THE PRICE OF ADMISSION, YOU KNOW?

THE MORE YOU LOVE SOMETHING, THE MORE YOU OPEN YOURSELF UP TO THE PAIN OF LOSING IT. THAT'S NOT *FOOLHARDY...*

THAT'S *BRAVE.*

AREN'T AVENGERS SUPPOSED TO BE *BRAVE?*

WHAT ABOUT YOUR BABIES? WILL THEY BE OKAY WITHOUT YOU?

THERE ARE 117 OF THEM AND THEY'RE IN THE FINEST RESCUE CENTER IN THE GALAXY.

THEY'LL BE FINE.

ALL RIGHT THEN...HARRISON, SET A COURSE FOR *ADVENTURE.*

NO MATCH FOR "ADVENTURE." DO YOU MEAN: ADVENTURRA? THE ADVENSIO FORMATION, ADV--

JUST... HEAD BACK IN THE GENERAL DIRECTION OF THE GUARDIANS, OKAY?

PLOTTING FOR RENDEZVOUS...

YOU'RE A *TERRIBLE* MOTHER, YOU KNOW THAT?

MRF

ALLIES AND ENEMIES

BECOMING AN AWESOME BEACON OF POWER HAS ITS BENEFITS AND DRAWBACKS. CAROL DANVERS HAS FRIENDS AND FOES IN EQUAL MEASURE! HERE'S A TASTER OF THOSE SHE'S ENCOUNTERED IN HER TIME AS CAPTAIN MARVEL...

ALLIES

WAR MACHINE

James 'Rhodey' Rhodes also served in the United States Air Force albeit at a higher rank than Carol Danvers. The two briefly became lovers before tragedy struck as War Machine battled Thanos, only to lose his life in the struggle.

MS. MARVEL (KAMALA KHAN)

Kamala was always a huge fan of Captain Marvel, so when she was transformed by the power of the Terrigen Mists (a short-cut to super powers as used by the Inhumans), Khan adopted Captain Marvel's old moniker of Ms. Marvel. The name was going spare anyhow! Fortunately, Danvers had no problem with it, and they've since teamed-up to battle their foes.

WOLVERINE

Carol Danvers and Wolverine go way back – to a time when Wolverine was simply called 'Logan' and they were operating for the CIA. They became good friends and they saved each other's lives a few times while on dangerous missions. Notably, this included a daring breakout by Logan when Carol was held at a secure Russian KGB installation in Lubyanka. The ordeal ended her desire to work for the CIA again, but they've remained close ever since.

ROGUE

During her time in the Brotherhood of Mutants, Rogue absorbed Carol Danvers' powers as they battled it out, but unintentionally absorbed her mind, too! This affected them both terribly, with Rogue having trouble distinguishing her own memories from Danvers'. They remain bitter enemies because of this traumatic event.

YON-ROGG

The Kree commander is both Danvers' enemy, and also the reason she has her amazing powers! During a fight between Mar-Vell and Yon-Rogg, his Psyche-Magnitron device exploded, causing damage to Carol, but also with the side-effect of altering her genetic structure to a human-Kree hybrid. Their mutual hatred rages on! He has superhuman strength, agility and stamina, and is a fearsome fighter.

THE OTHERS!

CAROL DANVERS HASN'T BEEN THE ONLY SUPER HERO TO BEAR THE NAME OF CAPTAIN MARVEL. THERE HAVE BEEN OTHERS! READ ON TO FIND OUT ABOUT THEM...

MONICA RAMBEAU

Hailing from New Orleans, Monica Rambeau was a lieutenant in the Harbor Patrol when her life changed for ever. Unlike Carol Danvers, her super powers came not from the extraterrestrial Kree, but via a bombardment of extra-dimensional energy from a disruptor weapon, created by a criminal scientist she was pursuing. This gave her the power to convert her own body into pure energy at will, enabling complete mastery over this new form. After a stint with the Avengers battling foes such as Dracula and Plantman, she relinquished the name Captain Marvel and has since adopted several super-heroic names including Photon, Pulsar and currently Spectrum.

First appearance:
The Amazing Spider-Man
Annual #16 (1982)

MAR-VELL

This Kree warrior was the very first to bear the name 'Captain Marvel' after being sent to monitor the space-flight capabilities of humans on Earth. His Kree name was mis-heard by the humans he was sent to observe and the name 'Captain Marvel' stuck. As a relative outcast to the Kree hierarchy (his commander and arch-rival Yon-Rogg tried to have him killed many times), Mar-Vell grew to love the human race and became a champion to their cause, aiding Earth's super heroes in many battles and even saving Carol Danvers' life on several occasions. His powers were also increased significantly by a being known as Zo during this time. He was ultimately undone by exposure to a dangerous nerve gas, which eventually caused his terminal cancer, during an entanglement with the foe named Nitro. He is undoubtedly the most significant figure in the history of Captain Marvel!

MOONSTONE

Karla Sofen literally 'stole' the moniker of Captain Marvel from Carol Danvers, much to her chagrin. Unsurprisingly, they consider each other as mortal enemies, especially since she joined forced with Norman Osborn in the Dark Avengers' team. Karla received her abilities from a similar source – a mysterious Kree life stone that gave her a range of powers not too dissimilar from Carol's own, including gravity manipulation, flight, and superhuman strength. She can fire photon blasts, and can become intangible at will. Moonstone has formerly been a member of the Thunderbolts and the Masters of Evil.

**First appearance:
Captain America
#192 (1975)**

**First appearance:
Marvel Super-
Heroes #12 (1967)**

THE ADVENTURE CONTINUES...

IF YOU'VE ENJOYED READING ALL ABOUT CAROL DANVERS' INCREDIBLE COMICBOOK HISTORY AND WANT TO DISCOVER MORE OF HER AMAZING TALES, HERE ARE SOME GRAPHIC NOVELS WE RECOMMEND:

CAPTAIN MARVEL: RISE OF ALPHA FLIGHT
ISBN: 9781846537332

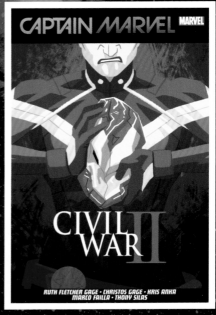

CAPTAIN MARVEL: CIVIL WAR II
ISBN: 9781846537707

MARVEL PLATINUM: CAPTAIN MARVEL
ISBN: 9781846539534

THE LIFE OF CAPTAIN MARVEL
ISBN: 9781846539503

OpenSource

Volume: 03 | Issue: 10 | Pages: 108 | July 2015

THE COMPLETE MAGAZINE ON OPEN SOURCE

ForYou

An **EFY**GROUP Publication

The Latest In Network Monitoring

Monitorix: The Lightweight
System Monitoring Tool

**Distributed Network
Monitoring:** An Overview

Observium: The Tireless
Network Monitor

Everything You Want
To Know About Nagios Core

**Selecting The Right
Multi-functional Printers**

**A Primer On Evil Twin
Wireless Attacks**

Enabling your Business for the Digital Age

100% GUARANTEE · CUSTOMER SATISFACTION

"ORAHI is India's most trusted and widely used ridesharing and carpool app. To support instant and LIVE transactions for thousands of members, we chose ESDS as our datacenter hosting partner". For all requirements in the past 2 years (of a rapidly growing start-up), ESDS' sales, service & support teams have been impeccable.

Mr. Sameer Khanna
MD, Orahi.com

Mr. Sanjeev Kumar
CIO, KafilaTravel

"Thank you for all the good work ESDS has provided to us recently. Your staff was courteous and professional as always".

"The extremely dynamic traffic pattern that our brand websites see throughout the year, the elasticity provided by eNlight is a blessing. Combined with variety of deployment options, security and exuberant support, eNlight fits the bill perfectly and Pay-per-consume works as the icing on the cake".

Mr. Ankur Jain
Head IT Infrastructure,
Yum Restaurants

Mr. Rajjesh Mittal
CEO,
Capricorn Infotech India

"I can finally say, we have caught up with the American ISPs in having a world class Hosting company in ESDS".

---

esds
enabling futurability

Mumbai | Delhi | Bengaluru | Nashik | Leeds (UK)

ESDS SOFTWARE SOLUTION PVT. LTD.
Toll Free No. : 1800 209 3006 | Fax : +91 95 95 247 247
Email : relationship@esds.co.in | Website : www.esds.co.in

Contents

REGULAR FEATURES

Contents

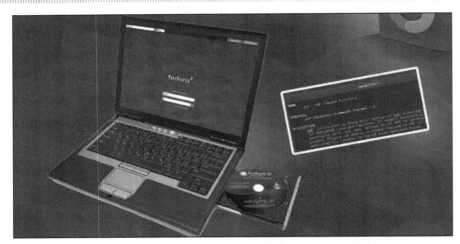

100 Things to do After Installing Fedora 22

Editor
RAHUL CHOPRA

Editorial, Subscriptions & Advertising
DELHI (HQ)
D-87/1, Okhla Industrial Area, Phase I, New Delhi 110020
Ph: (011) 26810602, 26810603; Fax: 26817563
E-mail: info@efy.in

Missing Issues
E-mail: support@efy.in

BENGALURU
Ph: (080) 25260394, 25260023
E-mail: efyblr@efy.in

Customer Care
E-mail: support@efy.in

Back Issues
Kits 'n' Spares
New Delhi 110020
Ph: (011) 26371661, 26371662
E-mail: info@kitsnspares.com

Advertising
CHENNAI
Ph: (044) 42994363
E-mail: efyenq@efy.in

HYDERABAD
Ph: (040) 67172633
E-mail: efyenq@efy.in

KOLKATA
Ph: (033) 22294788
E-mail: efyenq@efy.in

MUMBAI
Ph: (022) 24950047, 24928520
E-mail: efymum@efy.in

PUNE
Ph: (020) 40147882
E-mail: efypune@efy.in

GUJARAT
Ph: (079) 61344948
E-mail: efyahd@efy.in

JAPAN
Tandem Inc., Ph: 81-3-3541-4166
E-mail: tandem@efy.in

SINGAPORE
Publicitas Singapore Pte Ltd
Ph: +65-6836 2272
E-mail: publicitas@efy.in

UNITED STATES
E & Tech Media
Ph: +1 860 536 6677
E-mail: veroniquelamarque@gmail.com

CHINA
Power Pioneer Group Inc.
Ph: (86 755) 83729797, (86) 13923802595
E-mail: powerpioneer@efy.in

TAIWAN
J.K. Media, Ph: 886-2-87726780 ext. 10
E-mail: jkmedia@efy.in

Exclusive News-stand Distributor (India)
IBH BOOKS AND MAGAZINES DISTRIBUTORS LTD
Unit No.10, Bezzola Complex, Opp. Suman Nagar,
Sion Trombay Road, Chembur,
Mumbai – 400 071
Phones: 022 – 40497401 /02
E-mail: info@ibhworld.com

SUBSCRIPTION RATES			
Year	Newstand Price (₹)	You Pay (₹)	Overseas
Five	6000	3600	—
Three	3600	2520	—
One	1200	960	US$ 120

Kindly add ₹ 50/- for outside Delhi cheques.
Please send payments only in favour of **EFY Enterprises Pvt Ltd.**
Non-receipt of copies may be reported to support@efy.in—do mention your subscription number.

OFFERS of THE MONTH

YOUSAIDIT

 A request for articles on IoT

I have started reading *OSFY* magazine since a few months and I am very fascinated by the articles published in it.

I am particularly interested in the Internet of Things (IoT) domain. Would it be possible to get expert advice on IoT and its scope in the near future? And also about the impact of open source on IoT? Have previous editions carried articles on IoT?

–N. Durga Prasad,
ndprasad09@gmail.com

ED: Thanks a lot for the feedback. It really makes us feel good to know that OSFY *has been helpful to you. We cherish our readers' views. Regarding your query, with every edition of* OSFY, *we have covered news on IoT and open source software. Based on your request, we will try to come up with more articles on the topic. We love to hear from our readers and try our best to match their expectations. Keep sending us your views!*

 On writing guest posts for the *OSFY* website

I happened to visit your site - *http://opensourceforu. com/* - and found your blog very relevant and useful. This has motivated me to enquire if we could do guest blogging on your blog. We can post unique and highly-useful content that is relevant to your website as well as our website. We maintain high-content standards and we do follow a legitimate guest blogging process. We would be pleased to give your audience the more advanced content on the topics your blog covers. Looking forward to guest blogging for you.

–Manav,
manav.fatepuril@landmarkit.in

ED: Thanks a lot for writing to us! It feels great when enthusiastic authors like you wish to write for us. Before doing so, you can send us the detailed Table of Contents (ToC) at osfyedit@efy.in giving details of the topic your blog will be on. Our team will review it and once they give you the thumbs-up, you can go ahead with writing it. Do ensure that the blog has an open source angle and caters to our target audience.

 Where do I get *OSFY*?

I have been an OSS fan and have been reading *OSFY* for a long time. I used to buy the copies from news stands when I was at Delhi. I have shifted to Patna and am not able to get the copies. Can you please let me know where I can get the magazine?

—Sushovan.
suban13@rediffmail.com

ED: Thanks for writing to us. Check out our website dealers.efyindia.com. You may be able to locate some dealers selling OSFY *close to your home. We have tried to provide the phone numbers of as many dealers as possible, so that you can call before visiting. Also, you can subscribe to our magazine so that it gets delivered to you every month. You can visit http://electronicsforu.com/ electronicsforu/subscription/subsc2scheme.asp for details on how to subscribe.* END

Please send your comments or suggestions to:

The Editor,
Open Source For You,
D-87/1, Okhla Industrial Area, Phase I,
New Delhi 110020, **Phone:** 011-26810601/02/03,
Fax: 011-26817563, **Email:** osfyedit@efy.in

OSFYClassifieds

Classifieds for Linux & Open Source IT Training Institutes

WESTERN REGION

Linux Lab (empowering linux mastery)
Courses Offered: Enterprise Linux
& VMware

Address (HQ): 1104, D' Gold House,
Nr. Bharat Petrol Pump, Ghyaneshwer
Paduka Chowk, FC Road, Shivajinagar
Pune-411 005
Contact Person: Mr.Bhavesh M. Nayani
Contact No.: +020 60602277,
+91 8793342945
Email: info@linuxlab.org.in
Branch(es): coming soon
Website: www.linuxlab.org.in

Linux Training & Certification
Courses Offered: RHCSA,
RHCE, RHCVA, RHCSS,
NCLA, NCLP, Linux Basics,
Shell Scripting,
(Coming soon) MySQL

Address (HQ): 104B Instant Plaza,
Behind Nagrik Stores,
Near Ashok Cinema,
Thane StationWest - 400601,
Maharashtra, India
Contact Person: Ms. Swati Farde
Contact No.: +91-22-25379116/
+91-9869502832
Email: mail@ltcert.com
Website: www.linuxlab.org.in

NORTHERN REGION

GRRAS Linux Trainingand Development Center
Courses Offered: RHCE, RHCSS, RHCVA,
CCNA, PHP, Shell Scripting (online training
is also available)

Address (HQ): GRRAS Linux Trainingand
Development Center, 219, Himmat Nagar,
Behind Kiran Sweets, Gopalpura Turn,
Tonk Road, Jaipur, Rajasthan, India
Contact Person: Mr. Akhilesh Jain
Contact No.: +91-141-3136868/
+91-9983340133,9785598711,9887789124
Email: info@grras.com
Branch(es): Nagpur, Pune
Website: www.grras.org,www.grras.com

SOUTHERN REGION

Advantage Pro
Courses Offered: RHCSS, RHCVA,
RHCE, PHP, Perl, Python, Ruby, Ajax,
A prominent player in Open Source
Technology

Address (HQ): 1 & 2 , 4th Floor,
Jhaver Plaza, 1A Nungambakkam
High Road, Chennai - 600 034, India
Contact Person: Ms. Rema
Contact No.: +91-9840982185
Email: enquiry@vectratech.in
Website(s): www.vectratech.in

Duestor Technologies
Courses Offered: Solaris, AIX,
RHEL, HP UX, SAN Administration
(Netapp, EMC, HDS, HP),
Virtualisation(VMWare, Citrix, OVM),
Cloud Computing, Enterprise
Middleware.

Address (HQ): 2-88, 1st floor,
Sai Nagar Colony, Chaitanyapuri,
Hyderabad - 060
Contact Person: Mr. Amit
Contact No.: +91-9030450039,
+91-9030450397.
Email: info@duestor.com
Website(s): www.duestor.com

IPSR Solutions Ltd.
Courses Offered: RHCE, RHCVA,
RHCSS, RHCDS, RHCA,
Produced Highest number of Red Hat
professionals in the world

Address (HQ): Merchant's Association
Building, M.L. Road, Kottayam - 686001,
Kerala, India
Contact Person: Benila Mendus
Contact No.: +91-9447294635
Email: training@carnaticindia.com
Branch(es): Kochi, Kozhikode,
Thrissur, Trivandrum
Website: www.ipsr.org

Linux Learning Centre
Courses Offered: Linux OS Admin
& Security Courses for Migration,
Courses for Developers, RHCE,
RHCVA, RHCSS, NCLP

Address (HQ): 635, 6th Main Road,
Hanumanthnagar,
Bangalore - 560 019, India
Contact Person: Mr. Ramesh Kumar
Contact No.: +91-80-22428538,
26780762, 65680048 /
+91-9845057731, 9449857731
Branch(es): Bangalore
Email: info@linuxlearningcentre.com
Website: www.linuxlearningcentre.com

Eastern Region

**Academy of Engineering and
Management (AEM)**
Courses Offered: RHCE, RHCVA,
RHCSS, Clustering & Storage,
Advanced Linux, Shell
Scripting, CCNA, MCITP, A+, N+

Address (HQ): North Kolkata, 2/80
Dumdum Road, Near Dumdum Metro
Station, 1st & 2nd Floor,
Kolkata - 700074
Contact Person: Mr. Tuhin Sinha
Contact No.: +91-9830075018,
9830051236
Email: sinhatuhin1@gmail.com
Branch(es): North & South Kolkata
Website: www.aemk.org

Micromax launches a new phablet

Micromax recently launched the fourth variant of its Canvas Doodle series—the Canvas Doodle 4 phablet. It comes with a large 15.24cm (6 inch) IPS screen protected by Corning Gorilla Glass 3 and a 540x960 pixel resolution. The phablet runs on Android 5.0 Lollipop and is powered by a 1.3GHz quad-core ARM Cortex A7 processor. The device comes with 1GB RAM, 8GB inbuilt memory that's expandable up to 32GB via microSD card. The Canvas Doodle is equipped with an 8 megapixel rear camera and a 5 megapixel front camera, and is supported by a 3000mAh battery. The connectivity options of the device include 3G, Bluetooth and Wi-Fi.

The device is available at all Micromax stores.

Price: ₹ 9,499

Address: Micromax Informatics Limited, 90B, Sector-18, Gurgaon 122015; **Ph:** +91-124-4811000; **Email:** info@micromaxinfo.com

D-Link's ultra-fast router launched in India

D-Link recently announced the availability of its high performance 11AC, ultra-fast Wi-Fi router—the DIR-890L. Resembling a spaceship, the DIR-890L is equipped with a wide array of advanced features including wireless 11AC beamforming, which enhances signal strength and throughput. The router comes with a 1GHz dual-core processor along with gigabit WAN/LAN Ethernet ports for high speed wired connectivity, and is enabled with WPA or WPA2 security. Some of the features of the DIR-890 include:

- **Tri-band Wi-Fi:** Two 5GHz and one 2.4GHz bands for maximum possible speed for each device.
- **Ultimate Wi-Fi performance:** Up to 1300Mbps on both 5GHz bands and 600Mbps on 2.4GHz bands.
- **Media sharing:** Mydlink Shareport app to stream and share pictures/videos to mobile devices.
- **Advanced AC smartbeam:** Tracks connected devices for enhanced Wi-Fi speed and range.
- **Smarter bandwidth:** Distributes traffic using band steering technology for optimal Wi-Fi performance.
- **Remote access and management:** Enables you to manage the network through your smartphone or tablet.

DIR-890L is available in two colour variants — red and black via D-Link's wide network of channel partners and resellers across the country and comes with a three-year warranty.

Price: ₹ 18,500

Address: D-Link (India) Limited, Kalpataru Square, 2nd Floor, Kondivita Lane, Off Andheri Kurla Road, Andheri (E), Mumbai – 400059; **Ph:** +91-90046 72817; **Website:** www.dlink.co.in

Asus introduces all-in-one power bank

Asus has launched its latest power bank in India—the Asus ZenPower—which weighs only 215 grams and is no larger than a credit card. The ZenPower is powered by a built-in 10050mAh battery. It is capable of charging nearly all smartphones with battery capacities of 1500mAh and 2000mAh, and tablets of battery capacities 4000mAh, 4500mAh or more. The power bank offers high-speed and efficient charging with an output of up to 2.4A. The Asus ZenPower is equipped with many safety features such as protection against temperatures, short circuits and comes with an extra layer of tactile toughness. The power bank is available in silver, pink, blue and gold at exclusive Asus stores and via Flipkart.

Price: Starting from ₹ 1,499

Address: Asus Technology Pvt Ltd, 4C, Gundecha Enclave, Kherani Road, Sakinaka, Andheri-E, Mumbai-400072; **Ph:** 91-22-67668800; **Website:** www.asus.com

Sony launches Xperia M4 Aqua in India

Sony has launched its next generation mid-range smartphone, Xperia M4 Aqua in India. The phone features a 12cm (5 inch) HD (1280×720 pixel) display with Corning Gorilla Glass 3 for amazing picture quality. It runs on the latest Google Android 5.0 (Lollipop) and is powered by a 64-bit Qualcomm Snapdragon 615 octa-core processor. It is waterproof and dust resistant (up to IP65 and IP68 standards). The device comes with 2GB RAM, and 8GB/16GB internal memory that's expandable up to 32GB via a microSD card. Xperia M4 Aqua is equipped with 2400mAh battery, 13MP auto-focus primary camera with LED flash, and a 5MP secondary camera.

The smartphone supports Wi-Fi, Bluetooth, USB, GPS and FM radio. It is available in three colours—white, black and coral.

Price: Approximately ₹ 22,000

Address: Sony India Pvt Ltd, A-31, Mathura Road, Mohan Co-Operative Industrial Estate, New Delhi – 110044; **Ph:** 18001037799; **Website:** www.sonyindia.co.in

LG's latest version of Android Wear

LG has launched its latest Android Wear device called LG Urbane. The classy watch is IP67 standard dust and water resistant, and comes with a 3.3cm (1.3 inch) P-OLED display. It is crafted in stainless steel with a gold and silver finish, and is powered by the 1.2GHz Snapdragon 400 quad-core processor. It is Wi-Fi enabled and comes with 4.1LE Bluetooth. The stylish watch is equipped with 512MB RAM, 4GB eMMC and is compatible with devices running on Android 4.3 OS and higher. The LG Urbane comes with a 410mAh battery and features like OK Google. The LG Urbane is available via Amazon.

Price: ₹ 29,990

Address: LG Electronics India Pvt Ltd, A Wing (3rd Floor), D-3, District Centre, Saket, New Delhi -110017; **Ph:** 1800 180 9999; **Website:** www.lg.com

Xiaomi's highest capacity battery power bank

Chinese manufacturer, Xiaomi, has launched its highest capacity battery power bank of 16000mAh, based on its study of Indian customers' needs.

The power bank features two USB 2.0 ports, one micro USB port and gives a maximum of 5.1V/3.6A dual output. The device measures 145mm x 60.4mm x 22mm, weighs 350 grams and delivers a conversion rate of up to 93 per cent. The portable charger can offer 3.5 full charges to any device powered by a 3100mAh battery and 2.5 full charges to mini pads. The power bank is available via *mi.com* and on all Mi stores.

Price: Rs 1,399

Address: Xiaomi India Pvt Ltd, 8th Floor, Tower-1, Umiya Business Bay, Marathahalli-Sarjapur Outer Ring Road, Bengaluru, Karnataka 560103; **Email:** service.in@xiaomi.com; **Website:** www.mi.com

Intex launches its first LTE smartphone

Intex has launched the Aqua 4G+ in India. The dual SIM phone features a 12.7cm (5 inch) high definition display with scratch resistant Dragontrail glass for protection and runs on Android 5.0 Lollipop. The smartphone is powered by a quad-core MediaTek MT6735 processor coupled with 2GB RAM and 16GB inbuilt storage that's expandable up to 32GB via microSD card. The Intex Aqua 4G+ is equipped with a 13 megapixel rear camera with LED flash, full HD (1080p) video recording and a 5 megapixel front camera. The phone also features good connectivity options like 4G, GPRS/EDGE, GPS/A-GPS, Wi-Fi, Bluetooth v3.0 and USB OTG. The smartphone is available in white and black at retail stores.

Price: ₹ 9,499

Address: Intex Technologies, D 18/2, Okhla Industrial Area, Phase-II, New Delhi; **Ph:** 011 4161 0225; **Website:** www.intextechnologies.com

Fedora Project launches Fedora 22

Fedora Project has recently launched the Fedora 22 Linux operating system.
Apparently, Fedora 22 is based on the
Lightweight X11 Desktop Environment
(LXDE) project, which makes this latest
LXDE edition the most lightweight Fedora
22 flavour yet. Designed from the outset
to be deployed on computers with low-end
machines, the latest version of Fedora
comes with a traditional desktop layout.

It also comes embedded with open source applications like the Yum Extender
graphical package manager, the Midori Web browser, the AbiWord word processor,
the Pidgin instant messenger, the Asunder audio-CD ripper, GnomeBaker CD/DVD
burning software and the Gnumeric spreadsheet editor.

LXDE can be replaced with LXQt in Fedora 22 Linux. The release note of
Fedora 22 Linux defines LXQt as the integration of the LXDE-Qt and the Razor-
qt projects. Version 0.9.0 is reportedly available in Fedora 22. One can easily
download Fedora 22 LXDE from the official website of Fedora Project.

Debian GNU/Linux 8.1 (Jessie) officially released

This much-anticipated Debian version has
finally been released with a lot of hype. The first
maintenance version of Debian GNU/Linux 8
(Jessie) is now available for download. Debian
8.1 was released with a lot of new features and
fixes on June 8. The previous version of Debian,
i.e., Debian GNU/Linux 8.0, had many annoying
issues which have supposedly been resolved in
the latest version. The problems were reported in
April 2015, during the initial release of Jessie.

The fixes have been released for various packages including Caja, ClamAv,
BlackBox, Debian Installer, DBus, didjvu, feed2imap, ejabberd, fai, FreeOrion,
GNOME Shell, gdnsd, ganeti, GnuTLS, libav, Mutter, MATE, mew, node-groove,
pdf2DjVu, Perl, open-iscsi, OpenCV, PHP and systemd.

Debian GNU/Linux 8.1 comes embedded with Linux kernel version 3.16.7-
ctk11, which fixes the EXT4 data corruption issue. Apparently, it supports XHCI on
APM Mustang USB and updates Crucial/Micron blacklist in libata.

Mouser launches enhanced open source hardware technology site

Mouser Electronics Inc., the global authorised distributor that offers the newest

semiconductors and electronic components, has
announced the update of its popular open source
hardware (OSHW) technology site. Mouser's updated
technology site provides developers with the resources
they need to quickly learn about the latest advances
in open source hardware, and the newest open source
hardware products available from Mouser Electronics.
This newly enhanced site, accessible on Mouser.com, reduces the time spent
selecting the best OSHW boards by providing days' worth of research in one
convenient location. The updated Product Selector is a powerful tool, allowing

Dr Rajeev Papneja receives Bharat Gaurav award

The India International Friendship
Society (IIFS), New Delhi, has
conferred Dr Rajeev Papneja with
the Bharat Gaurav Puraskar for
2015. Dr Papneja, who is one of
the youngest candidates to have
received this award, hails from
Deolali Camp, a small town in
Nashik district in Maharashtra.
In a very short span of time he
completed a remarkable journey

from a small Indian town to New
York, where he served for more
than a decade in Fortune 100
organisations as a technology
leader. He is now back in his home
town in pursuit of making the
generation future-ready.

Dr Papneja holds a bachelor's
and a master's degree in computer
science from India and a Ph. D
in business administration from
USA. With more than 20 years of
extensive technology experience
at the national and international
levels, Dr Papneja now serves
as the COO and executive VP at
ESDS Software Solutions Pvt Ltd
and also as the COO of bodHost
(USA), a fast growing Web hosting
company that is a subsidiary of
ESDS. He is a mentor to many
students and is a guest lecturer
at many renowned technology
and management colleges. The
India International Friendship
Society has honoured him for
his meritorious services and
outstanding performance in the
field of technology.

developers to quickly select a board using a visual matrix of important features. Thirty different parameters can be selected and sorted including processor type and speed, memory and expansion capabilities, wireless and wired networking, user interface options, video connectivity, and more. Online materials include user guides, PCB files, schematics and complete documentation. Supporting software for each board is available for fast, direct download.

Under the *Hardware* section is a listing of available OSHW boards by category, including the newest Arduino and Arduino-compatible, BeagleBoard, Intel and TI LaunchPad boards. The site makes it easy to find related hardware such as BeagleBone Capes, Arduino Shields and other useful accessories. In the *Featured Products* section, developers can find the newest OSHW boards including the Intel Edison miniature computer, Texas Instruments' MSP-EXP432 LaunchPad, and the Arduino Lilypad for wearables. All hardware is available for same-day shipping from Mouser.com.

The *Articles* section contains new articles, including a discussion on open source vs proprietary hardware. Last, the *Technical Resources* section has new, related resources including updated application notes, white papers, and more to further assist developers.

Google Maps for Android offers offline search and navigation

Considering that many nations in the world are struggling with data connectivity issues, particularly when users are on-the-go, Google has launched offline search and navigation options for Google Maps for Android. The support for offline maps comes with voice-enabled  turn-by-turn directions and search support, and all this can be accessed with data connectivity. This new feature will arrive in India some time later this year. So, once this feature is enabled in Google Maps for Android, you will just need to save the map of a particular area in order to navigate and enjoy a local experience, even without any data connectivity.

Another new feature that will make Google Maps for Android an interesting offering is when searching for places, users will benefit from auto-complete suggestions, reviews and opening hours.

Red Hat introduces the Red Hat Cloud Suite for Applications

Red Hat Inc., one of the world's leading providers of open source solutions, has launched the Red Hat Cloud Suite for Applications, an accelerated way to develop, deploy and manage applications at scale using open source technologies. As organisations move to the cloud, many are evolving toward micro-services architectures that run within containers to increase scalability, portability and efficiency. These new architectures require massively scalable infrastructure in order to realise their full  potential. However, many organisations also have high-volume workloads that are not yet compatible with micro-services or container based architecture, but which could benefit from having a solution that supports both applications running within virtual machines and new container based application architectures. For example, developers may require storage services that are necessary for stateful application

Open Web device Compliance Review Board (CRB) certifies the first round of handsets

The open Web device Compliance Review Board (CRB) and its members, Alcatel One Touch, Deutsche Telekom, Mozilla, Qualcomm Technologies Inc. and Telefonica, have announced the first devices to be certified by CRB, which is an independent firm established to encourage the open Web device ecosystem by promoting API compliance and ensuring competitive performance. The two handsets are Alcatel ONETOUCH Fire C and Alcatel ONETOUCH Fire E.

Established in 2004, Alcatel Mobile Phones is a joint venture between Alcatel-Lucent and TCL Communication. The validation process includes OEMs applying to the CRB for their handsets to be approved. CRB's labs not only check the device for open Web APIs and key performance benchmarks, but also compare the results with the benchmarks set by the CRB.

The process is open to all device vendors including CRB members and non-members. The certification process has been published on the CRB website: *www.openwebdevice.org*

Jason Bremner, senior vice president of product management, Qualcomm Technologies, said that he was glad to know that the board has accomplished one of its major objectives in certifying Firefox OS devices on a standard set of Web APIs and performance metrics. The expectation is that other firms will improve their product development cycle time and ensure a convincing user experience with compliance to standard Web APIs.

Calibre 2.30.0 supports automatic conversion of newly added books

Calibre 2.30.0 introduces a new option that allows users to automatically convert printed books to e-books immediately after they have been added in the library, enabled by using *Preferences -> Adding Books*.

The e-book viewer component of Calibre has been improved to display the full text of a truncated Table of Contents (ToC) in a pop-up menu when the user moves the mouse cursor over the respective item. Additionally, Calibre 2.30.0 adds support for disabling verification of SSL (Secure Sockets Layer) certificates in individual recipes in the *News downloader* component of the software.

In Calibre 2.30.0, some of the most annoying bugs that have been reported by users since the previous version of the application, Calibre 2.29.0, have also been fixed. For example, two issues in the *DOCX Output* component have been patched, one related to the aspect ratio of images and the other to extra page breaks.

Besides, the broken *smarten punctuation* in the *LIT Input* component has been patched to work for text based LIT files instead of HTML based ones, the *Book details* panel has been improved for Windows users, and the EPUB metadata extraction functionality works better for cover images from EPUB 3 and EPUB 2 files.

Last but not the least, there's a fix for the broken *Saved Searches* panel in the *Edit Book* component. Calibre 2.30.0 also adds a workaround for a Mac OS X bug that caused the application to display multiple 'email to selected recipients...' messages when the users attempted to change the preferences in the *Connect/Share* menu.

development, alongside a new container based service.

Red Hat Cloud Suite for Applications helps solve these challenges by providing both Infrastructure-as-a-Service (IaaS) for massive scalability and Platform-as-a-Service (PaaS) for faster application delivery, combined with a unified management framework that supports hybrid deployment models. As the industry's first fully open source, integrated IaaS and PaaS solution, the Red Hat Cloud Suite for Applications enables customers to avoid cloud silos and empowers them to select their service model to best meet changing business requirements.

By integrating OpenShift with OpenStack, users not only have access to a faster way to develop, deploy and manage applications, they also have access to a full suite of middleware and mobility services. In addition, Red Hat Cloud Suite for Applications also supports a broad range of certified hardware, servers and third-party plugins, offering users expanded choices for their cloud stack.

Says Paul Cormier, president, products and technologies, Red Hat, "Combining these powerful cloud offerings addresses a significant customer need to reduce silos and enable more efficient OpenStack cloud deployments. While other companies can provide one or two of the building blocks for a cloud, Red Hat is the only vendor that can offer IaaS, PaaS and management in an open environment, backed by the strength of Red Hat Enterprise Linux and the ability to leverage certified hardware of their choice."

Gary Chen, research manager, cloud and virtualisation system software, IDC, reports, "Open source is driving significant innovations in cloud computing. Today, we see increasing convergence between IaaS and PaaS. By bringing these open source solutions together, along with integrated management, Red Hat is enabling customers to take advantage of this cloud convergence with a fully open source, integrated stack offering."

Red Hat extends enterprise management for OpenStack with CloudForms

Red Hat Inc. has announced Red Hat CloudForms 3.2, the latest version of its award-winning solution for managing private and hybrid clouds. CloudForms 3.2 delivers innovative management features that enable customers to automate  the deployment and management of OpenStack infrastructures, using the advanced management instrumentation available in the Red Hat Enterprise Linux OpenStack Platform 7 release (based on OpenStack Kilo). CloudForms 3.2 comes with additional OpenStack workload management capabilities including automated discovery, Web based console support, service catalogue publishing and user dialogue generation for OpenStack Orchestration (Heat) templates. It also has deeper image and workload introspection capabilities with OpenStack Image Service (Glance) and OpenStack Compute (Nova) integration, and improved capacity and utilisation management through expanded OpenStack Telemetry (Ceilometer) integration. These new capabilities in CloudForms represent a step forward in the manageability of OpenStack in the enterprise. CloudForms is the industry's first open source cloud management platform that manages both the OpenStack infrastructure as well as workloads from a single, integrated platform.

In addition, CloudForms is able to integrate OpenStack based private clouds together with other public clouds and a variety of virtualisation platforms, including VMware vSphere, Red Hat Enterprise Virtualization, Amazon Web Services (AWS) and Microsoft System Center Virtual Machine Manager. Advanced capabilities including a self-service portal, policy based control, governance, chargeback, showback, orchestration, capacity/utilisation planning, optimisation, and bottleneck analysis and reporting allow enterprises to more effectively manage hybrid cloud environments.

CloudForms has significantly helped customers accelerate their OpenStack implementations, and these new capabilities in CloudForms 3.2 provide an efficient and scalable migration framework across traditional virtualisation platforms and private clouds based on OpenStack. They enable enterprises to implement a bi-modal IT set-up, in which a new agility-optimised infrastructure coexists with traditional efficiency-optimised data centres and with workloads unified by a common management platform.

Other improvements in CloudForms 3.2 include support for the AWS Config service enabling near-real-time monitoring of changes in workloads deployed to AWS, Japanese language support, IPv6 support, and improved bare-metal provisioning and management through integration with Red Hat Satellite 6.

CloudForms 3.2 has become available to existing CloudForms customers in June 2015. OpenStack infrastructure management features in CloudForms 3.2 require OpenStack Kilo capabilities, which are scheduled to be available in the upcoming release of Red Hat Enterprise Linux OpenStack Platform 7.

Oracle and the community celebrate 20 years of Java

Oracle users and the development community worldwide are celebrating 20 years of Java. "Today, Java serves as the critical backbone of software that touches both our work and personal lives. From innovations in enterprise Big Data, the cloud, social media, the mobile and the Internet of Things, to connected cars, smartphones and

video games, Java continues to help developers push the boundaries in technology innovation. Java has grown and evolved to become one of the most important and dependable technologies in our industry today. Those who have chosen Java have been rewarded many times over with increases in performance, scalability, reliability, compatibility and functionality," said Georges Saab, vice president of development, Java Platform Group at Oracle. "The Java ecosystem offers outstanding libraries, frameworks, and resources to help programmers from novices to experts, alike. The development of Java itself occurs in the transparent OpenJDK community. With the considerable investment from Oracle and others in the community, we look forward to the next 20 years of Java's evolution and growth," Saab continued.

"IBM is celebrating Java's 20th anniversary as one of the most important industry-led programming platforms spanning mobile, client and enterprise software platforms. IBM began its commitment to Java at its inception over two decades ago, and has seen the Java ecosystem and developer community bring unsurpassed value to the investments our clients have made in their Java based solutions," said Harish Grama, vice president, middleware products, IBM Systems.

Introduced in 1995, Java is the programming language of choice for 9 million developers and today powers 7 billion devices. Improving road and air safety, collecting information from the world's oceans for science applications, increasing grain crop quality and quantity to help feed the hungry, simulating

Mozilla officially launches Thunderbird 31.7.0 with security and memory fixes

The development of the Thunderbird email client is no longer in the hands of the Mozilla developers, but in those of its dedicated community. Mozilla no longer considers Thunderbird to be an attractive project and doesn't want to invest any more time and money on it, so the reins have been handed over to some developers willing to do this on the side. This means that most of the updates usually just integrate security fixes, although some fixes do slip in, from time to time. According to the changelog, a privilege escalation issue through IPC channel messages has been fixed, a buffer overflow that occurred when parsing compressed XML has been fixed, and the 'use-after-free' feature during text processing with vertical text has been enabled. Also, a buffer overflow that happened with SVG and CSS content has been fixed, various memory safety hazards have been corrected, and a buffer overflow that occurred when parsing H.264 videos with Gstreamer on Linux has been repaired.

Play Store update for Android TV arrives!

The Play Store client for Android TV devices has got a new version, courtesy Google. The latest Play Store update for Android TV comes with over 600 applications and games. In addition, it expands the visible app catalogue considerably. Before the update, most of the apps of Android TV were accessible only via search on Play Store. Only a handful of applications were available otherwise. A Venture Beat report states that the latest version of Play Store offers 20 new curated collections like multiplayer games, everyday apps, et al, making app-discovery convenient on Android TV devices.

Protecode audit dissects a typical software portfolio

Protecode has recently compiled data that displays the consolidated findings from an audit of more than a million software files that belong to over hundred technology enterprises. Located in Ontario, Canada, Protecode is an open source licence management solution, which offers code auditing services to identify all open source, third party and related licensing obligations before a product release or acquisition. The audits were performed, fulfilling M&A due diligence, between 2010 and 2014. Much heed was paid to detection of open source versus proprietary and commercial software, and open source software with licences that could force publication of proprietary code, highlighting security vulnerabilities, and in some cases, focusing on potential exposure to export control policies mainly due to the encryption functions in the software.

According to the recently released report, in small portfolios, 18 per cent of software files contain copyleft OSS licences; in medium-sized portfolios, 13 per cent of software files contain copyleft OSS licences; and in large portfolios, 7 per cent of software files contain these licences. On the other hand, in small portfolios, 50 per cent of proprietary files are with no header information. This figure is almost 17 per cent and 4 per cent for medium portfolios and large portfolios, respectively.

While 0.1 per cent of files have been found with security vulnerabilities in small portfolios, 0.5 per cent of such files have been found in medium portfolios, which increased to 8.8 per cent in large portfolios.

If we talk about the percentage of software files containing encryption functions, 5.6 per cent of files in small portfolios contain these functions. The figures are 2.1 per cent and 38.1 per cent of files in medium portfolios and large portfolios, respectively.

the human brain and musculo-skeletal system, and gaming are some of the intriguing projects worldwide that use Java.

Enterprise developers can choose from an ecosystem of 30 Java EE 6 and Java EE 7 compatible implementations from 12 vendors. Additionally, more than 125 million Java based media devices have been deployed and over 10 billion Java Cards have been shipped since Java's introduction.

BQ set to launch second Ubuntu phone this month!

Although the Ubuntu OS for mobiles has not been able to make much of an

impact, this hasn't discouraged BQ, the company supporting the operating system. The Spanish firm has revealed its plans of coming up with its second Ubuntu phone this month. The BQ Aquaris E5 HD Ubuntu Edition, as the phone will be known as, will be available in Europe in mid-June, state some online reports. The smartphone will be priced at 199.99 euros. Alberto Méndez of BQ, said, "Working with Canonical on bringing out the Aquaris E5 Ubuntu Edition has been very satisfying. We share the same philosophy, along with the same commitment to open source initiatives. At BQ, our goal is to help people understand technology, encourage them to use it and inspire them to create it. That's why the opportunity for creation that Ubuntu affords is fundamentally important to us."

According to the team at Ubuntu, "The new device comes with a host of impressive features including a 12.7cm (5 inch) display with IPS HD technology, an HD screen resolution of 720 x 1280 pixels and 380 cd/m2 maximum brightness. It also includes a MediaTek quad-core Cortex A7 processor that runs at up to 1.3GHz, an internal memory of 16GB and 1GB of RAM. Additionally, it features a 5 megapixel front camera and a 13 megapixel rear camera, and is equipped with high quality Largan lenses and BSI sensors. Other features of note include dual flash and full HD video recording (1080p)."

The Aquaris E5 Ubuntu Edition comes fully unlocked and its dual SIM functionality allows users to select their operator. They can use SIMs from two different operators, the official website states.

BQ is not the only company working on the Ubuntu operating system. Chinese smartphone maker Meizu will soon offer competition to BQ's device in Europe (it's only available in China so far). The Meizu MX4 Ubuntu edition will be available for the price of 299.99 euros.

Meizu MX4 Ubuntu Edition comes packed with a 13.5cm (5.3 inch) full HD IPS display, a 2GHz octa-core MediaTek MT6595 processor, 2GB of RAM, a 20.7MP rear camera, a 2MP front-facing shooter, and a 3100mAh battery.

HP unveils developer-focused testing solution to help businesses accelerate application delivery

HP has announced a new functional test automation solution, the HP LeanFT, which allows software developers and testers to leverage continuous testing and continuous delivery methodologies to rapidly build, test and deliver secure, high quality applications. The solution enables organisations to achieve faster time to market, higher predictability and quality, and lower overall costs throughout the development lifecycle. "Modern approaches like agile and continuous delivery empower developers and help businesses unlock creativity," said Jonathon Wright, director, testing and quality assurance at Hitachi.

Businesses today must act with speed and agility, to continuously capitalise on opportunities to deliver new solutions and experiences, business models and revenue streams. In software development, this has fuelled the rise of the agile methodology, which embraces a continuous delivery process, rather than a phased, sequential approach. For software testing, this means developers and testers seek to 'shift left' and continuously test their applications much earlier in the application development lifecycle.

HP LeanFT is cost-effective and fits naturally into existing ecosystems (such as Microsoft TFS, GIT and Subversion) and frameworks that support test driven and behaviour driven development. It has powerful test automation authoring with either C# or Java, and IDE integration. Together, HP Software and HP Enterprise Services deliver a solution that is designed to provide customers with the following benefits.

Faster time-to-market: HP LeanFT provides a comprehensive set of tools designed to accelerate test design and maintenance, including an Object Identification Centre, used to automatically generate code and abstraction models for applications under test.

High predictability: HP LeanFT provides project templates for standard unit-testing frameworks, including NUnit, MSTest and JUnit, to improve collaboration and alignment between software developers and test automation engineers. This enables a reduction in the time needed to test applications, and allows developers to predict and identify defects earlier in the software development lifecycle.

Lower costs: HP LeanFT fully integrates with and provides plugins for popular IDEs such as Microsoft Visual Studio and Eclipse. Tests are authored in the IDEs using C# (in Visual Studio) or Java (in Eclipse). This allows developers and testers to work in the same environments utilising the same tools.

Built-in security: In conjunction with HP LeanFT, HP Application Defender enables the rapid discovery of software vulnerabilities during both the development and test phases, where code changes are less costly. Using runtime technology from HP

Fortify, HP Application Defender does not require specialised security expertise and offers continuous, real-time vulnerability testing.

Trusted expertise: In support of this latest launch, HP Enterprise Services has updated its Testing and Quality Assurance Services to support HP LeanFT projects. The new services help clients working in agile and DevOps environments to deliver key applications faster, cheaper, and with higher quality. The services expand HPES' testing and quality assurance capabilities for identifying and eliminating defects in the application development lifecycle management process, ultimately helping businesses accelerate time to market and deliver winning applications.

Nitin Gadkari launches indigenous software for small enterprises

India's transport minister recently launched the Kalculate Business Desktop for small and medium enterprises. Based on the Linux platform, this indigenous software is in keeping with the Indian government's vision to 'Make in India' and export to the world.

Transport minister Nitin Gadkari recently released indigenous software called Kalculate Business Desktop, which is aimed at small and medium enterprises. Also known as KBD, the software will apparently enable firms to do their accounting, inventory, sales and purchase functions in an economical way.

The event was attended by Virender Singh, MP from Bhadohi; Ashwini Mahajan, co-convenor, Swadeshi Jagran Manch; Vishwas Tripathi, chairman, UNI; Naresh Sirohi, advisor, Kisan Channel; Shabir Ali, MP; and Babu Dev Apte, ex-MP, apart from many others.

Addressing the gathering at the event, the minister said that 'Make in India' and Made in India would go hand in hand in the years to come. He pointed out the significance of biotechnology and information technology for the country's future, and stressed on reducing dependence on imports, promoting exports and transforming knowledge into wealth.

KBD is built on the Linux platform in accordance with the government's new open source policy. As it is integrated with the Openlx Linux operating system, the user gets an office suite, operating system, graphics and multimedia applications, and an Internet suite of applications.

Additionally, the software allows business users to get the advantages of an inexpensive, secure, virus-free environment with a user-friendly GUI by merging Openlx Linux with Kalculate business accounting software.

KBD is aimed at companies that are compelled to use pirated software as they cannot afford the high cost of proprietary software. By using KBD, the total cost of business software for a firm will drop to Rs 9999.

Addressing the audience, Gadkari said that Prime Minister Modi had often emphasised the importance of the Digital India drive, e-governance and other technological innovations for the development of the country. While the Digital India initiative aims to make government services available to Indian citizens electronically, e-governance ensures that the services reach citizens through the electronic media. The Digital India programme also intends to connect rural areas with high-speed Internet networks.

Gadkari mentioned that lack of knowledge is the biggest problem in India, and added that *'gyan, vigyan and tantra vigyan'* are significant for a nation's progress.

Sudhir Gandotra, CEO, Openlx, said, "Being an Indian company, we have always looked forward to manufacturing products in our country, which will be exported. The vision is to create Indian products that will become renowned across the world. Creating IT products in our country will help to create infrastructure and jobs. Indian technological innovations will push us towards progress."

The 'Make in India' initiative of the government of India was introduced by Prime Minister Narendra Modi on September 25, 2014, in a function at the Vigyan Bhawan in New Delhi. It aims to turn India into a global manufacturing hub, and focuses on 25 sectors of the economy for job creation and skills enhancement. These include industries like automobiles, pharmaceuticals, chemicals, mining, biotechnology, IT, leather, textiles, ports, aviation, tourism and hospitality, auto components, design manufacturing, wellness, railways, electronics and renewable energy.

It is the concept of 'Make in India' that is driving initiatives like Openlx, which has been launched with the aim of helping SMEs and SOHOs in India. END

By: Anurima Mondal

The author is a member of the EFY Times team at the EFY Group. She loves to explore new innovations in the technology world.

SELECTING THE RIGHT MULTI-FUNCTIONAL PRINTERS

Printing and managing documents has become one of the most important functions for any business. Today, in an era in which technology offers so many choices, selecting a multi-functional printer to suit your business can be confusing. Here are a few tips...

With huge amounts of information being shared even in small, start-up offices every day, having a cost-effective printing solution is a must. There are several solutions available in the market to meet your printing and document management requirements. Here's a guide to minimise your confusion and help you to take the right decision. It is always recommended that SMEs invest in a device that has capabilities beyond just printing. Such devices are commonly referred to as all-in-one printers (AIOs), multi-functional printers (MFPs) or even multi-functional devices (MFDs).

There are several aspects that need to be looked into while selecting a good MFP. The first thing to figure out, before you start exploring different options, is the printing, copying, scanning and other document handling requirements of the office. When searching for solutions for office use, you probably have to concentrate more on the quality of the text printing, rather than that of photos, which means you may need a laser printer that has a copier and scanning facility. An MFP with a fax, an automatic document feeder (ADF) to scan and the capability to send email will be an added advantage.

Features that you need to know about

All MFPs come with the basic features of printing, copying and scanning. A few have fax and emailing facilities too. Which one you opt for would depend on specific requirements. You have to decide whether you need an MFP with a fax, or whether you need a printer to just take colour and black and white prints, or whether the requirement is of a good quality scanner. If you need a good scanner, then you have to also decide on your scanning requirements, such as, whether you need an ADF or a flatbed scanner or a flatbed with ADF.

Apart from the features of the MFP you also need to have a look at the features available in the software bundled with it. There are many devices available in the market that can perform well only when connected to PCs with the relevant software installed.

Capacity, paper size and speed

While looking for printers, we must be clear about the exact capacity of the paper-holding trays. It would be very inconvenient to keep replenishing papers every now and then. One should also check the paper size supported. Speed of printing is the next thing we should look at while selecting any MFP. While you might assume that the printers capable of printing faster are better for your business, the reality is, your company's requirements might only justify purchasing a printer of a certain speed. Since features like high speed come at a price, it makes no sense paying for something you do not require. It's always recommended that you select a device that gives you the best ROI.

Connectivity

MFPs have various connectivity options. You can connect them to a system using a USB device or can connect through an Ethernet port. Most printers are also now available with Wi-Fi options. If you select a printer with Wi-Fi connectivity, do remember to ensure that you have a Wi-Fi network in place. There are other options too, but the most common are the ones mentioned above.

A few factors that may influence your decision are:

- The average number of prints that you need per month
- The quality of the scanner
- Connectivity options for communicating with the MFP
- Availability of duplex printing option
- Software compatibility with different operating systems
- Fax capability
- Printing cost per page
- Cost of toner/ink

SOME OF THE MFPS
AVAILABLE IN THE MARKET THAT YOU COULD CHOOSE FROM

HP LaserJet Pro 400 MFP M425dn

Price: ₹ 43,623

Functions: Print, copy, scan and fax
Print technology and type: Laser and mono
Duty cycle (monthly): 50,000 pages
Print speed: 35 ppm (normal, letter)
Duplex printing: Automatic
ADF: Yes
Connectivity: USB and Ethernet

Ricoh SP 310SFN

Price: ₹ 28,354

Functions: Print, copy, scan and fax
Print technology and type: Laser and mono
Duty cycle (monthly): 50,000 pages
Paper size: A4, B5, A5, B6, A6, legal, letter, HLT, executive and folio
Print speed: 28 ppm (A4)
Duplex printing: Automatic
ADF: Yes
Connectivity: USB and Ethernet

Canon imageCLASS MF229dw

Price: ₹ 32,744

Functions: Print, copy, scan and fax
Print technology and type: Laser and mono
Duty cycle (monthly): 10,000 pages
Paper size: A4, letter, oficio, B-oficio, M-oficio, Indian legal and foolscap
Print speed: 27 ppm (A4)
Duplex printing: Automatic
ADF: Yes
Connectivity: USB and Ethernet

Samsung SL-M2876ND

Price: ₹ 15,999

Functions: Print, copy, scan and fax
Print technology and type: Laser and mono
Duty cycle (monthly): 12,000 pages
Paper size: A4, A5, A6, letter, legal, executive, folio and oficio
Print speed: 28 ppm (A4)
Duplex printing: Automatic
ADF: Yes
Connectivity: USB and Ethernet

Note: Details regarding products have been taken from the Internet.

By: Aashima Sharma

The author is a member of the editorial team at EFY.

Sandya Mannarswamy

In this month's column, we take a break from our discussion on natural language processing (NLP) to feature a set of questions in computer science for our student readers.

In the last few columns, we have been discussing different aspects of NLP. This month, we feature a set of interview questions. While the questions generally cover the areas of algorithms and operating systems, I was requested by a couple of students to feature questions relating to machine learning, data science and NLP. So this month's question set features questions from all these areas.

1. Most of you will be familiar with Netflix's contest, in which the company offered a prize for a system that could suggest movies automatically for a user. Basically, given a movie and a particular user, it asked you to predict what would be the user's ratings for that movie. Contestants were given 480,189 users who had rated 17,770 movies. The training data set consisted of tuples of the form (user ID, movie ID, date of grade, grade given). For the test data set which consisted of tuples of the form (user ID, movie ID, date of grade), contestants had to predict the rating for each tuple in the test data set.

   a) Can you come up with an algorithm that would be able to do the prediction?

   b) The above problem belongs to the domain known as 'recommender systems', which applies to many domains including e-commerce, health care, education, etc. Let's assume that you have designed an algorithm for the above problem of movie ratings which works well. Now you are given a data set consisting of educational courses and users. The training data consists of the ratings given by the users for the courses. Just as in the earlier problem, you are asked to predict the rating for a course in the test data set for a given user. Would you be able to use the solution you created for question (a), as it is? If not, what are the changes that you would need to make?

   c) Consider problem (a) again, for which you are given large amounts of training data. But consider a scenario in which you have just started a movie rental company. So you have only 1000 samples of training data. In that case, how can you handle the problem 'cold start'?

2. In question (1) above, we considered the problem of collaborative filtering, in which users who have rated certain items in the past are now given suggestions on what items they might like in the future. Basically, consider the rating values represented in a two dimensional matrix of the form (Users X Movies), where each user is represented by a row in the movie and each column in the matrix stands for a movie. In the problem given above, the matrix is of the form (480,189 X 17,770) elements.

   • Given that each matrix element takes 4 bytes (an integer rating value), what would be the amount of memory needed to hold this matrix in memory?

   • Since each user would have watched only some of the movies among the total number of 17,740, he/she can provide ratings only for a few movies. Let us assume that a non-rated movie is given a special value of 0 whereas the valid ratings are from 1 to 5. In such a case, most of the matrix elements would be zero. So instead of occupying (480,189 X 17,770 X 4) bytes in memory, can you come up with an efficient way of storing the sparse matrix in memory and manipulating it?

3. What is A/B testing? If you are designing a website, how would you use A/B testing?

4. Most of you would be familiar with Map Reduce architecture and Hadoop, which is the most popular implementation of the former. Why is Map Reduce known as 'Shared Nothing' architecture? Can you give a high level overview of Hadoop architecture?

5. Following up on the above question, what are the performance bottlenecks associated with a traditional Hadoop cluster? In other words, is it CPU bound, memory bound or I/O bound? Consider that you have a Map Reduce application running on a four-node Hadoop cluster. You are given the following options:

a) You are allowed to increase the number of CPUs in each node from one to four.

b) You are allowed to increase the physical memory of each node from 8GB to 16GB.

c) You are allowed to use a different network communication channel, which has lower network latency.

d) You are allowed to use a different network communication channel, which has a higher network bandwidth.

e) You are allowed to replace the HDDs in each node with SSDs.

If you can choose only one of the above options, which would you choose? Explain the rationale behind your choice. Is your choice application dependent?

6. Can you explain the difference between linear regression and logistic regression? Can you use a linear regression technique to solve a logistic regression problem?

7. Let us consider the problem of predicting house prices in Bengaluru. Consider that your data set has a large number of features, say around 10,000. But you have training data only for 100 data points.

   a) How would you address the problem of overfitting the model to the limited training data?

   b) Are you familiar with L1 and L2 regularisation? What is the difference between the two?

8. What are the different machine learning algorithms that you have used? Can you compare decision trees, neural networks and support vector machines?

9. What is the well-known 'kernel trick' in machine learning? (We are not talking about the Linux kernel here.)

10. You are given a set of newspaper articles, which you have to categorise into four different categories such as politics, entertainment, sports and miscellaneous. What classification algorithm would you use to solve this problem for the following two cases?

    a) Your data set contains training data, for which you are given labelled categories for a set of documents.

    b) Your data set does not have any labelled instances.

11. Let us consider a binary classification problem in which you are asked to label emails as spam or non-spam. You are given a large enough training data set (100,000 emails), where the emails are already classified as spam or non-spam. Using this training data, you are asked to train a binary classifier, which can mark an incoming email as spam or non-spam. However, there is one problem with the training data that you have been given. Among the 100,000 emails, only 100 are labelled as spam. All other training data are of the non-spam category. What would be the problem if you train your model with such an unbalanced training data set? How would you address this issue?

12. We have all heard a lot about IBM's Watson system beating human contestants in the TV question and answer game 'Jeopardy'. Watson employs what is known as a 'deep parsing' pipeline for text processing. What is the difference between shallow parsing and deep parsing in natural language processing?

13. Consider the following two sentences:

    a) John bought a car.

    b) A car was bought by John.

    Can a shallow parsing system figure out that the two sentences are semantically equivalent? If not, what part of the NLP can determine that these two sentences are equivalent?

14. You are all familiar with product review systems used in various websites such as Amazon product reviews, TripAdvisor's review of hotels or Yelp's review of restaurants. We also know that many of the reviews can be fake, having been seeded by sellers themselves or by a competitor (if it is an adverse review). How would you design a system to filter only the 'useful' reviews for a given product? While filtering out fake reviews is a basic necessity, among the non-fake reviews, how would you give different weightage to different users?

15. You are given a large text document and asked to create a summary of it. There are two types of summarisation algorithms, namely, extractive vs abstractive summarisation. In extractive summarisation, the summary would contain sentences extracted from the text. In abstractive summarisation, the summary would contain the gist of the original text, without including the exact sentences from the text. What kind of summarisation algorithm would you choose? Explain the rationale behind your choice. Now assume that there is a real-time conversation that is going on. How would you create a running summary of it?

If you are interested in doing some data science experiments, Kaggle (*www.kaggle.com*) is a good place to start. There are generally a number of active competitions on, some of which are for learning purpose only. Currently, it's running a competition on sentiment analysis of movie reviews, which you may want to enter (*https://www.kaggle.com/c/word2vec-nlp-tutorial*).

If you have any favourite programming questions/software topics that you would like to discuss on this forum, please send them to me, along with your solutions and feedback, at *sandyasm_AT_yahoo_DOT_com*. Till we meet again next month, happy programming! END

By: Sandya Mannarswamy

The author is an expert in systems software and is currently in that happy land between jobs. Her interests include compilers, storage systems and natural language processing. If you are preparing for systems software interviews, you may find it useful to visit Sandya's LinkedIn group *Computer Science Interview Training India* at *http://www.linkedin.com/ groups?home=HYPERLINK "http://www.linkedin.com/groups? home=&gid=2339182"&HYPERLINK "http://www.linkedin.com/ groups?home=&gid=2339182"gid=2339182*

As personal, corporate and even national computer systems get subjected to stealthy, continuous cracking processes, it makes sense to be warned and armed. Read on to find out more about one high profile case of a silent malicious cyber attack (APT) that brought a country's nuclear programme to its knees – Stuxnet.

Advanced persistent threats or APTs are a kind of cyber attack that can go undetected for a long period of time. The objective of the attack is:

- To extricate vital data rather than cause damage.
- To gain access to the network or host.

The typical characteristics of APTs are listed below.

Advanced: They are highly sophisticated and targeted.

Persistent: They put in a lot of effort to achieve their goal and to reach the target.

Threatening: They have a newly generated payload compared to the conventional, target-specific payloads — something not known to security personnel.

In an APT, the attackers deface the network, plant advanced malware and hide themselves until they receive the command to get off the target. An advanced persistent threat uses a step-by-step approach.

Intrusion kill chain

"Intrusion kill chain is crucial, but it's not enough." -Peter Tran.

The intrusion kill chain (also known as a 'kill chain', a 'cyber kill chain' or 'attack cycles') is a model used to execute the successful pathway towards segmenting, analysing and mitigating the cyber attack. Various stages of attacks are performed in order to gain access to the target.

1. **Reconnaissance:** This is the initial stage of identifying and selecting the target. All the relevant information about the target is obtained by crawling the Internet (social engineering) to get personal information like email, social media ID, etc.
2. **Weaponisation:** At this stage, a RAT (remote administration tool or a Trojan) is encapsulated with any client application which is likely to be an executable.
3. **Delivery:** During this stage, the weaponised executable

is transferred to the target via email, suspicious links, USB media, etc.

4. **Exploitation:** Once the executable is delivered to the victim, the payload triggers the Trojan and exploits the operating system's vulnerability or targets a specific app.

5. **Installation:** Installation allows the Trojan and attacker to remain in close proximity.

6. **Command and control server:** A command and control server is used to control the Trojan installed in the target via remote access.

7. **Actions and goals:** After six stages of progress, the goal is accomplished by compromising the host.

The intrusion kill chain often takes many days for a successful attack to take place. It is very hard to identify these chain processes due to their 'stepping stone' behaviour (compromising multiple hosts to reach the target). It's very difficult to identify the first three stages of the attack cycle.

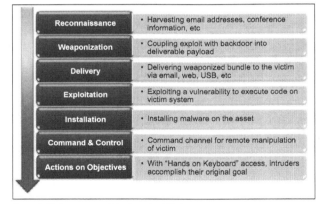

Figure 1: APT anatomy

APT vs traditional malware

Traditional viruses/ malware	APT
Targets random networks/ hosts	Targets specific networks/ hosts
Probability of getting detected by antivirus is high as signatures get detected	A combination of malware is used. Signatures go undetected because of this
The effects become visible over a period of time, as large networks/hosts get infected	The idea is to lie low over a significant period of time
A good firewall or intrusion detection system can prevent entry by signature checking	It is carried mostly through content, which uses well known ports (80, 443, etc) and known protocols like http, https, etc

Reconnaissance	• Harvesting email addresses, conference information, etc
Weaponization	• Coupling exploit with backdoor into deliverable payload
Delivery	• Delivering weaponized bundle to the victim via email, web, USB, etc
Exploitation	• Exploiting a vulnerability to execute code on victim system
Installation	• Installing malware on the asset
Command & Control	• Command channel for remote manipulation of victim
Actions on Objectives	• With "Hands on Keyboard" access, intruders accomplish their original goal

Figure 2: Various stages of the intrusion kill chain

Zero day exploits

A zero day exploit is a computer application vulnerability which is unpatched and previously not known to security vendors. These security holes are exploited by the attacker before the vendor becomes aware of the exploits. Zero day attacks include data infiltration and exfiltration malware, malicious code, etc. The best example of a zero day exploit is *Stuxnet*, which was named 'the first digital weapon'.

Stuxnet

Stuxnet, the first digital weapon, ranks No. 1 among zero day

vulnerabilities when it comes to causing collateral damage to computers in the real world. Stuxnet was first discovered in June 2010, and reportedly destroyed one-fifth of the centrifugal pumps of the Iranian nuclear facility. Stuxnet is specific to PLC boards and targets the rotator which spins them up and down. It has unique characteristics which differ from traditional payloads of various malware and Trojans. According to the Kaspersky report, once the Trojan hits the system, it automatically compromises the host PLC boards and sparks chaos.

Components of Stuxnet

Various aspects of Stuxnet differentiate it from other

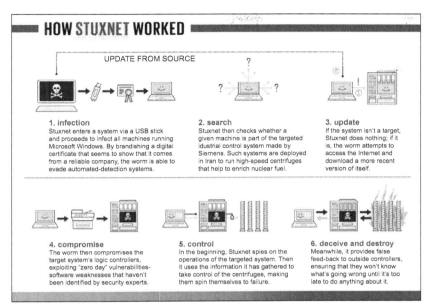

Figure 3: How Stuxnet worked

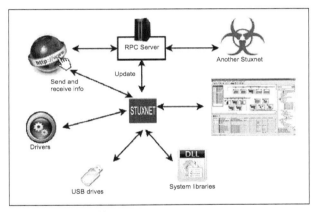

Figure 4: Components of Stuxnet

malicious software. These range from modifying system libraries, targeting the Step 7 SCADA controller, the use of a command and control server (via RPC), installation of malicious driver code in system software like drivers, etc. Stuxnet is also capable of downloading auto updates, which update an older version installed in a system. It recursively communicates to the command and control server covertly, to pass on information about its spread, the devices affected and possible ways of getting updated. Stuxnet auto updates via a built-in peer-to-peer network. This kind of auto updating leads to different versions and different attack vectors. The recent version of Stuxnet uses 'LNK vulnerabilities', whereas the older version uses *Autorun.inf*.

LNK vulnerability: Stuxnet registers the code in an infected Windows computer. Whenever USB drives are inserted, Stuxnet automatically copies the code to the drive. A very interesting fact is that the code will work to infect any of three machines. If the drive is already infected, a new version

of Stuxnet is updated to the drive for further infection. An LNK vulnerability contains four files with the *.lnk* extension in addition to Stuxnet DLL, which are used to execute the payload in different versions of Windows.

Autorun.inf: Autorun.inf is an auto run file which automatically runs the code in USB drives whenever the drive is inserted in a Windows machine. Here, the command and code for infection is inserted and configured in the *autorun.inf* file. Hence, the Windows OS ignores the Stuxnet data portion in the *autorun.inf* file.

WinCC

WinCC is an interface to SCADA systems; Stuxnet searches for WinCC and connects to the database via a hard-coded password. It then attacks the database using SQL commands by uploading and replicating a copy of code on a WinCC computer.

Network shares

Stuxnet can use Windows' shared folders to propagate itself in a LAN. It drops and schedules a dropper file to execute it on remote computers.

Print spooler vulnerability (MS10-061)

Stuxnet copies and shares itself to remote computers using this vulnerability and then executes itself to infect the remote computers. In general, Stuxnet replicates into two, and then it copies itself into the *C:\Windows\system* folder with zero day privilege escalation and infects the computer.

SMB vulnerability (MS08-067)

Server message block (SMB) is a network file-sharing protocol. Stuxnet modifies the path and sends data through a malformed path between remote computers.

Step7 project vulnerability

Stuxnet infects the executable of WinCC Simatic manager and modifies the shared libraries, DLLs, libraries for shared objects, code and data. Then it copies the additional code into the step7 directory, and connects to the command and control server for remote execution of payloads.

The attack phase

Stuxnet consists of two modules—the user module and kernel module.

User module: In the user module, there are several functions to do the following operations. First, Stuxnet itself injects malware code into the actual running process. This results in the execution of the malware code in the target address

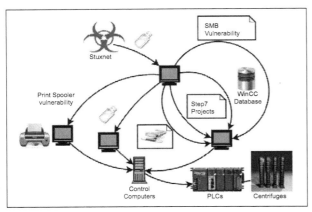

Figure 5: Stuxnet makes use of vulnerabilities to reach the target PLCs

How to figure out if you are a victim of APT attacks

Here's a list of things you must do to spot an APT attack before it is too late:

- An APT may go unnoticed by a single antivirus/intrusion detection system; multi-level defence is required.
- Analysing network layered packets is a good way to keep a check.
- Log analysis from various sources with co-relation may help in early detection.
- You must monitor end points for suspicious behaviour.
- Good asset management should be in place to guard critical systems.
- Monitoring critical assets is very important.

space. Then it checks for the appropriate platform (Export 15 Stuxnet routine to check for appropriate Windows version) to execute the code; if the machine is already infected, zero day vulnerabilities are used for escalating privileges. Finally, it installs (Export 16 Stuxnet routine for installation) two kernel drivers (*Mrxnet.sys* and *Mrxcls.sys*) - one for execution of Stuxnet after reboot and the other to hide the files.

Kernel module: Kernel module consists of two dropped driver files, namely, *Mrxnet.sys* and *Mrxcls.sys*. The latter is a driver used to mark itself as startup in the early stages of a boot. This driver takes responsibility for reading the registry and contains information for injecting Stuxnet code. *Mrxnet.sys* is used to hide the Stuxnet files; it creates the device object and attaches it to the system object (*s7otbxdx.dll*) of step7 to monitor all the requests.

Interestingly, as in the case of sabotaging the Iranian nuclear programme, Stuxnet monitored and recorded the normal operating frequency of centrifuges and fed the recorded data to the WinCC monitor during the attack. If the operator found the centrifuges are not operating normally, then Stuxnet shut itself down to a safe mode to remain undetected.

References

[1] https://blogs.sophos.com/2014/04/11/how-do-apts-work-the-lifecycle-of-advanced-persistent-threats-infographic/
[2] http://en.wikipedia.org/wiki/Zero-day_attack
[3] http://en.wikipedia.org/wiki/Advanced_persistent_threat
[4] http://www.stuxnet.net/
[5] http://www.wired.com/2014/11/countdown-to-zero-day-stuxnet/
[6] http://www.engadget.com/2014/11/13/stuxnet-worm-targeted-companies-first/
[7] Paul Mueller and Babak Yadegari, 'Report on The Stuxnet Worm'
[8] http://www.symantec.com/connect/w32_duqu_precursor_next_stuxnet

By: Sibi Chakkaravarthy Sethuraman

The author holds an M. Tech degree in computer science and engineering, and is currently pursuing a PhD at Anna University. Currently he is with AU-KBC Research Centre, MIT, Chennai. His research interests include network security, wireless security, wireless sensor networks, cloud security, etc. He can be reached at sb(DOT)sibi(AT)gmail(DOT)com.

OSFY Magazine Attractions During 2015-16

MONTH	THEME	BUYERS' GUIDE
March 2015	Open Source Firewall and Network security	SSD for Servers
April 2015	Web Development	Network Switches
May 2015	Virtualisation (containers)	Wireless Routers for SME
June 2015	Open source Databases	PaaS Solution
July 2015	Network Monitoring	MFD Printers for SMEs
August 2015	Mobile App Development	Hosting Solutions
September 2015	Backup and Data Storage	External HDD
October 2015	Mobile App Development	IaaS Solution
November 2015	Cloud Special	Firewall and UTMs
December 2015	Open Source on Windows	Online Backup solutions
January 2016	Android Special	Wifi Hotspot Devices
February 2016	Top 10 of Everything	External Storage

Monitorix: The Lightweight System Monitoring Tool

This article introduces readers to Monitorix, which can be a boon to systems administrators as well as those who like to keep tabs on their systems.

Administrators and, for that matter, typical users, often need to monitor servers for system resources like disk or CPU utilisation and other parameters to know how well the system is performing. There are many sophisticated system monitoring software such as Cacti, Munin and Nagios. Monitorix is a free, open source, lightweight system monitoring tool, designed to monitor many services and system resources.

Written in Perl, Monitorix has an inbuilt HTTP server. It consists of two programs—a collector called *monitorix,* which is a Perl daemon that is started automatically like any other system service, and a CGI script called *monitorix.cgi.*

Features

Here is a list of Monitorix's main features. For a more complete list, refer to the official site.
- System load and system service demand
- CPU/GPU temperature sensors
- Disk temperature and health

- Network/port traffic and netstat statistics
- Mail statistics
- Web server statistics (Apache, Nginx, Lighttpd)
- MySQL load and statistics
- Squid proxy statistics
- NFS server/client statistics
- Raspberry Pi sensor statistics
- Memcached statistics
- Fail2ban statistics
- Monitors remote servers (Multihost)
- Enables users to view statistics in graphs or in plain text tables on a daily, weekly, monthly or yearly basis
- Offers the capability to zoom graphs for a better view
- Has the capability to define the number of graphs per row

Prerequisites

For this article, I have chosen CentOS 6.6, 64-bit version, with minimal installation, which is equivalent to Red Hat 6.6. The steps are the same on CentOS 7 with just a few modifications in the commands.
1. Check the status of SELinux by using the command *sestatus.* If it is not disabled, then turn off SELinux, simply by changing *Enforcing* to *Disabled* in the */etc/selinux/config* file.

With **7500+** registrations, we lived up to our tag of

Asia's #1 Open Source Conference

Thank You

VISITORS, for making the event a huge success

SPEAKERS, for contributing your valuable thoughts

PARTNERS, for your support

  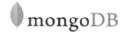

Announcing the 12th Edition

12th Edition

OPEN SOURCE INDIA

19 - 20 November 2015

NIMHANS Convention Center | BENGALURU

It's going to be **BIGGER & BETTER**

For more details, call on 011-40596605 or email us at info@osidays.com

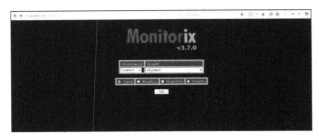

Figure 1: Monitorix Web interface

Figure 2: System load average, active processes and memory allocation

Figure 3: Global kernel usage

```
SELINUX=disabled
```

If it is in the enabled state, then graphs are not visible and you will get tons of error messages in the */var/log/messages* or */var/log/audit/audit.log* files about access denied to RRD database files.

Till rebooting the system, SElinux is in temporary disabled mode. After rebooting it is permanently get disabled.

2. Install the EPEL repository for extra package dependencies and enable it:

```
## RHEL/CentOS 6 64-Bit ##
# wget http://download.fedoraproject.org/pub/epel/6/x86_64/
epel-release-6-8.noarch.rpm
#rpm -ivh epel-release-6-8.noarch.rpm
```

If it is not enabled, set *enabled=1* in */etc/yum.repos.d/epel.repo*

Installing Monitorix on RHEL/CentOS

Log in with root privileges. Download the *monitorix rpm* package, as follows:

```
#wget -c http://www.monitorix.org/monitorix-3.7.0-1.noarch.rpm
```

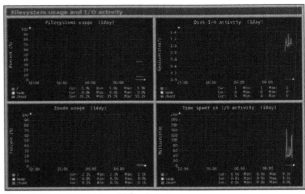

Figure 4: File system usage and I/O activity

Install the required packages:

```
#yum install rrdtool rrdtool-perl perl-libwww-perl perl-
MailTools perl-MIME-Lite perl-CGI perl-DBI perl-XML-Simple perl-
Config-General  perl-HTTP-Server-Simple perl-IO-Socket-SSL
```

Install *monitorix rpm:*

To install *monitorix rpm* using yum should be at the same path where *rpm* package is downloaded. Remaining at the same path where *monitorix rpm* downloaded, run below command:

```
#yum install monitorix-3.6.0-1.noarch.rpm
```

Start the Monitorix service:

```
#service monitorix start
```

To make Monitorix start at boot time, type:

```
#chkconfig --level 345 monitorix  on
```

Configuration

The main configuration file is */etc/monitorix/monitorix.conf.* Before changing parameters, take a backup of this file:

```
#cp -pRvf /etc/monitorix/monitorix.conf    /etc/monitorix/
monitorix.conf _org
```

We can change the various parameters like the title, hostname, authentication, host allow, host deny in the *config* file.

To make the changes, type:

```
title =                     <-------Set Title
hostname =              <----Set hostname
<httpd_builtin>
      enabled = y
      host =
      port = 8080         <--------Set to required port
      user = nobody
      group = nobody
```

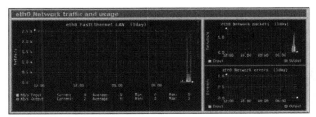

Figure 5: *eth0* interface traffic

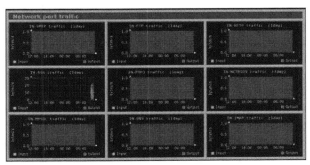

Figure 6: Network port traffic

```
log_file = /var/log/monitorix-httpd
hosts_deny =    <-------- Ip  from which not to allow
                          web link access
hosts_allow =   <-------- Ip  from which to allow web
                          link access

<auth>
enabled = n   <--------- set to "y"
msg = Monitorix: Restricted access
htpasswd = /var/lib/monitorix/htpasswd
              <-----------htpasswd file Location
</auth>
</httpd_builtin>
```

This is what you get after the changes are made:

```
title = diamond Monitorix
hostname =diamond
<httpd_builtin>
        enabled = y
        host = diamond
        port = 8080
        user = nobody
        group = nobody
        log_file = /var/log/monitorix-httpd
        hosts_deny =
        hosts_allow =
        <auth>
            enabled = y
            msg = Monitorix: Restricted access
            htpasswd = /var/lib/monitorix/htpasswd
        </auth>
</httpd_builtin>
```

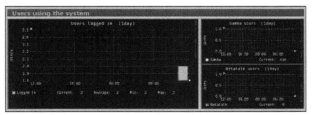

Figure 7: User using the system

To enable graph based statistics for a particular service, e.g., Apache, make the changes under *# Graphs (de)activation section* from *n* to *y.*

```
<graph_enable>
        apache          = y
. </graph_enable>
```

And, finally, restart the Monitorix service whenever the changes are made to the *config* file.

```
#service monitorix restart
```

How to secure Monitorix
To secure Web link access with authentication, set 'enabled = y' under the *<auth>* section and create a file */var/lib/monitorix/htpasswd...*

```
#touch  /var/lib/monitorix/htpasswd
#htpasswd -d /var/lib/monitorix/htpasswd   username
```

...which will add a user with Force SHA encryption of the password.

Now point your browser to *http://ip-address:8080/monitorix/*

In our case, *http://192.168.1.222:8080/monitorix*, it will ask for the user name and password. After entering both, you will be able to see the Monitorix main page, as shown in Figure 1.

You can check out the screenshots given in Figures 2 to 7 for system statistics. **END**

References

[1] Official site: *http://www.monitorix.org/*
[2] *http://www.tecmint.com/how-to-enable-epel-repository-for-rhel-centos-6-5*
[3] *http://www.tecmint.com/monitorix-a-lightweight-system-and-network-monitoring-tool-for-linux/*
[4] *http://linux.die.net/man/5/monitorix.conf*

By: Suresh M. Jagtap

The author is a Linux enthusiast who loves to explore various Linux distributions and open source software. He can be contacted at *smjagtap@gmail.com*

OBSERVIUM THE TIRELESS NETWORK MONITOR

Network monitoring involves constant monitoring of how the network functions by collecting useful data from its various parts, which helps to alert the network administrator in case of failures. Observium is an open source network monitoring platform that supports a range of operating systems. Let's take a look at how to install it on CentOS, its features and how it compares with other such platforms.

Observium is a network monitoring platform that supports a wide range of operating systems such as Windows, Cisco, Juniper, Dell, HP and Linux. It is open source and free, and based on PHP/MySQL. It collects data from devices by using the Simple Network Management Protocol (SNMP) and displays it through graphical presentation via a Web interface. It makes use of the RRDtool package, and requires no manual interpretation or very little of it. It can be integrated with some other open source tools for network monitoring such as Cacti or Nagios. Observium uses the GeSHi and jpgraph software packages to extend its features.

The platform supports IPv6 address tracking, VLAN tracking, VRF and pseudowire tracking, device inventory tracking, session tracking and so on. It also supports auto discovery of the network infrastructure, and finds the network section that needs to be monitored.

Installation of Observium on CentOS

The following steps will help you install Observium on the CentOS, x86_64 platform.
1. Install the RPM Forge and EPEL repositories as follows:

```
rpm --import http://apt.sw.be/RPM-GPG-KEY.dag.txt
rpm -Uvh http://packages.sw.be/rpmforge-release/rpmforge-
release-0.5.2-2.el6.rf.x86_64.rpm
rpm -Uvh http://download.fedoraproject.org/pub/epel/6/i386/
epel-release-6-8.noarch.rpm
```

2. Install the required packages for Observium as follows:

```
yum install wget.x86_64 httpd.x86_64 php.x86_64 php-mysql.
x86_64 php-gd.x86_64 php-posix.x86_64 php-mcrypt.x86_64 php-
pear.noarch \
vixie-cron.x86_64 net-snmp.x86_64 net-snmp-utils.x86_64
fping.x86_64 mysql-server.x86_64 mysql.x86_64 MySQL-python.
x86_64 \
rrdtool.x86_64 subversion.x86_64 jwhois.x86_64 ipmitool.
x86_64 graphviz.x86_64 ImageMagick.x86_64
```

3. Download the latest *.tar.gz* of Observium and uncompress it as follows:

```
wget http://www.observium.org/observium-community-latest.
tar.gz
```

Hardware and software prerequisites

Hardware	Software
Processor (Web) • A 2.13GHz Xeon E5506 will take ~2 seconds to generate /ports/ with 12k ports • A 3.4GHz i7-3770 will take ~0.24 seconds to generate /ports/ with 4.5k ports • A 3.4GHz i7-3770 will take ~0.05 seconds to generate /ports/ with 100 ports Processor (Poller) • A quad-core 2.13GHz Xeon E5506 that will scale to ~20k ports • A quad-core 3.4GHz i7-3770 that will scale to ~40k ports Memory • An 11k port installation uses ~220MB of RAM to generate /ports/ • A 4k port installation uses ~65MB of RAM to generate /ports/ • A 100 port installation uses ~5.5MB of RAM to generate /ports/ Storage capacity • A 5,000 port installation will generate ~8GB of RRDs • An 11,000 port installation will generate ~23GB of RRDs • Storage I/O throughput • A single 7200RPM drive will handle the RRD I/O of about 5,000 ports	• Apache • fping • MySQL 5 • Net-SNMP 5.4+ • RRDtool 1.3+ • Graphviz • PHP 5.4+

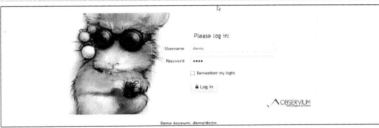

Figure 1: Demo login

Figure 2: Dashboard

Figure 3: Device alerts

```
tar zxvf observium-community-latest.tar.gz
```

4. Install the MySQL database and configure a root password to MySQLd, as follows:

```
service mysqld start /usr/bin/mysqladmin -u
root password 'yournrewrootpassword'
mysql -u root -p
CREATE DATABASE observium DEFAULT CHARACTER
SET utf8 COLLATE utf8_general_ci;
GRANT ALL PRIVILEGES ON observium.* TO
'observium'@'localhost' IDENTIFIED BY
'<observium db password>';
```

5. Configure Observium based on steps available in *http://www.observium.org/wiki/ RHEL_Installation*

6. Visit *http://<server ip>*

There is a live demo of Observium at *http://demo.observium.org/*. Log in with a demo account: *demo/demo*. Some screenshots from the live demo are given in this article (Figure 1).

The dashboard provides information on devices, ports, sensors and alerts (Figure 2).

The *Device Alerts* section provides related information and recent event log entries too (Figure 3).

Go to the *Devices* menu and click on *All devices*, which will provide you information on devices, the platform, operating system, etc (Figure 4).

Go to the *Ports* menu and click on *Traffic Accounting*. It will give information related to *Customer billing* (Figure 5).

A comparison of network monitoring tools

Name	Observium	Ganglia	Nagios	Zenoss
Platform	PHP	C, PHP	C, PHP	Python, Java
Licence	QPL, commercial	BSD	GPL	Free Core GPL, commercial enterprise
Latest release version	Continuous rolling release	3.71	4.0.8	4.2.5
Auto discovery	Yes	Via gmond check in	Via plug-in	Yes
Agentless	Supported	No	Supported	Supported
Syslog	Yes	No	Via plugin	Yes
SNMP	Yes	Via plugin	Via plugin	Yes
Triggers / Alerts	Yes	No	Yes	Yes
WebApp	Full control	Viewing	Yes	Full control
Distributed monitoring	No	Yes	Yes	Yes
Inventory	Yes	Unknown	Via plugin	Yes
Data storage method	RRDtool, MySQL	RRDtool	Flat file, SQL	ZODB, MySQL, RRDtool
Access control	Yes	No	Yes	Yes
IPv6	Yes	Unknown	Yes	Yes
Maps	Yes	Yes	Yes	Yes
Logical grouping	Yes	Yes	Yes	Yes
Trend prediction	No	No	No	Yes
Plugins	Yes	Yes	Yes	Yes

A few global users of Observium

1. Web4all.fr	This French Web hosting provider uses Observium to monitor its entire network and server infrastructure
2. ICANN	ICANN uses Observium to monitor L-Root instances
3. Jersey Telecom	Jersey Telecom uses Observium to monitor its IP/MPLS, data centre and VoIP platforms
4. Vostron	Vostron uses Observium to monitor its IP/MPLS, data centre and VoIP networks
5. Altercom	Altercom uses Observium to monitor its national VoIP network infrastructure
6. ThinFactory	ThinFactory uses Observium to monitor its cloud services and IP/MPLS infrastructure
7. Boxed IT Ltd	Boxed IT Ltd uses Observium to monitor its network and server infrastructure
8. SupraNet	SupraNet uses Observium to monitor its cloud services and IP/MPLS infrastructure

Figure 4: Device information

Figure 5: Traffic Accounting

Go to the *Health* menu and click on *Memory* to get information regarding devices, memory, usage, etc (Figure 6).

To get polling information and discovery timing, go to the main menu and select *Polling Information* (Figure 7).

Features of Observium

- Auto-discovery of SNMP based network monitoring tool
- Application monitoring, using SNMP
- Includes support for network hardware and operating systems such as Cisco, Juniper, Linux, FreeBSD, Foundry, etc.
- Metrics supported: CPU, memory, storage, IPv4, IPv6, TCP and UDP stack statistics, MAC/IP, users, processes,

Figure 6: *Health* menu

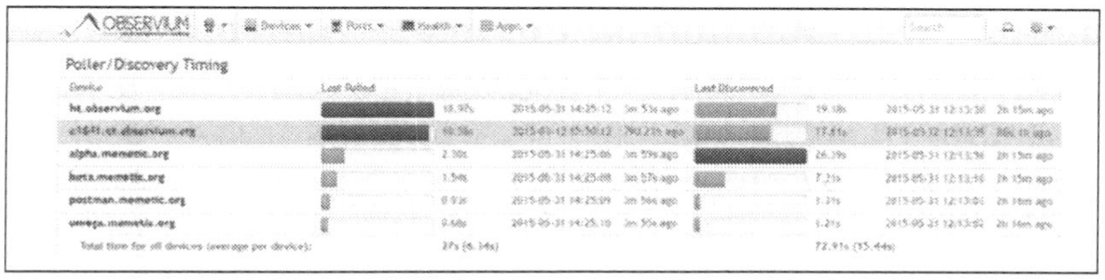

Figure 7: Polling Information

load average, amperage, power, humidity, temperature, fan speed, voltage, uptime statistics, device inventory collection and Linux distribution detection
- Host monitoring well supported using *check_mk* and support scripts
- Billing module
- Integration with Smokeping, collectd, Syslog, etc.

Due to these powerful features, system admins can totally depend on Observium to monitor their network 24x7. END

References

[1] *http://www.observium.org*
[2] *http://en.wikipedia.org/wiki/Observium*
[3] *http://en.wikipedia.org/wiki/Comparison_of_network_monitoring_systems*
[4] *http://www.observium.org/wiki/Users*

By: Priyanka Agashe and Mitesh Soni

Priyanka Agashe is a senior software engineer. Her professional interests include testing, Oracle apps, electronics and robotics.
Mitesh Soni is a technical lead. He loves to write about new technologies. Blog: *http://clean-clouds.com*

Relay Mails Using Gmail on RHEL6.1

This article explains the use of Postfix as a mail transfer agent to relay mails using Gmail.

In this article, lets explore how to configure RHEL 6.1 [x86] to relay emails using Gmail. In order to do so, we need to configure Postfix in RHEL 6.1. Postfix is a free and open source mail transfer agent [MTA] that routes and delivers emails. It's an alternative to Sendmail, which, to date, is the most widely used MTA that routes and delivers emails. It supports various mail transfer and delivery methods, which includes SMTP (Simple Mail Transfer Protocol).

Prerequisites

The settings given below are configured.

1. The operating system, host name and IP address used are RHEL 6.1, PILOTVM01.linuxrocks.org and 192.168.1.15, respectively.
2. The */etc/hosts* configuration file should look like what's shown below:

```
#cat /etc/hosts

127.0.0.1   localhost localhost.localdomain localhost4
localhost4.localdomain4
::1         localhost localhost.localdomain localhost6
localhost6.localdomain6
192.168.1.15        PILOTVM01        PILOTVM01.
linuxrocks.org
```

3. To set the IP address, type:
   [*GUI – System -> Preferences -> Network Connection*;
4. Now, turn 'OFF' the firewall:
   [*GUI – System -> Administration -> Firewall.*
   If you want to stop the firewall using command, we can run:

```
service iptables stop
chkconfig iptables off
```

5. Next, disable SELinux.
6. Now change the system's date and time [optional].
   To change date and time go to *System -> Administration -> Date & Time* and modify the value.

Postfix configuration on RHEL 6.1 x86

Before we start with the configuration, here are some points to consider. For office users, Internet connectivity to Postfix Server is a must. In case of limited Internet connectivity as part of organisational policy, at least Gmail must be accessible.

For home users, Internet connectivity to Postfix Server should not be an issue.

Since, in my environment, I have a separate colour coded cable for free Internet, I just needed to configure the IP address mode to be dynamic so as to receive the IP address automatically. In my case, the IP address received is 192.168.1.15

So, the network configuration depends upon the environment in which you are configuring Postfix Server.

Verify if the Postfix package is already installed, as follows:

```
#rpm -qa | grep postfix*
postfix-2.6.6-2.1.el6_0.i686
```

As observed, the package is already installed.

If not installed, please install the package from the RHEL 6.1 DVD with the following command:

```
#rpm --ivh --aid --force postfix-2.6.6-2.1.el6_0.i686.rpm
```

In case of package dependencies, keep appending the dependent package name with the above command till all dependencies are resolved and Postfix is installed.

Once the package is installed, open the primary configuration file of Postfix with the Vi Editor:

```
#vi /etc/postfix/main.cf
```

Now add the following lines at the end of the configuration file [precisely after Line 676]:

```
#EDITED BY ARINDAM MITRA
smtp_sasl_security_options = noanonymous
#sasl [Simple Authentication and Secure Layer]
            #option, no anonymous login.
relayhost = smtp.gmail.com:587
#Setting Gmail as relay
smtp_use_tls = yes
#Use TLS [Transport Layer Security]
smtp_tls_CAfile = /etc/postfix/cacert.pem
#Trusted Server Certificate while verifying
smtp_sasl_auth_enable = yes
#Use of sasl [Simple Authentication and Secure Layer]

#while authenticating to foreign SMTP Server, in our
```

```
#case, it is GMAIL
smtp_sasl_password_maps = hash:/etc/postfix/sasl/passwd
#Location of Hash Password File [as its more Secure]
```

Now follow the steps given below:

```
[root@pilotvm01 ~]#cd /etc/postfix/
```

Verify if the directory named *sasl* exists:

```
[root@pilotvm01 postfix]#ll
total 140
-rw-r--r--. 1 root    root    19579 Mar 9 2011       access
-rw-r--r--. 1 root    root    11681 Mar 9 2011       canonical
-rw-r--r--. 1 root    root    9904  Mar 9 2011       generic
-rw-r--r--. 1 root root       18287 Mar 9 2011 header_checks
-rw-r--r-- 1 root     root    27256 May 18 10:51     main.cf
-rw-r--r--. 1 root    root    5113  Mar 9 2011       master.cf
-rw-r--r--. 1 root    root    6816  Mar 9 2011       relocated
-rw-r--r--. 1 root    root    12500 Mar 9 2011       transport
-rw-r--r--. 1 root    root    12494 Mar 9 2011       virtual
```

As observed, no directory named *sasl* exists.

Proceed further by creating a directory named *sasl* and re-verify:

```
[root@pilotvm01 postfix]#mkdir sasl
[root@pilotvm01 postfix]#ll
total 144
-rw-r--r--.  1 root root  19579 Mar 9 2011  access
-rw-r--r--.  1 root root  11681 Mar 9 2011  canonical
-rw-r--r--.  1 root root  9904  Mar 9 2011  generic
-rw-r--r--.  1 root root  18287 Mar 9 2011 header_
checks
-rw-r--r--   1 root root  27256 May 18 10:51  main.cf
-rw-r--r--.  1 root root  5113  Mar 9 2011  master.cf
-rw-r--r--.  1 root root  6816  Mar 9 2011  relocated
drwxr-xr-x   2 root root  4096  May 18 11:03  sasl
-rw-r--r--.  1 root root  12500 Mar 9 2011  transport
-rw-r--r--.  1 root root  12494 Mar 9 2011  virtual
```

Browse to directory *sasl*, create a 0 byte file named *passwd*, open it with the Vi editor and add the following lines:

```
[root@pilotvm01 postfix]#cd sasl/
[root@pilotvm01 sasl]#touch passwd
[root@pilotvm01 sasl]#cat passwd
[root@pilotvm01 sasl]# vi passwd
[root@pilotvm01 sasl]#

[root@pilotvm01 sasl]#cat passwd
smtp.gmail.com:587 arindam0310018@gmail.com:GMAIL PASSWORD
[root@pilotvm01 sasl]#
```

Note: 1. You need to provide an existing Gmail user name and password.

2. The user name should be of the format '*arindam0310018@gmail.com*'.

3. For the purpose of this article, I have used *arindam0310018@gmail.com* as the Gmail user ID.

Now change the permissions so that only the owner [in our case, root] can read and write the *passwd* file:

```
[root@pilotvm01 sasl]#chmod 600 passwd
[root@pilotvm01 sasl]#ll
total 4
-rw------- 1 root root 52 May 18 11:08 passwd
[root@pilotvm01 sasl]#

HASH the passwd file so that it is more secure.

[root@pilotvm01 sasl]#postmap passwd
```

As observed, after HASHING, *passwd* and *passwd.db* both reside in the same location.

```
[root@pilotvm01 sasl]#ll
total 12
-rw------- 1 root root    52    May 18 11:08  passwd
-rw------- 1 root root    12288 May 18 11:10  passwd.db
[root@pilotvm01 sasl]#
```

Now generate the TRUSTED SERVER CERTIFICATE for verification.

```
[root@pilotvm01 sasl]#cd /etc/pki/tls/certs/
[root@pilotvm01 certs]#ll
total 1220
-rw-r--r--.  1 root root   578465 Apr 7 2010  ca-bundle.
crt
-rw-r--r--.  1 root root   658225 Apr 7 2010  ca-bundle.
trust.crt
-rwxr-xr-x.  1 root root   610    Feb 10 2011  make-
dummy-cert
-rw-r--r--.  1 root root   2242   Feb 10 2011  Makefile
[root@pilotvm01 certs]#

[root@pilotvm01 certs]#make pilotvm01.pem
umask 77 ; \
        PEM1=`/bin/mktemp /tmp/openssl.XXXXXX` ; \
        PEM2=`/bin/mktemp /tmp/openssl.XXXXXX` ; \
        /usr/bin/openssl req -utf8 -newkey rsa:2048 -keyout
$PEM1 -nodes -x509 -days 365 -out $PEM2 -set_serial 0 ; \
        cat $PEM1 >  pilotvm01.pem ; \
        echo ""    >> pilotvm01.pem ; \
        cat $PEM2 >> pilotvm01.pem ; \
```

```
        rm -f $PEM1 $PEM2
Generating a 2048 bit RSA private key
..........+++
.............+++
writing new private key to '/tmp/openssl.4L2n3J'
-----
```

You will be asked to enter information that will be incorporated in your certificate request.

What you will enter is called a 'distinguished name' or a DN. There are quite a few fields but you can leave some blank. For some fields, there will be a default value. If you enter '.', the field will be left blank.

```
Country Name (2 letter code) [XX]:IN
State or Province Name (full name) []:MAHARASHTRA
Locality Name (eg, city) [Default City]:PUNE
Organization Name (eg, company) [Default Company Ltd]:OSFY
Organizational Unit Name (eg, section) []:PUBLISHING
Common Name (eg, your name or your server›s hostname)
[]:PILOTVM01
Email Address []:arindam0310018@gmail.com
[root@pilotvm01 certs]#
```

```
[root@pilotvm01 certs]#ll
total 1224
-rw-r--r--.  1 root root   578465 Apr  7   2010   ca-
bundle.crt
-rw-r--r--.  1 root root   658225 Apr  7   2010   ca-
bundle.trust.crt
-rwxr-xr-x.  1 root root      610 Feb 10 2011   make-
dummy-cert
-rw-r--r--.  1 root root     2242 Feb 10 2011   Makefile
-rw-------   1 root root     3141 May 18 11:14
pilotvm01.pem
[root@pilotvm01 certs]#
```

Now rename the certificate from *pilotvm01.pem* as *cacert. pem* while copying it to */etc/Postfix/*:

```
[root@pilotvm01 certs]#cp pilotvm01.pem /etc/Postfix/cacert.pem
[root@pilotvm01 certs]#cd
[root@pilotvm01 ~]#
```

Verify if the Postfix Service is running, as follows:

```
[root@pilotvm01 ~]#service Postfix status
master (pid 2093) is running...
[root@pilotvm01 ~]#
```

After verification, restart the Postfix Service:

```
[root@pilotvm01 ~]#service postfix restart
```

```
Shutting down postfix:                        [  OK  ]
Starting postfix:                       [  OK  ]
[root@pilotvm01 ~]#
```

Now, let's try sending email.
1. To send email as the root user, type:

```
echo "This is message body" | mail -s "This is Subject"
<VALID EMAIL ADDRESS>
```

Example:

```
[root@pilotvm01 ~]#echo "This is the message body" | mail -s
"This is the Subject" mail2arindam2003@yahoo.com
```

Observation:
On receiving email, the 'From Address' is displayed as '*root arindam0310018@gmail.com*'.
2. Now let's create a normal user 'adminlinux' and then send email:

```
[root@pilotvm01 ~]#useradd adminLinux
[root@pilotvm01 ~]#su - adminLinux

[adminLinux@pilotvm01 ~]$pwd
/home/adminLinux
[adminLinux@pilotvm01 ~]$

[adminLinux@pilotvm01 ~]$echo «This is the message body» |
mail -s «This is the Subject» mail2arindam2003@yahoo.com
[adminLinux@pilotvm01 ~]$
```

Observation:
On receiving email, the 'From Address' is displayed as <*arindam0310018@gmail.com*>.
3. To send email with attachments as user *adminlinux*, type:

```
[adminLinux@pilotvm01 ~]$echo "This is message body" | mail
-s "This is Subject" -r "Arindam<arindam0310018@gmail.com>"
-a /root/df.txt mail2arindam2003@yahoo.com
```

Note: 1. With the *-r* option, the 'from' name and address can be specified.

2. With the *-a* option, attachments can be added.

By: Arindam Mitra

The author is assistant manager in a Pune-based IT company. You can contact him at *mail2arindam2003@yahoo.com* or *arindam0310018@gmail.com*

Installing and Configuring
Nagios Core on Linux

Here's a comprehensive guide on the Nagios network and system monitoring software application, which covers the installation and configuration of Nagios Core on a Linux system. It also includes the creation of custom Nagios plugins using the Bash script.

A network monitoring system is an essential constituent of any enterprise, small or large. A substantial amount of money is spent on establishing the entire network infrastructure, mainly servers and network components, expanding it as per changing needs and most important, keeping it alive all the time. With the network infrastructure constantly growing, it becomes a tedious job for network and systems administrators to continuously keep an eye on every device, all the time. Hence, there's a need for a network monitoring system that does this job for them.

A network monitoring system can show the live statuses of all the devices - whether they are up or down, the resources being consumed by them, services running on them, etc - in one place. Moreover, it notifies the administrators immediately in case of a malfunction by sending them emails, SMSs or even phone calls, so that admins are always aware of what has gone wrong and at which point in the network.

When it comes to selecting the best monitoring tool, there are many alternatives to choose from, but Nagios is one of the finest options. It is available in two versions – Nagios Core, which is open source and free, and Nagios XI, which comes with some added features and capabilities, but needs to be purchased. However, both deal with monitoring critical servers and network devices, both provide indications of problematic situations, and both report the issues to the admins through mails and/or messages to help minimise downtime, reduce commercial losses and improve SLA.

This article is about installing and configuring Nagios Core on a Linux system. To demonstrate this, I have used the framework mentioned below.

Nagios server: 192.168.0.109
Operating system: Red Hat Enterprise Linux 6.5
Nagios client: 192.168.0.108
Operating system: Red Hat Enterprise Linux 6.5
Nagios Core version: 4.0.8
Nagios plugins version: 2.0.3

Nagios Core installation

Installing the necessary packages and their dependencies:
The required packages mainly include Apache, PHP, C
compilers, C libraries and development libraries. These packages
can be installed using the Yum install as shown below:

```
$ yum install wget httpd php gcc glibc glibc-common gd gd-devel
make net-snmp
```

In order to make sure that the service 'httpd' starts after
every system reboot, it should be added to the startup as
follows:

```
$ chkconfig httpd on
$ service httpd start
```

**Downloading the Nagios Core and Nagios plugins
packages:** After the installation of the required packages, it's
time to download Nagios Core and Nagios plugins, which are
available in the form of tarballs, from the official website.

```
$ cd /root
$ wget http://prdownloads.sourceforge.net/sourceforge/nagios/
nagios-4.0.8.tar.gz
$ wget http://nagios-plugins.org/download/nagios-plugins-
2.0.3.tar.gz
```

Adding the 'nagios' user and 'nagios' group: In order
to submit and process external commands from the graphical
user interface, we need to create a group, say 'nagios', and
add a user, say 'nagios', to that group.

```
$ groupadd nagios
$ useradd -g nagios nagios
```

Nagios Core installation: Having downloaded the Nagios
Core tarball file from the source, we will have to extract it in
order to proceed with the installation.

```
$ tar -xvzf nagios-4.0.8.tar.gz
```

Change to the *nagios-4.0.8* directory to begin the
configuration part. After executing the 'configure' script, we
have to compile the source code and then install it.

```
$ cd nagios-4.0.8
$ ./configure --with-command-group=nagios
```

Figure 1: Nagios-Web console

```
$ make all
$ make install
$ make install-init
$ make install-config
$ make install-commandmode
$ make install-webconf
```

Now, restart the httpd service for the changes to take effect.

```
$ service httpd restart
```

To make sure that the 'nagios' service starts after every
system reboot, we must add it to the startup services as follows:

```
$ chkconfig nagios on
```

Nagios plugins installation: In order to monitor remote
hosts and the services running on them, we need to install
Nagios plugins. For this, we need to change to the 'nagios-
plugins-2.0.3' directory, run the 'configure' script, make and
install the binaries.

```
$ cd nagios-plugins-2.0.3
$ ./configure --with-nagios-user=nagios --with-nagios-
group=nagios
$ make
$ make install
```

Nagios Web access: We are almost done with the installation
part and to verify if it is correct, you can open your Web browser
and enter *http://<NAGIOS-SERVER-IP-ADDRESS>/nagios*
You will find a dialogue box asking for your credentials in
order to access the Nagios Web interface (Figure 1).
So far, we've not created any login to access the Nagios
Web interface. Let's
create it now.

```
$ htpasswd -c /
usr/local/nagios/
etc/htpasswd.users
<USERNAME>
```

You'll be asked to
enter the password and
then confirm it before a
login is created.

Nagios®
Core™
✗ **Unable to get process status**

Nagios® Core™
Version 4.0.8
August 12, 2014
Check for updates

Figure 2: Nagios unable to get process status

If you try logging in with the newly created credentials, you might encounter the following error displayed on the Nagios Core Web console: 'Unable to get process status' (Figure 2).

This error is displayed as SELinux is enabled on the system. It can be verified as shown below:

```
$ getenforce
Enforcing
```

In order to disable SELinux, you can execute the following command, verify the status again and restart the Nagios service:

```
$ setenforce 0
$ getenforce
Permissive
$ service nagios restart
```

And the outcome is shown in Figure 3.

Again, you can verify the Nagios configuration file for its correctness using the following command:

```
/usr/local/nagios/bin/nagios -v /usr/local/
nagios/etc/nagios.cfg
```

Nagios Core configuration

We have now installed Nagios Core and we can access it from a Web console. On the left pane, a link named 'Hosts' can be observed, which when clicked on displays the list of hosts currently being monitored (Figure 4).

Clearly, we have not added any hosts to Nagios, so it will just show 'localhost' in the list of hosts being monitored.

The same can be observed in the 'Host Status Details' shown in Figure 5. It gives us a brief How To of all the hosts configured to monitoring Nagios and their statuses – the total number of hosts, the number of hosts that are up/down/unreachable, etc.

NRPE installation on a Nagios client: In order to monitor any Linux hosts using Nagios, we need to install the NRPE (Nagios Remote Plugin Executor) client on the host, so that the Nagios server can execute Nagios plugins remotely to fetch the host/service information.

To proceed with the NRPE installation, we need to download the NRPE tarball from the sources, as follows:

```
$ wget http://liquidtelecom.dl.sourceforge.net/project/
nagios/nrpe-2.x/nrpe-2.15/nrpe-2.15.tar.gz
```

In the next step, we have to extract the tarball, compile the binaries and install them. Prior to that, make sure that 'xinetd' is installed in the system; otherwise, install it manually using Yum.

```
$ yum install xinetd
$ tar -xvzf nrpe-2.15.tar.gz
$ cd nrpe-2.15
$ ./configure
$ make all
$ make install-plugin
$ make install-daemon
$ make install-daemon-config
$ make install-xinetd
```

In the next step, we need to open port 5666 for the NRPE service.

```
$ echo "nrpe    5666/tcp    # NRPE" >> /etc/services
```

In the last step, we need to allow requests from the Nagios server. For this, edit the /etc/xinetd.d/nrpe file and mention the IP address of the Nagios server in front of 'only_from' as follows:

```
only_from = 127.0.0.1, <NAGIOS-SERVER-IP-ADDRESS>
```

For the changes to take effect, restart the *xinetd* service as follows:

```
$ service xinetd restart
```

To verify the installation of NRPE on the Nagios client, execute the following command from the Nagios server:

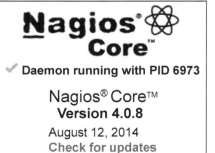

Figure 3: Nagios daemon running

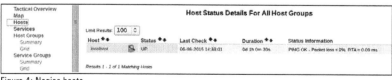

Figure 4: Nagios hosts

Figure 5: Nagios host status details

```
$ /usr/local/nagios/libexec/check_nrpe -H <REMOTE-HOST-IP-
ADDRESS>
NRPE v2.15
```

The output should display the NRPE version installed on the remote host, as shown above.

Adding hosts to Nagios monitoring: In order to add new servers to Nagios monitoring, let's create a directory with name servers inside the */usr/local/nagios/etc/objects* directory. Configuration files for all the servers we add will reside in this directory.

```
$ mkdir /usr/local/nagios/etc/objects/servers
```

In order to add this directory in the configuration file, edit the */usr/local/nagios/etc/nagios.cfg* file and uncomment the following line:

```
# cfg_dir=/usr/local/nagios/etc/servers
```

Now, change to the 'servers' directory and create a new configuration file for our new Nagios client. Add the following details to the configuration file, for which you can take help from the *templates.cfg* file:

```
$ cd usr/local/nagios/etc/servers
$ vi MyLinuxServer.cfg
define host {
name                      MyLinuxServer
address       192.168.0.110
use                       generic-host
check_period              24x7
check_interval            5
retry_interval            1
max_check_attempts        5
check_command             check-host-alive
notification_period       workhours
notification_interval     60
contact            nagiosadmin
register                  1
}
```

Adding services for the hosts: To add any service to the hosts, one might need to create a command to monitor that service. This can be done by editing the */usr/local/nagios/etc/objects/commands.cfg* file.

```
define command{
        command_name check_nrpe
        command_line $USER1$/check_nrpe -H $HOSTADDRESS$ -c
$ARG1$
        }
```

Similar to the hosts, we should create a directory called

'services' in order to keep custom services configuration files. Again, the necessary changes should be made to the */usr/local/nagios/etc/nagios.cfg* file.

```
$ mkdir /usr/local/nagios/etc/objects/services
$ echo "cfg_dir=/usr/local/nagios/etc/services" >> /usr/
local/nagios/etc/nagios.cfg
```

To add services for the host *MyLinuxServer*, let's create a configuration file *MyLinuxServer.cfg* in the *services* directory as shown below:

```
$ cd /usr/local/nagios/etc/objects/services
$ vi MyLinuxServer.cfg
define service {
        use                    generic-service
        host_name              MyLinuxServer
        service_description    Server Uptime
        check_command          check_nrpe!check_
uptime
        notifications_enabled        1
        }
```

Note: Whenever changes are made to the */usr/local/nagios/etc/nagios.cfg* file, execute the following command to check for any errors in the configuration:

```
/usr/local/nagios/bin/nagios -v /usr/local/nagios/etc/nagios.
cfg
```

After adding the host to the Nagios configuration, restart the Nagios service once on the Nagios server, and observe the changes in the Nagios Web console (Figure 6).

In a similar manner, many more hosts and services can be added to the Nagios configuration.

Creating custom Nagios plugins using the Bash script: Even though the Nagios plugins that we have already installed offer a wide variety, one might need to create one's own Nagios plugin in order to monitor a specific service. The Nagios plugin supports a wide range of programming languages including Bash, Python, Perl, C/C++, etc. But one common fact that needs to be remembered while creating a Nagios plugin using any of the mentioned programming languages is the syntax of the output, which is as follows:

```
<STATUS> - <DATA TO BE DISPLAYED ON WEB CONSOLE> | <DATA
NEEDED FOR GENERATING GRAPHS>
```

Figure 6: Nagios host added

A service's 'STATUS' can be 'OK', 'WARNING', 'CRITICAL', or 'UNKNOWN', which entirely depends upon the corresponding threshold values defined in the script.

Exit status 0 denotes an 'OK' status for the service, which is responsible for highlighting the service check with green on the Nagios Web console. Similarly, *exit status 1* denotes the 'WARNING' status of the service highlighted with yellow; *exit status 2* denotes the 'CRITICAL' service status highlighted with red; and *exit status 3* denotes the 'UNKNOWN' service status highlighted with grey.

Consider that we have to create a custom Nagios plugin to monitor the load average on a Linux server. For this, we need to decide the WARNING and CRITICAL thresholds, which are usually 80 per cent and 90 per cent, respectively, of the number of processor cores available in the system.

The live status of the load average can be obtained from the 'uptime' command, which can then be compared with the threshold levels, to decide the status of the service. Thresholds can be set using the */proc/cpuinfo* file, which possesses the necessary information related to the processor installed in the system. There are some conditional statements to compare live values with the threshold values. The echo statements display the service check in the proper format, and a few exit commands help to colour the service check on the Nagios Web console, accordingly.

The sample Bash script will look like what's shown below:

```
#!/bin/bash

UPTIME=`uptime | awk -F "average:" '{print $2}'`
load1=`echo $UPTIME | awk -F, '{print $1}' | xargs`
load5=`echo $UPTIME | awk -F, '{print $2}' | xargs`
load15=`echo $UPTIME | awk -F, '{print $3}' | xargs`

intload1=`echo "scale=1; $load1*100" | bc -l | cut -d "." -f 1`
intload5=`echo "scale=1; $load5*100" | bc -l | cut -d "." -f 1`
intload15=`echo "scale=1; $load15*100" | bc -l | cut -d "." -f 1`

Nprocs=`grep "processor" /proc/cpuinfo | wc -l`

warn=`scale=1; echo "80 * $Nprocs" | bc -l | cut -d "." -f 1`
crit=`scale=1; echo "90 * $Nprocs" | bc -l | cut -d "." -f 1`

actwarn=`echo "scale=1; $warn/100" | bc -l`
actcrit=`echo "scale=1; $crit/100" | bc -l`

if [ "$intload1" -le "$warn" -a "$intload5" -le "$warn" -a
"$intload15" -le "$warn" ]
then
        STATUS="OK"
        EXIT="0"
elif [ "$intload1" -gt "$warn" -o "$intload5" -gt "$warn" -o
"$intload15" -gt "$warn" ]
then
        if [ "$intload1" -gt "$crit" -o "$intload5" -gt
```

```
"$crit" -o "$intload15" -gt "$crit" ]
        then
                STATUS="CRITICAL"
                EXIT="2"
        else
                STATUS="WARNING"
                EXIT="1"
        fi
else
STATUS="UNKNOWN"
EXIT="3"
fi

echo "$STATUS- Load Average: $load1, $load5, $load15 |
load1=$load1;$actwarn;$actcrit;; load5=$load5;$actwarn;$actc
rit;;
load15=$load15;$actwarn;$actcrit;;" && exit $EXIT
```

When the script is created, it has to be put in the */usr/local/nagios/libexec* directory of the Nagios server as well as the clients to be monitored.

To create a command using the custom script, the *commands.cfg* file needs to be edited.

```
$ vi /usr/local/nagios/etc/objects/commands.cfg
define command{
        command_name check_load_average
        command_line $USER1$/check_nrpe -H $HOSTADDRESS$ -c
load_average
        }
```

Now, add the above command to the remote host's service configuration file.

```
$ vi /usr/local/nagios/etc/objects/services/MyLinuxServer.cfg
define service {
        use                     generic-service
        host_name               MyLinuxServer
        service_description     Load Average
        check_command           check_load_average
        }
```

Restart the Nagios service and perform a check from the command line:

```
$ /usr/local/nagios/libexec/check_nrpe -H 192.168.0.108 -c
load_average
```

Your custom Nagios plugin has been created. END

By Mandar Shinde

The author works in the IT division of one of the largest commercial automotive organisations in India. His technical interests include Linux, networking, backups and virtualisation.

A Detailed Review of Distributed
Network Monitoring

Distributed network monitoring involves receiving performance reports about the state of the network from various locations in it, via different types of pollers. This article deals with the concept at great length.

istributed monitoring involves the use of the underlying distributed infrastructure and communication protocols. Each server or device runs a client that acts as a node in the distributed monitoring network. The node collects metrics, is topology aware, uses gossip protocol for communication and contributes in monitoring other servers. This approach promises robustness and low latency failure detection.

Overlay network monitoring enables distributed Internet applications to detect and recover from path outages and periods of degraded performance, within seconds. This makes it possible to manage distributed systems such as VPN's (virtual private networks) and CDN's (content distribution networks). Accurate loss rate monitoring is critical to building adaptive overlay systems like streaming media frameworks.

In this article, we discuss the various building blocks of monitoring infrastructure, highlight feature capabilities, the significance of 'probe' vs 'router' models and look at new approaches to distributed network monitoring like packet doppler, gossip based monitoring and network tomography.

Network monitoring is the practice of monitoring infrastructure over a computer network to ensure service delivery to meet service level agreement (SLA) requirements and performance metrics for hardware infrastructure, networking equipment and repositories of virtual servers and software infrastructure.

With the convergence of telecommunications infrastructure with IP infrastructure to deliver seamless services over the network, operational practices have seen an overlap of frameworks, practices and protocols.

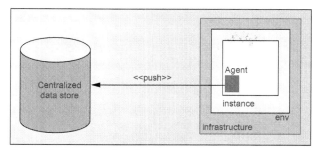

Figure 1: Distributed network monitoring

Protocols

With the introduction of carrier-grade Ethernet, the problem management lifecycle as captured by OAMPT (operations, administration, maintenance, provisioning and troubleshooting) has gained importance. The telecommunication management network model has FCAPS (fault management, configuration, accounting/administration, performance and security) capabilities. Since service delivery and service support is what the end users focus on, ITIL (Information Technology Infrastructure Library) captures the workflows.

CMIP (Communication Management Information Protocol) is a network management protocol standardised by the ITU (International Telecommunication Union). CMIP models management information in terms of managed objects. With the establishment of the IETF (Internet Engineering Task Force), a much more simplified yet comprehensive ASN.1 based network management protocol that could be used to design a hierarchy of managed objects was created. This is the Simple Network Management Protocol (SNMP).

Managed objects

In a network, a managed object is a device (router, switch), a system (server, blade chassis), a service (PostgreSql, Squid or HA-proxy), an entity (it could even be virtual machine or Docker instance) or a QoS (quality of service) metric that requires some form of monitoring and management.

A managed object is an abstract representation of network resources that are managed. It is defined in terms of the attributes it possesses, the operations that can be performed on it, and its relationship with other managed objects.

SNMP architecture

Simple Network Management Protocol (SNMP) is an IETF (Internet Engineering Task Force) ratified (multiple RFCs) standard for the Internet Management Protocol.

The notion of SNMP is expressed in terms of two complementary approaches:
1. The SNMP model of how to access the same information (communication over UDP and BER for encoding).
2. The SMI (structure of management information), which is a data model for representing a managed object as a MIB (management information base).

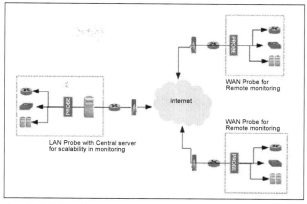

Figure 2: Probe based network monitoring approach

SNMP verbs

The basic verbs of the SNMP protocol are GET, SET, GETNEXT and GETBULK. An SNMP entity can also send asynchronous events, such as a TRAP and a NOTIFICATION. The verbs like GET and SET operate on individual variables of simple types, which can be scalar or located in tables.

Each SNMP data entity is expressed in terms of an OBJECT-IDENTIFIER encoded using TLV and a subset of ASN.1, which represents a node in a global tree. All SNMP definitions - MIBs, objects, etc - are identified by their OID in the global tree.

Thus, as part of the network monitoring strategy, it is common to define SMI for each of the network elements that need to be monitored and measured. An illustrative MIB fragment from *mibdepot.com* for D-Link is shown below.

D-Link: DLINKMGMT-MIB (SMIv2)
```
agentIpIfAddress OBJECT-TYPE
-- 1.3.6.1.4.1.326.2.20.1.11.1.3.2.1.2
-- iso(1). org(3). dod(6). internet(1). private(4).
enterprises(1). marconi(326). systems(2). external(20).
dlink(1). dlinkMgmtMIB(11). agentConfigInfo(1).
agentIpProtoConfig(3). agentIpIfTable(2). agentIpIfEntry(1).
agentIpIfAddress(2)
SYNTAX  IpAddress
MAX-ACCESS read-only
DESCRIPTION
"The IP address of the interface ."
::= { agentIpIfEntry 2  }
```

JMX architecture

Java Management Extensions (JMX) is a framework and technology platform for building distributed and modular solutions to manage and monitor devices, applications and service-driven networks. Legacy systems can be adapted with the JMX infrastructure. While it is a Java based technology, JMX Beans and mbean server can be used to manage complex network topologies.

OpenNMS is an open source project that offers a feature-rich network management application platform.

Internet infrastructure

Architecturally speaking, most of the conventional models of network and system monitoring are (semi) centralised and can suffer from a single point of failure.

Measuring the characteristics of network traffic is critical to identify and diagnose performance problems. Some of the metrics are traffic volume, delay, delay distribution, packet loss rate, etc. The insight we gain is useful for designing distributed services.

The Internet is one of the most important distributed network infrastructures today. Interestingly, performance was not a design goal at the time of its conception.

Most network measurement models utilise a monitoring approach that is either 'probe based' (active) or 'router based' (passive).

P2P network monitoring

The static design and rigidity of Internet architecture makes it difficult to innovate or deploy technologies in the core.

Consequently, most of the research and innovation has focused on 'overlay' and 'peer-to-peer' systems. A data structure like distributed hash tables (DHT) is used to implement protocols that keep track of the changes in membership and thus the attendant changes in the route. Tapestry, Chord, Kelips and Kademlia are the common implementation protocols.

In order to monitor such topology, lookup performance has often been measured with hop count, latency, success rate and probability of timeouts. For applications, lookup latency is used as a unified performance metric.

Cloud and container infrastructures

The rapid development of sensor technologies and wireless sensor network infrastructure has led to the generation of huge volumes of real-time data traffic. Cloud infrastructure needs to elastically handle the data surge, and provide computing and storage resources to applications in real-time.

As a result, software infrastructure that supports analytics for real-time decision support must have the ability to enable traffic data acquisition, and distributed and parallel data management. Intrusive network monitoring practices will neither work nor scale in dense cloud infrastructures. Cloud lifecycle management integrated with measurement is a value proposition.

Networked storage infrastructure

Storage networking infrastructures like SAN (storage area networks), NAS (network attached storage), NAS filers, VTL (virtual tape libraries), pNFS (parallel Network File System), DRBD (distributed replicated block device) clusters and RDMA (remote direct memory access) zero-copy networking have very stringent network performance requirements supported by backplane fabric technologies like data centre Ethernet, fibre channel (FC) and Infiniband. The common

theme is very high throughput and very low latency.

Advanced Telecommunications Computing Architecture (ATCA)

Mobile data will grow ten times each year for the rest of this decade. A typical ATCA platform offers a mix of CPU, DSP, storage and I/O payload blades, together with up to four switch blades. The network and server infrastructure for mobile and fixed line services requires many line rate functions.

The functions include security, deep packet inspection (DPI), packet classification and load balancing. Line rate DPI enables advanced policy management and gives service providers full control of network resources. As network capacity increases, the line rates must increase from 10 Gbps and 40 Gbps to hundreds of Gbps, in the future.

Existing approaches of probe based network monitoring will not work and require the monitoring models to deeply integrate with line rate functions. Techniques like Packet Doppler represent a promising solution as they monitor SLA metrics.

Analytics based approaches

The current data-driven approach to defining metrics has led to operation analytics and route analytics, among other techniques, being used to manage and monitor heavy bandwidth overlay networks.

While topology discovery products are established, there are also many logical network 'overlays' for the topology, including network routes. As a result, device-centric discovery mechanisms cannot capture the routes through the network.

Route analytics solves the configuration management requirements of organisations with highly meshed networks. By capturing the complex network topology relationships, route analytics systems can perform advanced configuration management, incident correlation and root-cause identification.

Performance metrics like latency, throughput and cost can be calculated since the analytics systems participate in the cooperative negotiations between routers. Real-time alerts can be generated as route paths become modified or there is a problem related to routing protocol. This can trigger polling, which leads to root-cause analysis through the event correlation system.

Packet Doppler

Delay and loss sensitive applications such as telecommuting, streaming media, gaming and live conference applications require stringent monitoring of service level agreement (SLA) metrics.

The traditional methods of end-to-end monitoring are not effective, as they are based on active probing and thus inject measurement traffic into the network.

Packet Doppler is used to measure and monitor the *delay distributions* of origin-destination (OD) pairs in an ISP network. A node could be an end-host, link, router or point of presence (PoP).

For each OD pair, tiny digests of real traffic (at both origin and destination) are listened to and recorded. The digests encode the time series information of the packets passing by.

Next, to extract all of the useful information out of packet digests, two decoding techniques are applied:
1. Sequential hypothesis testing (SHT) with Viterbi decoding
2. Sequential hypothesis testing (SHT) with iterative proportional fitting (IPF)

Keeping the structural constraints in the SLA measurements in mind, delay distributions are constructed, which are quite accurate.

The key advantages of Packet Doppler are:
- Passive technique
- Does not perturb real traffic
- Low storage and bandwidth overhead
- Detects burst events
- Detects packet loss events

Gossip protocol based monitoring

Gossip or epidemic protocols have emerged as a useful model to implement highly scalable, and resilient and reliable broadcast primitives. For reasons of scalability, participants in a gossip protocol maintain only a partial view of the system, from which they select peers to perform gossip exchanges.

The monitoring algorithm works by creating a network of nodes. Each server that is monitored represents a node. It also participates in monitoring the other nodes, by gossiping with them. Each node will periodically gossip its knowledge about the other nodes with a random node in the network.

The key concepts used by the algorithm are:
- *Heartbeat value:* Indicates the number of gossip rounds passed since the last communication with that node
- *Gossip list:* Contains a heartbeat value for each node
- *Gossip interval:* Time between two gossip messages sent by a node
- *Cleanup time:* Threshold value of the heartbeat before a node will be suspected to have failed
- *Suspect list:* List of suspects for each node, if the node is suspected to have failed
- *Suspect matrix:* 2D matrix, where each row is the suspect list of a node

When a node receives a message, it will update its own gossip list and suspect matrix if the received data is recent.

The protocol is generic enough and is used in NoSQL database design, in Akka router and cluster formations, among others, not to speak of distributed monitoring infrastructure.

Alerting

When a node detects that consensus is reached about a failure, it broadcasts this across the network. This can happen multiple times for a single failure, as the consensus can be detected by multiple nodes simultaneously.

In order to prevent multiple alerts, only the live node with the lowest identifier will send the consensus broadcast and alert. In case this node fails, the next live node will take this role. The other nodes will know an alert has been sent when they receive the consensus broadcast.

With this approach, the failure detection time can be significantly reduced as there is no single point of failure.

Since the monitoring software is running on each node instead of being an external entity, the resource usage of the server can be monitored as well. This can potentially provide more information in case of a failure, and by monitoring the system health, possible failure causes can be detected early, helping to prevent downtime.

Network tomography

Network tomography (NT) is the study of the internal characteristics of the Internet using information derived from end nodes. According to the type of data acquisition and performance parameters being tracked, network tomography can be classified as:
1. Link-level parameter estimation based on end-to-end, path-level traffic measurements
2. Sender-receiver path level traffic intensity estimation based on link-level traffic measurements

NT is a comprehensive model for building inferential network monitoring techniques that require minimal cooperation from network elements.

Network Coding (NC) was developed with the aim of improving the throughput of networks. NC packets introduce topology-dependent correlation, which can be used to improve the accuracy and reduction of complexity in choosing monitoring paths. The introduction of NC to NT extends the bottleneck discovery to P2P networks. This has implications on traffic routing and other network performance metrics.

Network monitoring capabilities

What started as a model of end-point monitoring has grown to span a spectrum of network leveraged monitoring and management capabilities, largely driven by the complexity of the entire network and infrastructure. The various aspects of monitoring categorised below are seen in metrics driven service level agreements (SLA).

Availability and uptime monitoring:
- Network device monitoring
- Cisco monitoring
- Device health monitoring
- Switch monitoring
- Network mapping
- Custom network maps
- WAN RTT monitoring
- VoIP monitoring

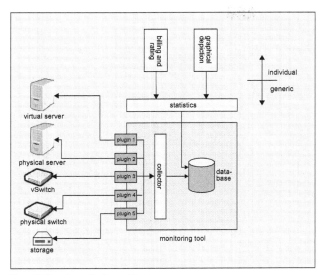

Figure 3: Generic monitoring architecture

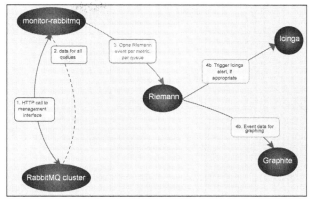

Figure 4: Riemann deployment

- Network traffic analysis
- Network configuration management
- IP address management
- Switch port management

Server management:
- Server management
- Server performance management
- Server monitoring
- VMware monitoring
- Hyper-V monitoring
- Citrix XenServer monitoring
- System health monitoring
- Service monitoring
- Windows service monitoring
- Process monitoring
- File/folder monitoring

Fault management:
- Network fault management
- IT workflow automation
- Email alerts
- SMS alerts
- Network monitoring tools
- Real-time graphs
- Switch port mappers
- Remote connection support
- SNMP trap processing
- Syslog monitoring
- Event log monitoring
- Threshold based alerting
- Integration with helpdesk
- Advanced alert management
- Customisable dashboard
- Service level management dashboards

- Network performance monitoring
- Prioritised reports
- Line of business teports
- Scheduled emailing of periodic reports

Data centre management:
- 3D data centre floor visualisation
- Systems management
- Data centre management
- Root cause analysis
- CMDB (configuration management database)
- Social connected IT

Enterprise grade scalability:
- Enterprise network monitoring
- Scalability in enterprise monitoring
- Remote network monitoring

Failover support:
- Third-party integrations and plugins
- Add-ons and plugins
- REST APIs
- Integration with industry frameworks (HP OpenView, Tivoli, etc)
  Plugins extend the scope of management to include network changes, configuration management and IP address management.

Deployments:
- Automatic network discovery
- Discovery engine rule
- Monitoring templates
- Bulk configuration tools

Mobile dashboards:
- Android apps
- iOS apps

Productivity workflows:
- Automated workflows

- Intelligent alerting engines
- Configurable discovery rules
- Flexible templates

Open source tools

Now that we have an overview of the technology, protocols, practices and the key drivers for SLA driven network monitoring, let us take a quick look at some of the interesting open source monitoring tools. The generic architecture is seen in Figure 3.

collectd

collectd is a daemon which collects system performance statistics written in plain C for performance and portability. Everything in collectd is done in plugins, and its memory footprint is so small that it runs even on embedded WLAN routers with OpenWRT.

collectd uses a 'data push' model, wherein the data is collected and then pushed to a multi-cast group or server. It also implements a lightweight binary TLV based network protocol that works for data collection even over slow networks. Since data transmission and reception can be configured separately, the resultant models of network operation are - no networking, uni-cast, proxy and multi-cast.

collectd uses an in-memory self-balancing binary search tree to cache values in memory. This approach results in high resolution statistics being processed at scale. The multi-threaded design of collectd allows for multiple plugins to be queried simultaneously. It must be mentioned that influxDB, a time-series database, and Javascript based client-side frameworks like Grafana can also be used to build feature-rich custom dashboards.

Riemann

Another way to visualise the network is in terms of events raised by the various network elements, servers and applications as part of their processing capabilities. An outbound packet on a network interface constitutes an event —a http reply is an event, a log entry written is an event, processing stage completed in Apache spark is an event, etc. Thus, any changes to CPU, memory, disk, database, application, services, infrastructure, IPMI, HT bus, etc, are events.

Riemann is an event stream processor with an asynchronous event model. It aggregates events and processes them with a stream language.

Figure 4 shows a typical deployment scenario, wherein Riemann is used to monitor a message queue cluster using multiple technology components.

OpenNMS

While we discuss OpenNMS architecture, an interesting feature beyond monitoring is its capability for log correlation. A Java-centric infrastructure will lean towards OpenNMS rather than Riemann.

Other monitoring tools that should be mentioned are Munin, Shinken, Sensu, Consul and Icinga2. Interested readers are welcome to explore them at leisure.

Networks, going forward

Carrier network infrastructure (CNI) and telecom operations management systems are growing at a compounded annual growth of 2.6 per cent, resulting in a US$ 2.7 trillion market. The speed of smartphone and tablet adoption, coupled with cloud infrastructure and video streaming, is disrupting centralised systems, driving network traffic and changing traffic patterns.

New technologies like software defined networking (SDN), network function virtualisation (NFV), 100Gbps+, Data Centre Ethernet, Packet Optical Transport Systems (P-OTS), 5G, LTE-advanced and small cell technology have the potential to change network cost structures, and improve network flexibility and resilience.

Tools and products that provide distributed network monitoring with tomography and real-time route analytics capabilities have the potential to be game changers. END

References

[1] OATCA, Advanced Telecommunications Computing Architecture: *http://www.atca.org/*
[2] Jinyang Li et' al (2004) Comparing the performance of Distributed Hash tables under churn. *https://pdos.lcs.mit.edu/~strib/docs/dhtcomparison/dhtcomparison-iptps04.pdf*
[3] Chen et' al (2004) An algebraic approach to practical and scalable overlay network monitoring. SIGCOMM. *http://dl.acm.org/citation.cfm?id=1015475*
[4] Birman (2007) The promise, and limitations, of gossip protocols, ACM SIGOPS 41(5). *http://dl.acm.org/citation.cfm?id=1317382*
[5] Subramanian et' al (2006) Gossip Enabled monitoring services for scalable heterogenous distributed systems, Cluster computing. *doi:10.1.1.160.2604*
[6] Wem Qiang Wang et' al (2012), Smart Traffic Cloud: an infrastructure for Traffic Applications, Proc. of 2012 IEEE 18th Intl Conf on Parallel and Distributed Systems.
[7] Tongqing Qiu et' al (2008) Packet Doppler: Network monitoring using Packet Shift Detection. ACN CoNext 2008, Madrid Spain.
[8] O'Donnell, G (2004), Route Analytics enrich technology relationships, META group publication.
[9] Peng Qin et' al (2014) A Survey on Network Tomography with Network Coding *http://arxiv.org/abs/1403.5828*

By: Saifi Khan

The author is the founder of Containerlogic, which is focused on building solutions using micro services, Docker and real-time analytics. He is passionate about open source software, and believes that it is one of the most enduring ways to build flexible, scalable and feature-rich infrastructure platforms. He can be reached at *saifi@containerlogic.co*.

In a scenario where we are using freely available public wireless networks all the time, security considerations are vital. Wireless attacks can be launched on the unwary and unprepared in several ways. An evil twin attack is one such serious threat.

The era of wireless connectivity offers us flexibility and mobility, but also comes with security issues. With wired connectivity, the user is more secure due to the physical connectivity. In wireless connectivity, however, the user is completely dependent on the AP or the SSID. In this article, I will discuss a very serious attack called the 'evil twin'.

Before proceeding further, you will need to get familiar with the terminology used in this article.

Service Set Identifier (SSID): An SSID is a 32-character (maximum) alphanumeric key identifying the name of the wireless local area network (WLAN).

AP (Access Point): This is used to connect the wireless device to the wireless network.

BSSID: This is the MAC address of the AP.

In an evil twin attack, the attacker makes a clone of a legitimate AP, and tries to route the user traffic from the cloned AP by means of any kind of DOS of the legitimate AP.

An evil twin attack can be launched in a cafe, hotel or any open wireless access area. Consider a scenario in which you connect to the familiar AP's SSID -- you know only its name. Next time, when you start your PC, it searches for the known AP. Evil twin attacks leverage preferred network lists, which enable automatic re-association with previously-used networks.

In this article, I will demonstrate how to make a clone of an AP, then its association with the client and finally, I will

discuss the defence techniques suggested by researchers.

Launching an evil twin attack

To launch the attack, I used the following:
- Kali Linux as the attacker
- Windows 7 as the victim
- A wireless AP

Kali Linux was installed in a VMware machine with a USB wireless card (Atheros-based), and it successfully recognised the card. I then followed the steps given below to launch the attack.

Step 1: To know the name of the wireless card, I typed the command *airmon-ng* as shown in Figure 1.

The wireless card's name is wlan0.

Step 2: The next command *airmon-ng start wlan0* set the wireless card in monitor mode 0, which means mon0 as shown in Figure 2.

Step 3: Then I ran the command *airdump-ng mon0*. Figure 3 shows the effect of the command. It also shows all the APs in the vicinity of the attacker. The red rectangle shows the target AP's SSID (L4wisdom.com), channel number (1) and BSSID (0C:D2:B5:01:0F:E6).

Step 4: Here, I set mon0 to Channel 1, using the following command (as shown in Figure 4):

```
airodump-ng mon0 -c <channel>  --bssid  <mac address of AP>
```

It's Good To Have A Choice!

ASSURED GIFT WITH EACH SUBSCRIPTION

GET DISCOUNTS

1 OR 2

Toaster Oven
(Worth Rs 2000)

Coffee Maker
(Worth Rs 1400)

EFY Round Neck T-Shirt
(worth Rs 300)

OSFY Collered T-Shirt
(Worth Rs 500)

Popcorn Maker
(Worth Rs 1100)

SUBSCRIBE TO YOUR FAVOURITE MAGAZINES NOW!

Free e-zine Access With Every Subscription

Option 1: Assured Gifts with every subscription

Magazine	Duration	Issues	Cover Price (₹)	You Pay (₹)	Assured Gift
Electronics Bazaar	1 Year	12	1200	1200 ☐	☐ EFY Round Neck T-Shirt (worth Rs 300)
	3 Years	36	3600	3600 ☐	☐ Popcorn Maker (Worth Rs 1100)
	5 Years	60	6000	6000 ☐	☐ Toster Oven (Worth Rs 2000)
Open Source For You	1 Year	12	1200	1200 ☐	☐ OSFY Collered T-Shirt (Worth Rs 500)
	3 Years	36	3600	3600 ☐	☐ Coffee Maker (Worth Rs 1400)
	5 Years	60	6000	6000 ☐	☐ Toaster Oven (Worth Rs 2000)

Option 2: Upto 40% Discount Offer

Magazine	Duration	Issues	Cover Price (₹)	Discount	You Pay (₹)	You Save
Electronics Bazaar	1 Year	12	1200	20%	960 ☐	240
	3 Years	36	3600	30%	2515 ☐	1080
	5 Years	60	6000	40%	3595 ☐	2400
Open Source For You	1 Year	12	1200	20%	960 ☐	240
	3 Years	36	3600	30%	2520 ☐	1080
	5 Years	60	6000	40%	3600 ☐	2400

Offer Valid till 31st July 2015

Introducing EFY's Premium Edition

Electronics For You PLUS
(With software-packed DVD)

☐ 1 Year (12 Issues) ~~1280~~ ₹ **960**

☐ 2 Yrs (24 Issues) ~~2400~~ ₹ **1800**

Free e-zine Access With Every Subscription

- Don't Miss A Single Issue!
- Ensure Regular Supply
- FREE Replacement Policy*
- Order Now For FREE Home Delivery

* Replacement will be made if intimation of damaged / non-receipt
of copies is received within 30 days of its publication
** If you are not satisfied with the magazine & services
your balance amount will be returned

To Subscribe Online, Visit: http://subscribe.efyindia.com   **For Online Renewal,** Visit: http://renew.efyindia.com

Name_____Designation_____Organisation_____

Mailing Address_____City_____

Pin Code_____State_____Phone_____Email_____

Subscription No. (for existing subscribers only_____. I would like to subscribe to the above (✓)marked magazine(s) starting with the next

issue. Please find enclosed a sum of Rs_____by DD/MO/crossed cheque*bearing the No._____dt._____in favour of

EFY Enterprises Pvt Ltd, payable at Delhi. (*Please add Rs 50 on non-metro cheque)

Send this filled-in form or its photocopy to :   **EFY Enterprises Pvt Ltd** D-87/1, Okhla Industrial Area, Phase 1, New Delhi 110 020
Ph: **011-26810601-03**; Fax: **011-26817563**; e-mail: **info@efy.in**   **EFY**GROUP   www.efy.in

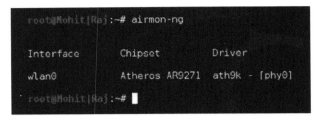

Figure 1: The wireless card

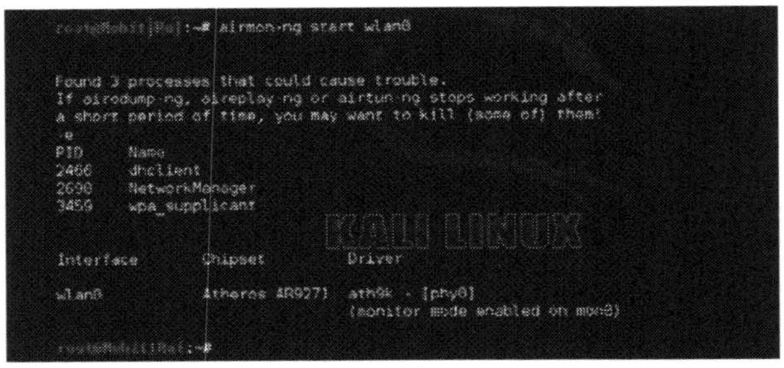

Figure 2: Setting Wlan0 to mon0

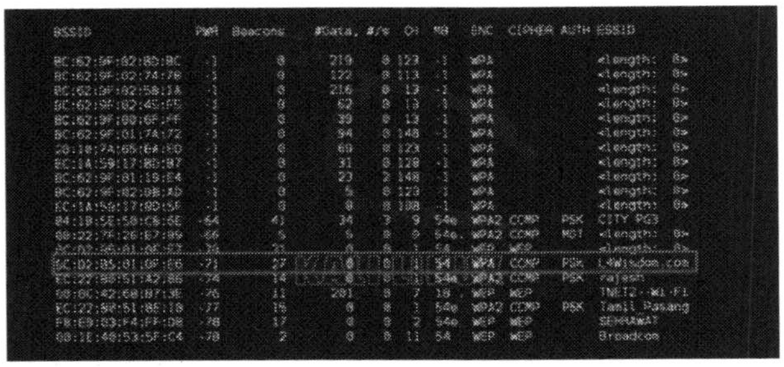

Figure 3: List of APs

Figure 4: Setting mon0 to Channel 1

Figure 5: Clients associated with the AP (*L4wisdom.com*)

The clients associated with the AP have BSSID 0C:D2:B5:01:0F:E6 (as shown in Figure 5).

Step 5: To clone the *L4wisdom.com* AP, I used the following command:

```
root@Mohit|Raj:~# airbase-ng -a bb:bb:bb:bb:bb:bb --essid
"L4wisdom.com" -c 1 mon0
```

The attack was launched. After a few seconds, the client disassociated the legitimate AP due to the confusion between the original and fake AP.

Attack scenario

I repeated this experiment thrice.

The attack was successful in the following cases:

1. When the victim's PC was equidistant from the AP and attacker PC.
2. The distance between the AP and the victim was 1 metre, and the distance between the victim's PC and attacker's PC was 6 metres.
3. The distance between the AP and victim was 1 metre, and the distance between the victim's PC and attacker's PC was 9 metres.

In each instance, the victim's PC got confused and was not able to detect the real AP.

Practical defences against evil twin attacks

Trust based on location: In this approach, the client records all the APs in the vicinity. These recorded APs act as wireless landmarks, so that the client can recognise the correct location for a particular network. During association, the client must compare the new location with the previous location, and if these match, the client can trust this AP.

Establishing cryptographic identity: When trust is based on location, one cannot make any strong assertions about an AP's identity. This is addressed in the research paper 'Practical Defences for Evil Twin Attacks in 802.11', Harold Gonzales, Kevin Bauer, Janne Lindqvist, and Damon McCoy, presented at the IEEE GlobeCom in December 2010 at Miami in Florida. The paper proposes that AP identities be bound to self-signed public keys using a new authentication module designed for the 802.1X extensible authentication protocol (EAP). In this defence technique, the researchers proposed that the client would have to trust the AP for the first time. However, this defence technique ensures that the AP is the same for each subsequent association.

In addition, it is possible for an attacker to impersonate a legitimate AP and present clients with a fraudulent public key. However, it is difficult to distinguish between an AP revoking a potentially compromised key and an evil twin attack. **END**

References

[1] Kevin Bauer, Harold Gonzales, and Damon McCoy; 'Mitigating Evil Twin Attacks in 802.11'
[2] Harold Gonzales†, Kevin Bauer, Janne Lindqvist, Damon McCoy, Douglas Sicker; 'Practical Defenses for Evil Twin Attacks in 802.11'

By: Mohit

The author is a CEH and ECSA with a master's degree in computer science engineering from Thapar University. He is the author of the book 'Python Penetration Testing Essentials'. He currently works at IBM India, and can be contacted at mohitraj.cs@gmail.com and on LinkedIn at: *https://www.linkedin.com/profile/view?id=104187708;* website: *www.L4wisdom.com*

The Pros and Cons of Polyglot Persistence

The design of a database determines its optimal use. A single database engine is inefficient and insufficient for all data searches. This is where polyglot persistence comes in - it helps to shard data into multiple databases to leverage their power.

Today, we have a large number of databases, which range from document databases like MongoDB and graphs like Neo4j, to search databases like ElasticSearch, caches like Redis and more. All of these databases are great at doing a few things well and other things not so well. For example, ElasticSearch is great for full-text search on large volumes of data, something that cannot be done well in MongoDB.

Polyglot persistence is the way to shard or divide your data into multiple databases and leverage their power together. For example, if you have some data on which a search has to be performed, you can store that data in ElasticSearch because it works on a data structure called *Inverted Index*, which is designed to allow very fast full-text searches and is extremely scalable.

What types of databases can I use?

Document databases (e.g., MongoDB): Document databases are used to store whole JSON documents and query with relevant fields. It's the go-to database for most developers. Document databases are usually bad at doing joins between collections/tables and doing a full-text search.

Graph databases (e.g., Neo4j): Graph databases are used for storing relations between entities, with nodes being

entities and edges being relationships. For example, if you're building a social network and if Person A follows Person B, then Person A and Person B can be nodes and the 'follows' can be the edge between them. Graphs are excellent in doing multi-level joins and are good for features that need the shortest-path algorithm between A and B.

Cache (e.g., Redis): Cache is used when you need superfast access to your data—for example, if you're building an e-commerce application and have product categories that load on every page load. Instead of hitting the database for every read operation (for every page load), which is expensive, you can store it in cache, which is extremely fast for reads/writes. The only drawback of using cache is that it is in-memory and is not persistent.

Search databases (e.g., ElasticSearch): If you want to do a full text search on your data (e.g., products in an e-commerce app), you need a search database like ElasticSearch, which can help you perform the search over huge volumes of data.

Row store (e.g., Cassandra): Cassandra is used for storing time-series data (like analytics) or logs. If you have a use-case that performs a lot of writes, less reads and is non-relational data, then Cassandra is the database to take a look at.

The advantages of polyglot persistence

Faster response times: You leverage all the features of databases in your app, which makes the response times of your app very fast.

Helps your app to scale well: Your app scales exceptionally well with the data. All the NoSQL databases scale well when you model databases properly for the data that you want to store.

A rich experience: You have a very rich experience when you harness the power of multiple databases at the same time. For example, if you want to search on 'Products' in an e-commerce app, then you use ElasticSearch, which returns the results based on relevance, which MongoDB cannot do.

Disadvantages of polyglot persistence

Requires you to hire people to integrate different databases: If you're an enterprise, you will have the resources to hire experts for each database type (which is good). But if you're a small company or a start-up, you may not have the resources to hire people to implement a good polyglot persistence model.

Implementers need to learn different databases: If you're an indie developer or start-up building apps on multiple databases, then you have no choice but to learn multiple types of databases and implement a good polyglot persistence model for your app.

It requires resources to manage databases: If you're running multiple databases for your app, then you need to take care of backups, replicas, clusters, etc, for each of those types of databases, which might be time consuming.

Testing can be tough: If you shard your data into many databases, then testing of your data layer can be complicated and debugging can usually be time consuming.

Automating polyglot persistence

The good thing is that there are solutions which automate polyglot persistence. Automating polyglot persistence frees you from learning different types of databases or hiring experts. The following such solutions also tend to manage mundane tasks like backups, replication and more, so that you never have to worry about them.

CloudBoost.io: Gives you one simple API to store and query your data, and it uses AI to automatically store your data into the database where it should naturally belong. It does auto-scaling, replication and backups for you too.

Orchestrate.io: This has a graph DB API, which you can use to store data. Orchestrate is a good database service if you've used Neo4j or any graph DB before. END

By: Nawaz Dhandala

The author works as a hacker at a company called HackerBay, which builds database services. He is also the worldwide winner of the Microsoft Imagine Cup, and has participated as a delegate in many international conferences like World Business Dialogue, South American Business Forum and more.

Check This New
Sorting Algorithm Design

In this article, which is aimed at those who love playing around with algorithms and data structures—programmers, developers and coders—the author shares a new sorting algorithm developed by him, which reduces sort time drastically. It assumes that the readers are aware about at least asymptotic analysis, worst and best case running time analysis and basic sorting algorithms.

Sorting algorithms, which arrange the elements of a list in a certain order (either ascending or descending), are an important category in computer science. We can use sorting as a technique to reduce search complexity. Vast amounts of research has gone into this category of algorithms because of its importance, particularly in database algorithms.

Classification

Sorting algorithms are generally classified into different categories based on various factors like the number of comparisons, memory usage, recursion, etc. Existing sorting algorithms include the *Selection, Bubble, Heap, Insertion, Quick, Merge, Counting, Bucket* and *Radix sort*. All these different algorithms have some advantages and disadvantages.

The description of each of these algorithms is beyond the scope of this article.

The following gives a glimpse of how sorting works (with the Bubble sort):

```
Void bubble_sort(int arr[], int n) {
    for(int pass=n-1;pass>=0;pass--)
                        // outer loop executed  n times
        {
         for( int i=0; i<pass-1;i++)
                        // inner loop execute  n times
            {
              if(arr[i]> arr[i+1])
                  { // swapping the elements
                        Int temp=arr[i];
                      arr[i]= arr[i+1];
                      arr[i+1]=temp;
                  }
            }
        }
}
```

The above algorithm takes $O(n^2)$ time even in the best case.

Try optimising it so that we can skip some extra swaps by introducing an extra flag.

The following is optimised code of the above:

```
Void bubble_sort(int arr[], int n)
{
Int pass, I, temp, swapped=1;
for( pass=n-1; pass>=0&& swapped; pass--)
    {
       Swapped=0;
            for( i=0; I<pass-1;i++)
                {
                    If(arr[i]> arr[i+1])
                        {
                            temp=arr[i];
                           arr[i]=arr[i+1];
                           arr[i+1]=temp;
                           swapped=1;
                        }
                }
    }
}
```

This optimised version finally improves the time of the worst and best cases of the Bubble sort to O(n). This is called an optimisation of the code.

My new sorting algorithm

Recently, I developed a sorting algorithm that is able to sort any input (i.e., not ask for input restrictions) in *O(n) time* with *O(n) Space Complexity*. Though there are several sorting algorithms out there, which I mentioned earlier, some like Merge, Quick and Heap sort take O(nlogn) time, and some like Bubble, Selection and Insertion sort, take O(n^2) time; but no algorithm takes O(n) time to throw up the result.

Of course, Counting, Radix and Bucket sort take O(n) time, but ask for input restrictions and finally cannot sort all the input given.

In this algorithm, we use a hash table implicitly to operate onto input elements, and only by doing two scans we are able to sort any kind of input (no input restriction) provided to us.

Implementation: How does it work?

Now, let us find a better solution to this problem. Since our objective is to sort any kind of input, what if we get the maximum elements and create the hash? So, create a maximum hash and initialise it with all zeros. For each of the input elements, go to the corresponding position and increment its count. Since we are using arrays, it takes constant time to reach any location.

> **Note:** All the code described in this algorithm was checked in 32-bit compilers (CodeBlocks) and in gcc-compilers.

Here is the main code implementation:

```
#include <stdio.h>
#include <conio.h>
#include <stdlib.h>

void main()
{
long int arr[]={62,4,8,423,43,4,432,44,23,2,55,12,3};
int n=sizeof(arr)/sizeof(arr[0]) ;
int i, j, k,l;
int min=arr[0];
int max=arr[0] ;
for(i=1;i<n;i++)          // run for n times
   {
     if(arr[i]<min)
       min=arr[i] ;       // required for optimization
     else if(arr[i]>max)
       max=arr[i] ;
   }
int *hash=(int*)calloc((max+1), sizeof(int)); //should be max+1

for(i=0;i<n;i++ )
   {
    hash[arr[i]]++; // storing the count of occurances of element
   }
   printf("\n");

   for(i=0;i<max+1;i++)    // loop to read the hash table...
   {
   if(hash[i]>0)
   {
   printf("%d\t", i) ; //print 1st time if the element has occured
   }
```

```
j=hash[i];       /* this requires if the count of the element
          is greater than one(if there is duplicates
          element in the array) otherwise dupplicated element
          will not be displayed more than once.*/
if(j==1 ||j==0)
continue;
   while(j!=1)
   {           // here we are printing till count not equal to 1
   printf("%d\t", i) ;
   j--;
   }
 }
getch();
}
```

The time complexity of the above algorithm is O(n) and with only two scans, we are able to arrive at the result. Its space complexity is O(n), as it requires extra auxiliary space (almost the maximum elements in an array) to get the result.

How is it better than other existing sorting algorithms?

Let's check how this new algorithm compares with other existing sorting algorithms in terms of time complexity and speedup, flexibility and elegance of code.

I have already given you a glimpse of the Bubble sort and its optimisation. Now let's take a look at the time complexity of existing algorithms:

Selection sort	Best case- O(n)	Worst case-O(n2)
Bubble sort	Best case O(n)	Worst case-O(n2)
Insertion sort	Best case- O(n2)	Worst case-O(n2)
Merge sort	Best case- O(nlogn)	Worst case-O(nlogn)
Quick sort	Best case- O(nlogn)	Worst case-O(n2)
Radix sort	Best case- O(n)	Worst case-O(n)
Bucket sort	Best case- O(n)	Worst case-O(n)
Counting sort	Best case- O(n)	Worst case-O(n)

> **Note:** Radix, Bucket and Counting sort make assumptions about the input provided, i.e., they cannot sort all the input provided. There is an input restriction, though (about which there will be no discussion in this article).

How the new sorting algorithm is better in terms of time-complexity and overhead

I am using *rand()*. The function *rand()* generates a pseudo-random integer number. This number will be in the range of 0 to RAND_MAX. The constant RAND_MAX is defined in the standard library *(stdlib)*.

```
#include<stdio.h>
#include<stdlib.h>
```

```
#include<time.h>
 main()
 {
  int arr[10000],i,j,min,temp;
  for(i=0;i<10000;i++)
   {
     arr[i]=rand()%10000;
   }
  //The  MySort Agorithm
  clock_t start,end;
  start=clock();

min=arr[0];
int max=arr[0] ;
for(i=1;i<10000;i++)
  {
    if(arr[i]<min)
    min=arr[i] ;      // required for optimization
    else if(arr[i]>max)
    max=arr[i] ;
  }
int *hash=(int*)calloc((max+1), sizeof(int)); //should be max+1

for(i=0;i<10000;i++ )
  {
   hash[arr[i]]++;  // storing the count of occurances of elements
  }
 printf("\n");
 end=clock();
 double extime=(double) (end-start)/CLOCKS_PER_SEC;
 printf("\n\tExecution time for the  MySort Algorithm is %f
seconds\n ",extime);


  for(i=0;i<10000;i++)
  {
   arr[i]=rand()%10000;
  }
 clock_t start1,end1;
 start1=clock();
 // The Selection Sort
 for(i=0;i<10000;i++)
  {
   min=i;
   for(j=i+1;j<10000;j++)
    {
     if(arr[min]>arr[j])
     {
     min=j;
     }
    }
   temp=arr[min];
   arr[min]=arr[i];
   arr[i]=temp;
```

Figure 1: Result - > speed up difference between two Sorting Algorithm

```
  }
 end1=clock();
 double extime1=(double) (end1-start1)/CLOCKS_PER_SEC;
 printf("\n");
 printf("\tExecution time for the selection sort is %f
seconds\n \n",extime1);
  if(extime1<extime)
   printf("\tSelection sort is faster than MySort Algorithm
by %f seconds\n\n",extime-    extime1);
  else if(extime1>extime)
   printf("\tMysort Algorithm is faster than  Selectionsort
by %f seconds\n\n",extime1-extime);
  else
   printf("\tBoth algo has same execution time\n\n");
 }
```

> **Note:** It is not always recommended to use *clock ()* since it is badly [not precise] implemented on many architectures. Precise optimisation can only be done by analysing the code. Asymptotic analysis is the perfect way for analysing algorithms. It evaluates the performance of an algorithm in terms of input size [we don't measure the actual running time].

How is this sorting algorithm better than Merge sort and Quick sort algorithms in terms of both time complexity and overhead spent?

Both Merge sort [O(nlogn)] and Quick sort [O(nlogn)-best case] use recursion to sort the input; also, the running time of Quick sort in the worst case is O(n^2). There are always certain overheads involved while calling a function. Time has to be spent on passing values, passing control, returning values and returning control. Recursion takes a lot of stack space. Every time the function calls itself, memory has to be allocated, and also recursion is not good for production code.

In the new sorting algorithm, we are getting rid of all issues—the recursion, the time and the overhead. In comparison with the Merge and Quick sort, we are almost cutting the time by logn and making the new algorithm to run in O(n) time.

It may happen that when you try to compare the execution time of Merge and Quick sort and the new sorting algorithm, they may give the same or equal execution time based on the above method by introducing *clock*, but again, you cannot measure the accurate running time by doing so.

I am providing a Merge sort algorithm here, so that you can refer to and trace the difference in both codes, and see how many recursions and function calls are involved:

```
/* Function to merge the two haves arr[l..m] and
arr[m+1..r] of array arr[] */
void merge(int arr[], int l, int m, int r)
{
    int i, j, k;
    int n1 = m - l + 1;
    int n2 =  r - m;

    /* create temp arrays */
    int L[n1], R[n2];

    /* Copy data to temp arrays L[] and R[] */
    for(i = 0; i < n1; i++)
        L[i] = arr[l + i];
    for(j = 0; j < n2; j++)
        R[j] = arr[m + 1+ j];
    /* Merge the temp arrays back into arr[l..r]*/
    i = 0;
    j = 0;
    k = l;
    while (i < n1 && j < n2)
    {
        if (L[i] <= R[j])
        {
            arr[k] = L[i];
            i++;
        }
        else
        {
            arr[k] = R[j];
            j++;
        }
        k++;
    }
    /* Copy the remaining elements of L[], if there are any
*/
    while (i < n1)
    {
        arr[k] = L[i];
        i++;
        k++;
    }
    /* Copy the remaining elements of R[], if there are any
*/
    while (j < n2)
    {
        arr[k] = R[j];
        j++;
        k++;
    }
}
/* l is for left index and r is right index of the sub-array
   of arr to be sorted */
void mergeSort(int arr[], int l, int r)
{
    if (l < r)
    {
        int m = l+(r-l)/2;
        //Same as (l+r)/2, but avoids overflow for large l and h
        mergeSort(arr, l, m);
        mergeSort(arr, m+1, r);
        merge(arr, l, m, r);
    }
}
```

Finally, as every algorithm has some pros and cons according to the input provided, some of the advantages and disadvantages of this new sorting algorithm are listed here.

Advantages

- Time efficient about O(n) in even the worst case, and has sorting flexibility
- Elegant and lucid code that is easy to understand
- Requires only two scans to get the result, and it is free from recursion and extra overhead
- Is an advantage in many problems that use sorting as pre-processing to arrive at the result

Disadvantages

- It requires extra space as per input provided
- Wastes much of the space if the input is short and has a large number at any point, e.g., {5, 1, 11, 395, 159, 64, 9,}, though situations like this rarely occur

Applications of this sorting algorithm

There are several applications and uses that require sorting as pre-processing before doing real computation to get the result, which takes O(nlogn) as the total running time. This particular problem can be decreased to a time of O(n) with the help of this new sorting algorithm. Some examples can be:

- Finding the majority element
- Finding the triplet in an array
- Finding two elements whose sum is closest to zero. **END**

By: Santosh Kumar

The author is an alumnus of NIT-Jamshedpur with a computer science and engineering background. He loves playing around with algorithm design and programming. He currently works for Cisco Systems as a software engineer, and can be contacted at *santoshnitjsr2010@gmail.com*

Reordering C Structure Alignment

The memory footprint of C programs can be reduced by manually repacking C structure declarations. This article is about reordering the structure members in decreasing lengths of variables.

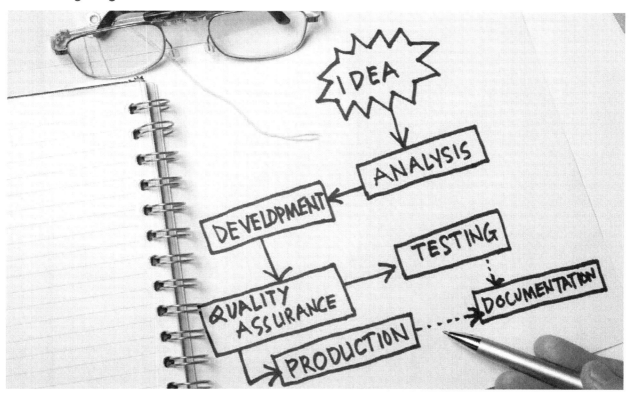

Computer memory is word-addressable. For every instruction, the CPU fetches one word data from the memory. This behaviour affects how basic C data types will be aligned in memory. For example, every short (2B) will start on an address divisible by 2; similarly, int(4B) or long(8B) start on addresses divisible by 4 and 8, respectively. But char(1B) can start on any address. This happens due to *self-alignment* by the processor. Be it X86, ARM or PPC—all display this behaviour.

The following example will explain self-alignment and its advantages. In this example, the size of the pointer is assumed to be 4B. Here, we will use a user-defined struct data type.

```
struct ESTR
{
    char c;            /*1B*/
    unsigned int* up;    /*4B*/
    short x;            /*2B*/
    int v;            /*4B*/
    char k;            /*1B*/
};
```

You may think this structure will take 12B memory space. But if you print *sizeof(struct ESTR)* you will find the result to be 20B. This is because of self-alignment. This structure will be placed in memory in the following way:

BYTE1	BYTE2	BYTE3	BYTE4
c			
Up	up	up	up
x	x		
v	v	v	v
k			

So, you can see all the variables are starting on word boundaries. It is good practice to explicitly mention the *padding* so that no places are left with junk values. With padding, the structure resembles the following:

```
struct ESTR
{
    char c;            /*1B*/
    char pad1[3];
```

```
    unsigned int* up;    /*4B*/
    short x;             /*2B*/
    char pad2[2];
    int v;               /*4B*/
    char k;              /*1B*/
    char pad3[3];
};
```

Now our structure looks like what's shown below:

BYTE1	BYTE2	BYTE3	BYTE4
C	pad1	pad1	pad1
Up	up	up	up
x	x	pad2	pad2
v	v	v	v
k	pad3	pad3	pad3

The best way to decrease the slope is by 'reordering the structure' members in decreasing lengths of variables. If we reorder the structure, we get the following:

```
struct ESTR
{
    unsigned int* up;    /*4B*/
    int v;               /*4B*/
    short x;             /*2B*/
char c;      /*1B*/
char k;      /*1B*/
};
```

Now, our structure looks like what's shown below:

BYTE1	BYTE2	BYTE3	BYTE4
Up	up	Up	up
v	v	v	v
x	x	c	k

You can see the structure has come down to 12B from 20B. But do not think that padding can be completely eliminated. In this specific example, it has happened with reordering. This may not happen always. But the right practice is to sort the members according to their size.

The disadvantage of reordering

Reordering may affect cache-locality. For example, in a structure, you refer to two variables very frequently. But because of reordering, they are placed very far in terms of word number. So when they are mapped in cache, they become part of different blocks which generate cache-miss and require very frequent cache block swapping. Hence, execution becomes slow.

'Structure packing' stops compilers from adding any pad but forces the use of a defined order. It can be achieved with '*#pragma pack*' in C. Then our first structure alignment looks like what follows:

BYTE1	BYTE2	BYTE3	BYTE4
c	up	up	up
up	x	x	v
v	v	v	k

This is called structure packing.

Now, if the CPU wants variable *v* or *up* it needs two word accesses for each word consisting of 4 bytes.

So it is the design, which will enable users to make a choice. In embedded systems, there is a performance versus memory size trade-off, because everybody expects faster responses but the size of the memory is fixed. Fragmentation may also not be handled in an embedded OS because of the size constraints. So, the designer has to be careful. END

By: Supriyo Ganguly

The author is an engineer working at the Electronics Corporation of India Limited, Hyderabad.

Unit Testing in Java Using the JUnit Framework

The JUnit Framework can be easily integrated with Eclipse. Unit testing accelerates programming speed.

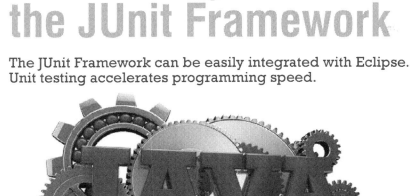

While software testing is generally performed by the professional software tester, unit testing is often performed by the software developers working on the project, at that point of time. Unit testing ensures that the specific function is working perfectly. It also reduces software development risks, cost and time. Unit testing is performed by the software developer during the construction phase of the software development life cycle. The major benefit of unit testing is that it reduces the construction errors during software development, thus improving the quality of the product. Unit testing is about testing classes and methods.

What is JUnit?

JUnit is a testing tool for the Java programming language. It is very helpful when you want to test each unit of the project during the software development process.

How to perform unit testing using the JUnit testing tool

To perform JUnit testing in Java, first of all, you have to install the Eclipse editor. Installation of the latest version is recommended. You can download the Eclipse IDE from the following link: *http://eclipse.org/downloads/*.

In the Eclipse editor, you can write any code. For example, let's suppose that I want to test the following code:

Code-1

```
1 package com;
2
3 public class Junit {
```

```
4
5    public String concatenate(String firstName, String
lastName) {
6
7        return firstName + lastName;
8    }
9
10    public int multiply(int number1, int number2) {
11
12        return number1 * number2;
13    }
14
15 }
```

After writing Code-1, let's write two test cases—one for the *concatenate* method and the other for the *multiply* method of the JUnit class defined in this code. To create JUnit test cases, you need to click on the Eclipse editor:
File→New→JUnit Test Case

Defining the test case for the *concatenate()* method of the JUnit class (Code-1)

Code-2

```
1 package com;
2 import static org.junit.Assert.*;
3 import org.junit.Test;
4
5 public class ConcatTest {
6
```

```
7    @Test
8    public void testConcatnate() {
9
10     Junit test = new Junit();
11
12     String result = test.concatenate("Vikas","Kumar");
13
14     assertEquals("VikasKumar", result);
15
16   }
17
18}
```

Code-2 is the test case for the *concatenate()* method defined inside the JUnit class in Code-1. The annotation *@Test* at Line 7 is supported by JUnit version 4. To add JUnit version 4, you can click on *Project directory* in the Eclipse IDE and go to *Java Build Path*, before clicking on *Add Library* and then on *JUnit*, where you select *Junit 4*.

The *assertEquals()* method is a predefined method, and it takes two parameters. The first parameter is called *expected output* and the second is *original output*. If the expected output doesn't match the original output, then the test case fails. To run the test cases, right click the Eclipse code and then click on *Run as JUnit Test*.

Defining the test case for the *multiply()* method of JUnit class (Code-1)

Code-3

```
1 package com;
2
3 import static org.junit.Assert.*;
4 import org.junit.Test;
5
6 public class MultiplyTest {
7
8    @Test
9    public void testMultiply() {
10
11     Junit test = new Junit();
12
13     int result = test.multiply(5, 5);
14
15     assertEquals(25, result);
16   }
17
18 }
```

Code-3 is the test case for the *multiply()* method of the JUnit class defined above.

Creating a test suite

A test suite is a combination of multiple test cases. To create a JUnit test suite, you need to click on the following in Eclipse:

File→Other→Java→JUnit→JUnit Test Suite

After creating the JUnit test suite, the code will look like what is shown in the Code-4 snippet.

Code-4

```
1 package com;
2
3 import org.junit.runner.RunWith;
4 import org.junit.runners.Suite;
5 import org.junit.runners.Suite.SuiteClasses;
6
7 @RunWith(Suite.class)
8 @SuiteClasses({ ConcatTest.class, MultiplyTest.class })
9 public class AllTests {
10
11 }
```

Understanding the *@Before* annotation

The *@Before* annotation is used to annotate the method that has to be executed before the actual test method gets executed. To understand this, let's look at Code-5.

Code-5

```
1 package com;
2
3 public class Calculator {
4
5    public int add(int x, int y) {
6
7      return x + y;
8    }
9
10   public int sub(int x, int y) {
11
12     return x - y;
13
14   }
15 }
```

Now let's create the test case for Code-5. The following code is the JUnit test case for the *Calculator* class defined in this code.

Code-6

```
1 package com;
2
3 import static org.junit.Assert.*;
4 import org.junit.Before;
5 import org.junit.Test;
6
7 public class CaculatorTest {
8
```

```
9    Calculator cal;
10
11   @Before
12   /*
13     the init() method will be called for each test, such
14     testAdd() as well as testSub()
15   */
16   public void init() {
17
18     cal = new Calculator();
19
20   }
21
22   @Test
23   public void testAdd() {
24
25     int x = 10;
26     int y = 20;
27     assertEquals(30, cal.add(x, y));
28
29   }
30
31   @Test
32   public void testSub() {
33     int x = 10;
34     int y = 20;
35     assertEquals(-10, cal.sub(x, y));
36   }
37
38 }
```

Parameterised unit test cases using JUnit

If you want to test any method with multiple input values, you would normally have to write multiple test cases for the same method. But if you use the parameterised unit testing technique, you don't need to write multiple test cases for the same method.

Let's look at the example of the *Calculator* class defined in Code-5. If you have to create parameterised test cases for the *add()* method of the Calculator class with multiple inputs, then consider the following code for that requirement.

Code-7

```
1    package com.emertxe;
2
3    import static org.junit.Assert.*;
4    import java.util.Arrays;
5    import java.util.Collection;
6    import org.junit.Assert;
7    import org.junit.Before;
8    import org.junit.Test;
9    import org.junit.runner.RunWith;
10   import org.junit.runners.Parameterized;
11   import org.junit.runners.Parameterized.Parameters;
```

```
12
13 @RunWith(Parameterized.class)
14 public class AddParamTest {
15
16    private int expectedResult;
17    private int firstVal;
18    private int secondVal;
19    Calculator cal;
20
21    @Before
22    public void init() {
23
24      cal = new Calculator();
25    }
26
27    public AddParamTest(int expectedResult, int firstVal, int
secondVal) {
28      this.expectedResult = expectedResult;
29      this.firstVal = firstVal;
30      this.secondVal = secondVal;
31    }
32
33    @Parameters
34    public static Collection<Object[]> testData() {
35
36      Object[][] data = new Object[][] { { 6, 2, 4 }, { 7, 4, 3 },
37           { 8, 2, 6 } };
38
39      return Arrays.asList(data);
40    }
41
42    @Test
43    public void testAdd() {
44    Assert.assertEquals(expectedResult, cal.add(firstVal,
secondVal));
45    }
46 }
```

When the test case written in Code-7 is executed, then an execution occurs in the following order:
1. Parameterised class at Line 11 is executed.
2. Static method at Line 32 is executed.
3. Instance of *AddParamTest* class at Line 12 is executed.
4. The data {6,2,4}, {7,4,3} and {8,2,6} at Lines 34-35 is passed to the constructor at Line 24.
5. *testAdd()* method at Line 41 is executed. END

By: Vikas Kumar Gautam

The author is a mentor at Emertxe Information Technology (P) Ltd. His main areas of expertise include application development using Java/J2EE and Android for both Web and mobile devices. A Sun Certified Java Professional (SCJP), his interests include acquiring greater expertise in the application space by learning from the latest happenings in the industry. He can be reached at *vikash_kumar@emertxe.com*

CakePHP: How to Create a Component

Here's a hands-on tutorial on creating a component in CakePHP—a must-read for those who like to learn through practical knowledge.

CakePHP is a free and open source PHP framework. Built with MVC (model-view-controller) pattern, it provides a powerful structure for the creation of well-organised Web applications.

There are many MVC frameworks available like CakePHP, Zend, Laravel, Yii, Codeigniter, etc. CakePHP is one of the top MVC frameworks. It is suitable for small, medium and large scale applications, and provides most of the tools we need to build an application. Instead of building from scratch, just copy CakePHP and start building your application. CakePHP has a very active development team and a large community for help. Its key features are inbuilt CRUD operations, automatic code generation, inbuilt validations, ACL, caching, etc.

In this tutorial, we will learn the basic concept of a component, how to create our own components and use them in our application. We will use the CakePHP 2.x version.

A CakePHP component

A component is a class file which contains the common code or logic. The component can be shared between the application's controllers. CakePHP comes with some good components, so you can perform various common tasks like session handling, cookies and security related things, etc.

A component is a good option when you need the same logic or functions in multiple controllers. It helps you to reuse the code and make your controllers tiny and clean. Apart from the built-in components of CakePHP, you can create your own components for common functionality such as handling file uploads, image processing or any common logic of our application.

Creating a component

Creating a component is a simple task. Just like a normal PHP class, you need to create a class file in your *Component* directory. The name of the class must be in *CamelCase* format and the word *Component* must be appended to it. For example, if you want to create a password component, the class name will be *PasswordComponent* and the file name will be *PasswordComponent.php*.

Let's continue with our password component example. As the name suggests, our component will be used for generating random passwords in our application.

Now, let's create a file in the *app/Controller/Component* directory and name it *PasswordComponent.php*. The basic structure of our component looks like what's shown below:

```
App::uses('Component', 'Controller');
class PasswordComponent extends Component {
// some code goes here
}
```

Now, our basic component is ready. Let's add a function to it that generates a random password string and returns it.

```
App::uses('Component', 'Controller');
class PasswordComponent extends Component {
public function generate() {
                    $length = 10;
$chars = 'ABCDEFGHIJKLMNOPQRS
TUVWXYZabcdefghijklmnopqrstuvwxyz' .'0123456789``-
=~!@#$%^&*()_+,./<>?;:[]{}\|';
$passwordStr = '';
$max = strlen($chars) - 1;

for ($i = 0; $i < $length; $i++) {
$passwordStr .= $chars[mt_rand(0, $max)];
}

                    return $passwordStr;
}

}
```

So we have now added our password generator function to the component. When we call this function, it will return a randomly generated password string.

If you see the *generate()* function, it generates a fixed length string of 10 characters. As with any normal PHP function, we can make it more dynamic by adding 'length' as a function parameter, so that we can pass the desired length for our password string.

Let's modify our function to use dynamic length:

```
function generate($length = 8) {
$chars = 'ABCDEFGHIJKLMNOPQRSTU
VWXYZabcdefghijklmnopqrstuvwxyz' .
'0123456789``-=~!@#$%^&*()_+,./<>?;:[]{}\|';

$passwordStr = '';
$max = strlen($chars) - 1;

for ($i = 0; $i < $length; $i++) {
$passwordStr .= $chars[mt_rand(0, $max)];
}

return $passwordStr;
}
```

We have set the default value of *$length* to 8. So, if we don't pass the length, it will generate an eight character long string.

Our final component code should look like what follows:

```
App::uses('Component', 'Controller');
class PasswordComponent extends Component {
public function generate($length = 8) {
$chars = 'ABCDEFGHIJKLMNOPQRST
UVWXYZabcdefghijklmnopqrstuvwxyz' .'0123456789``-
=~!@#$%^&*()_+,./<>?;:[]{}\|';
$passwordStr = '';
$max = strlen($chars) - 1;
for ($i = 0; $i < $length; $i++) {
$passwordStr .= $chars[mt_rand(0, $max)];
}

return $passwordStr;
}

}
```

Now our component is ready to be used in our application's controllers.

How to include the component in the controller

We can include our component in the controller by simply adding its name to the *$components* array. Here, *$components* is a public property of the *Controller* class. Please note that we only need to add the class name of the component, without the 'Component' suffix. For example, to use our *PasswordComponent* in any controller, add the following command:

```
public $components = array('Session', 'Password');
```

After adding this, we can access this component by using *$this->Password*, similar to other components.

If we include the component in our *AppController*, it will be available in all the other controllers and there is no need to include it in each controller file.

For example, to use our *PasswordComponent* and its *generate()* method in *UsersController*, issue the following code:

```
App::uses('AppController', 'Controller');

class UsersController extends AppController {

    public $components = array('Session', 'Password');

    public function some_action() {

      $password = $this->Password->generate(12);
    }

}
```

We can use this generated password in the *view* file by setting the view variable or saving it to the database.

> **Note:** In the latest version of CakePHP, which is 3.0, loading of a component is a little different. There is a method called *loadComponent()* to load any component in the controller. So, to include our password component, we can use *$this->loadComponent('Password')*. After this, we can use the component in the same way as we do in CakePHP 2.0: *$this->Password->generate()*.

Using other components in our component

We can use other components—built-in or custom—inside our own component. CakePHP provides an easy way to do this. Similar to controllers, we can define other components in the *$components* property of our component.

For example, if there is an existing component named *ExampleComponent*, and we want to use it in our *PasswordComponent*, we can issue the following code:

```
App::uses('Component', 'Controller');
class PasswordComponent extends Component {
public $components = array('Example');
public function some_function_name() {
    $foo = $this->Example->bar();
```

```
}

  /* other code goes here*/

}
```

As you can see, we can use another component and its methods in the same way using *$this->Component->method()*.

Magic methods of a component

CakePHP provides some callback functions known as magic methods for components. We can use these callback methods to fulfil our needs. These methods are automatically called by CakePHP, so we can define the logic that needs to be performed before or after some action or event.

Given below is a list of the available magic methods.

initialize (Controller $controller): This method is called before the controller's *beforeFilter* method. We can use this method to initialise our variables or objects and use them later.

startup (Controller $controller): This method is called after the controller's *beforeFilter* method, but before the controller executes its current action handler. This method can also be used to carry out some processes before our main action executes, like checking a session for a logged-in user, or setting cookies, etc.

beforeRender (Controller $controller): This method is called after the controller executes the requested action's logic, but before the controller renders its views and layout. Here we can set the view variables, so that we can use them in our *view/layout* files.

shutdown (Controller $controller): This method is called before the output is sent to the browser. We can use it to unset the unnecessary variables and objects to free up the memory.

beforeRedirect (Controller $controller, $url, $status=null, $exit=true): This method is called when the controller's redirect method is called but before any further action is taken. In this method, we can check some conditions and reset the redirect URL or disable the redirection from here. END

By: Narendra Vaghela

The author works as a tech lead in an IT company. He can be contacted at *narendravaghela4389@gmail.com.*

Network Monitoring and Programming Using Python

Python scripts and APIs can be tailor made into effective network monitoring and forensics tools. Their versatility makes them ideal in assorted applications including cyber security, data mining, Internet of Things, cloud simulation, grid implementation, etc.

and highly effective programming languages, which include Python, Java, PERL, PHP and many others. Python is one of the widely used languages for writing the special scripts for packet capturing, classification and machine learning.

It should be mentioned that a great deal of network monitoring and logging software has been developed in Python. Shinken and Zenoss are common tools used for monitoring the hosts, network data collection, alerts and messaging, and include lots of active and passive monitoring methods. Currently, Shinken, based on Python, is the open source framework used for monitoring. This software can perform a large set of operations related to digital forensics and logging.

Python scripts and libraries for network forensics

Here's a list of tools built with Python for network monitoring, logging, high security credential management and performance evaluation.

Eddie
The features of this tool include:
- System monitoring checks
- File system checking
- HTTP checks
- POP3 tests
- SNMP queries
- RADIUS authentication tests
- Monitoring of processes

Network monitoring and digital forensics are some of the prominent areas in the domain of cyber security. There are a number of software products and tools available in the technology market to guard network infrastructure and confidential data against cyber threats and attacks.

For a long time, the monitoring of servers and forensic analysis of network infrastructure has been done using packet capturing (PCAP) tools and intrusion detection systems (IDS). These activities are performed using PCAP and IDS tools available in the market, which include open source software as well as commercial products.

Despite the number of tools available for packet capturing and monitoring, professional programmers prefer to use their own software developed by coding and scripting. Self-developed and programmed code offers a lot of flexibility in customising the tool. Many organisations concerned about security, confidentiality and integrity, choose not to use any third party software. Rather, they develop their own tools using efficient

- System load
- Network configuration
- Ping checks
- Customised TCP port checks
- Watching files for changes
- Scanning of log files

Pypcap (Packet Capture Library)

Pypcap is a Python wrapper with object-oriented integration for libpcap. It can be installed easily:

```
$ pip install pypcap
```

Using Python pcap, the packets can be captured with the following few lines of code:

```
>>> import pcap
>>>   for ts, pkt in pcap.pcap():
print ts,  pkt`
```

LinkChecker

Recursive and deep checking of server pages can be done using the LinkChecker library in Python. Site crawling is made easy with its features for integrating regular expressions and filtering using LinkChecker. The output can be generated in multiple formats including HTML, XML, CSV, SQL or simply the sitemap graph.

WebScraping

Python is used by researchers and practitioners for collecting live data for research and development. For example, we can fetch live records of the stock market, the price of any product from e-commerce websites, etc. Data collected in this way forms the foundation of Big Data analytics. If a researcher is working on Big Data analysis, the live data can be fetched using a Python script and can be processed based on the research objectives.

Here is a code snippet written in Python to fetch live stock exchange data from the website *timesofindia.com*:

```
from bs4 import BeautifulSoup
import urllib.request
from time import sleep
from datetime import datetime
def getnews():
    url = "http://timesofindia.indiatimes.com/business"
    req = urllib.request.urlopen(url)
    page = req.read()
    scraping = BeautifulSoup(page)
    price = scraping.findAll("span",attrs={"class":"red14px"})
[0].text
    return price
with open("bseindex.out","w") as f:
    for x in range(2,100):
```

```
    sNow = datetime.now().strftime("%I:%M:%S%p")
    f.write("{0}, {1} \n ".format(sNow, getnews()))
    sleep(1)
```

Fetching live data from social media

In the same way, Twitter live feeds can be fetched using Python APIs. Using a Twitter developer account, a new app can be created and then a Python script can be mapped with the Twitter app, as follows:

```
from tweepy import Stream
from tweepy import OAuthHandler
from tweepy.streaming import StreamListener

#setting up the keys
consumer_key    = 'XXXXXXXXXXXXXXXXXXX'
consumer_secret = ' XXXXXXXXXXXXXXXXXXX '
access_token    = ' XXXXXXXXXXXXXXXXXXX '
access_secret   = ' XXXXXXXXXXXXXXXXXXX '

class TweetListener(StreamListener):
  # A listener handles tweets are the received from the stream.
  # This is a basic listener that just prints received tweets
to standard output

    def on_data(self, data):
        print data
        return True

    def on_error(self, status):

        print status

#printing all the tweets to the standard output
auth = OAuthHandler(consumer_key, consumer_secret)
auth.set_access_token(access_token, access_secret)

stream = Stream(auth, TweetListener())
stream.filter(track=['research'])
```

Using this Python code, the keyword 'research' is extracted from Twitter and the output is sent in JSON format. JSON (JavaScript Object Notation) is a special file format that is used by many NoSQL and unstructured data handling engines. Once the JSON is obtained, the required knowledge can be extracted by using the Refine or any other tool, and further predictions can be made. END

By: Dr Gaurav Kumar

The author is the managing director of Magma Research and Consultancy Pvt Ltd, Ambala. He is associated with a number of academic institutes, where he delivers lectures and conducts technical workshops on the latest technologies and tools. E-mail: *kumargaurav.in@gmail.com*

GENERATING COMPUTER GRAPHICS with OpenGL

OpenGL is the industry's most widely used environment for the development of portable, interactive 2D and 3D graphics applications. The OpenGL API is open source and is platform independent. This article introduces OpenGL to our readers.

OpenGL was ported from the archaic Graphics Library (GL) system developed by Silicon Graphics Inc. as the means to program the company's high-performance specialised graphics workstations. GL was ported to OpenGL in 1992 so that the technology would be platform-independent, i.e., not just work on Silicon Graphics machines. OpenGL is a software interface to graphics hardware. It's the specification of an application programming interface (API) for computer graphics programming. The interface consists of different function calls, which may be used to draw complex 3D scenes. It is widely used in CAD, virtual reality, scientific and informational visualisation, flight simulation and video games.

The functioning of a standard graphics system is typically described by an abstraction called the graphics pipeline.

The graphics pipeline

The graphics pipeline is a black box that transforms a geometric model of a scene and produces a pixel based perspective drawing of the real world onto the screen. The graphics pipeline is the path that data takes from the CPU, through the GPU, and out to the screen. Figure 1 describes a minimalist workflow of a graphics pipeline.

Every pixel passes through at least the following phases: vertices generation, vertex shading, generating primitives, rasterisation, pixel shading, testing and mixing. After all these stages, the pixel is sent to a frame buffer, which later results in the display of the pixel on the screen. This sequence is not a strict rule of how OpenGL is implemented but provides a reliable guide for predicting what OpenGL will do.

A list of vertices is fed into the GPU that will be put together to form a mesh. Information present with the vertices need not be restricted to its position in 3D space. If required, surface normals, texture coordinates, colours, and spatial coordinate values generated from the control points might also be associated with the vertices and stored. All data, whether it describes geometry or pixels, can be saved in a display list for current or later use.

The vertices that are processed are now connected to form the mesh. The GPU chooses which vertices to connect per triangle, based on either the order of the incoming vertices or a set of indices that maps them together. From vertex data, the next stage is the generation of primitives, which converts the vertices into primitives. Vertex data gets transformed by matrix transformations. Spatial coordinates are projected from the 3D space map onto a screen. Lighting calculations as well

Real-Time Graphics Pipeline

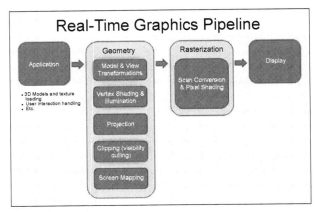

Figure 1: Graphics pipeline

as generation and transformation of texture coordinates can take place at this stage.

Next comes clipping, or the elimination of portions of geometry which don't need to be rendered on the screen and are an overhead. Once we have figured out which pixels need to be drawn to the screen, the varying values from the vertex shader will be interpolated across the surface and fed into the pixel shader. These pixels are first unpacked from one of a variety of formats into the proper number of components. The colour of each pixel is determined. Now, we can use this information to calculate lighting, read from textures, calculate transparency, and use some high level algorithms to determine the depth of the pixels in 3D space.

We now have all the information that we need to map the pixels onto the screen. We can determine the colour, depth and transparency information of every single pixel, if needed. It's now the GPU's job to decide whether or not to draw the new pixels on the top of pixels already on the screen. Note that, prior to this stage, various complexities in the pipeline can occur. If textures are encountered, they have to be handled; if fog calculations are necessary, they are to be addressed. We can also have a few stencil tests, depth-buffer tests, etc. Finally, the thoroughly processed pixel information, the 'fragment', is drawn into the appropriate buffer, where it finally advances to become a pixel and reaches its final resting place, the display screen.

Note that the above described 'fixed-pipeline' model is now obsolete on modern GPUs, which have grown faster and smarter. Instead, the stages of the pipeline, and in some cases the entire pipeline, are being replaced by programs called shaders. This was introduced from OpenGL version 2.1 onwards. Modern 3D graphics programs have vertex shaders, evaluation shaders (tessellation shaders), geometry shaders, fragment shaders and compute shaders. It's easy to write a small shader that mimics what the fixed-function pipeline does, but modern shaders have grown increasingly complex, and they do many things that were earlier impossible to do on the graphics card. Nonetheless, the fixed-function pipeline makes a good conceptual framework

on which to add variations, which is how many shaders are created.

Diving into OpenGL

As described, OpenGL is designed to be hardware-independent. In order to become streamlined on many different platforms, OpenGL specifications don't include creating a window, or defining a context and many other functions. Hence, we use external libraries to abstract this process. This helps us to make cross-platform applications and save the real essence of OpenGL.

The OpenGL states and buffers are collected by an abstract object, commonly called context. Initialising OpenGL is done by adding this context, the state machine that stores all the data that is required to render your application. When you close your application, the context is destroyed and everything is cleaned up.

The coding pattern these libraries follow is similar. We begin by specifying the properties of the window. The application will then initiate the event loop. Event handling includes mouse clicks, updating rendering states and drawing.

Here's how it looks:

```
#include <RequiredHeaders>

int main(){
createWindow();
createContext();

 while(windowIsOpen){
  while (event == newEvent()){
    handleThatEvent(event);
}

  updateScene();

  drawRequiedGraphics();
  presentGraphics();
 }
  return 0;
}
```

Coming to which libraries to use with OpenGL, we have a lot of options: *https://www.opengl.org/wiki/Related_toolkits_and_APIs.*

Here are a few noteworthy ones:
- The OpenGL Utility Library (GLU) provides many of the modelling features, such as quadric surfaces and NURBS curves and surfaces. GLU is a standard part of every OpenGL implementation.
- For machines that use the X Window System, the 'OpenGL Extension to the X Window System (GLX)' is provided as an adjunct to OpenGL. The X Window System creates a hardware abstracted layer and provides

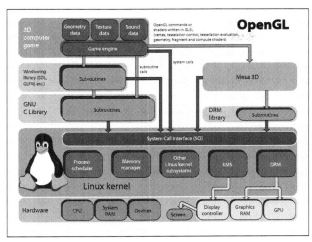

Figure 2: OpenGL commands on a Linux architecture

support for networked computers.

- The OpenGL Utility Toolkit (GLUT) is a Window System-independent toolkit, which is used to hide the complexities of differing window system APIs. We will be using GLUT in our sample program.
- Mesa helps in running OpenGL programs on an X Window System, especially Linux.
- OpenInventor is a C++ 3D graphics API that abstracts on OpenGL.

Now, let's see what the workflow of a C++ OpenGL program looks like. We have our application program, the compiled code at one end. At the other end is a 3D image that is rendered to the screen.

Our program might be written with OpenInventor commands (or in native C++). The function calls are declared in OpenGL. These OpenGL calls are platform-independent. On an X Window System (like Linux), the OpenGL calls are redirected to the implementation calls defined by Mesa. The operating system might also have its own rendering API at this stage, which accelerates the rendering process. The OpenGL calls might also redirect to the implementation calls defined by the proprietary drivers (like Nvidia drivers, Intel drivers, etc, that facilitate graphics on the screen). Now, these drivers convert the OpenGL function calls into GPU commands. With its parallelism and speed, GPU maps the OpenGL commands into 3D images that are projected onto the screen. And this way we finally see 3D images called by OpenGL.

Setting up Linux for graphics programming

For graphics programming on a Linux machine, make sure that OpenGL is supported by your graphics card—almost all of them do. OpenGL, GLX and the X server integration of GLX, are Linux system components and should already be part of the Debian, Red Hat, SUSE or any other distribution you use. Also make sure your graphics drivers are up to date. To update the graphics drivers on Ubuntu,

go to *System settings* >> *Software and Updates* >> *Additional drivers* and install the required drivers.

Next, install GLUT. Download the GLUT source from *http://www.opengl.org/resources/libraries/glut/glut_downloads. php* and follow the instructions in the package. If you're programming in C++, the following files need to be included:

```
#include <GL/glut.h> // header file for the GLUT library
#include <GL/gl.h> // header file for the OpenGL32 library
#include <GL/glu.h> // header file for the GLu32 library
```

To execute this file, an OpenGL program, you require various development libraries like GL, GLU X11, Xrandr, etc, depending on the function calls used. The following libraries would be sufficient for a simple 3D graphics program. Use *apt-get* or *yum* to install these libraries:

```
freeglut3
freeglut3-dev
libglew1.5
libglew1.5-dev
libglu1-mesa
libglu1-mesa-dev
libgl1-mesa-glx
libgl1-mesa-dev
```

Next comes the linking part. You can use a *Makefile* to do this. But for our example, we will link them manually while compiling. Let's say we want to execute a C++ OpenGL program called *main.cpp*. We can link OpenGL libraries as follows:

```
g++ -std=c++11 -Wall -o main main.cpp -lglfw3 -lGLU -lGL
-lX11 -lXxf86vm -lXrandr -lpthread -lXi
```

Note that the linking is done sequentially. So the order is important. You can now execute the program the usual way (./ main for the above).

A simple OpenGL based example

Let's now write a minimal OpenGL program in C++. We will use GLUT for windowing and initialising context.

We have already discussed what an OpenGL based workflow looks like. We create a window, initialise a context, wait for some event to occur and handle it. For this simple example, we can ignore event handling. We will create a window and display a triangle inside it.

The required headers are:

```
#include <GL/glut.h> // header file for the GLUT library
#include <GL/gl.h> // header file for the OpenGL32 library
```

The latest versions of GLUT include *gl.h*. So we can only include the GLUT library header.

The main function will look like what follows:

```
int main (int argc, char** argv){
      glutInit(&argc, argv);
// Initializing glut
      glutInitDisplayMode(GLUT_SINGLE | GLUT_RGB);
// Setting up display mode, the single buffering and RGB colors
  glutInitWindowPosition(80, 80);
// Position of the window on the screen
  glutInitWindowSize(400, 300);
// Size of the window
  glutCreateWindow("A simple Triangle");
// Name of the window
  glutDisplayFunc(display);
// The display function
      glutMainLoop();
}
```

All the above are GLUT calls. Since OpenGL doesn't handle windowing calls, all the window creation is taken care of by GLUT. We initialise a window and set up the display mode. The display mode specified above states that the window should display RGB colours and will require a single buffer to handle pixel outputs. We then specify the window position on the screen, the size of the window to be displayed and the display function. The display function takes a pointer to a function as an argument. The function would describe what is to be displayed inside the screen. The final function call loops the main forever, so that the window is always open until closed.

Now that a window is initialised, let's draw a triangle with OpenGL function calls. Here's how the display function looks:

```
void display(){
        glClear(GL_COLOR_BUFFER_BIT);
glBegin(GL_POLYGON);

glColor3f(1, 0, 0);
glVertex3f(-0.6, -0.75, 0.5);

glColor3f(0, 1, 0);
glVertex3f(0.6, -0.75, 0);

glColor3f(0, 0, 1);
glVertex3f(0, 0.75, 0);
```

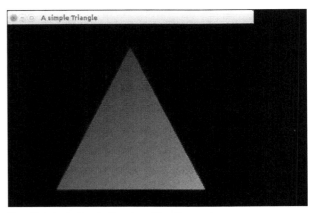

Figure 3: A simple triangle: C++ based OpenGL example program

```
glEnd();
glFlush();
}
```

All OpenGL based function calls begin with the letters *gl* in lowercase. We are planning to display a simple triangle defined by three vertices. We specify the colour and position of the vertices and map them on to the screen. For this, we first call the *glClear()* function which clears the display buffer. Next, we specify the type of primitive we are planning to draw with the *glBegin()* function. This is the primitive of our drawing until a *glEnd()* function is called. Next, between the *glBegin()* and *glEnd()* we draw three points (vertices) and form a triangle with them. We first have to specify the colour and then the position of the drawing. As OpenGL is platform independent, the C-style datatypes are specified as a function call. This can be seen with the *glColor3f()* function, which takes three float values.

Once the program is compiled, linked and called as described above, it would look like what's shown in Figure 3.

If you're interested in learning OpenGL based computer graphics, the old version of the official 'red book' is available for free at *http://www.glprogramming.com/red/*. END

By: Sricharan Chiruvolu

The author is a FOSS enthusiast, Web developer and a graphics programmer. He is a student at Amrita School of Engineering, Bengaluru, and a student developer for Copyleft games in association with Google, under Google Summer of Code – 2015. You can contact him at *sricharanized@gmail.com*

Creating Vehicular Traffic Simulation with OSS

Here is a tutorial on creating real-time vehicular traffic simulation using SUMO and OpenStreetMap.

S UMO stands for Simulation of Urban Mobility. It is designed as an open source package for microscopic road traffic simulation, while OpenStreetMap is an editable, open source map of the world. This article tells you how to simulate real-time traffic using SUMO and OpenStreetMap.

Prerequisites

I have used SUMO 0.22.0 and Ubuntu 12.04 for this simulation.

For installing SUMO in Ubuntu, follow the steps given below:

1. Download SUMO from *http://sourceforge.net/projects/sumo/files/sumo/*
2. Install some packages that are necessary to build SUMO with a GUI:

```
sudo apt-get install libgdal1-dev proj libxerces-
c2-dev
sudo apt-get install libfox-1.6-dev libgl1-mesa-
dev libglu1-mesa-dev
```

3. Ubuntu 12.04 does not ship with *libgdal.so*; it ships only with *libgdal1.7.0.so*. So, create a symbolic link:

```
sudo ln -s /usr/lib/libgdal1.7.0.so /usr/lib/
libgdal.so
```

4. Now decompress the downloaded file by using the following command:

```
tar xzvf filename.tar.gz
```

5. Enter into the source directory and call *configure*, *make* and *make install*:

```
cd sumo-0.22.0/
./configure --with-fox-includes=/usr/include/fox-
1.6 --with-gdal-includes=/usr/include/gdal --with-
proj-libraries=/usr --with-gdal-libraries=/usr
--with-proj-gdal
make
sudo make install
```

6. To start SUMO from the command line, run the following command:

```
sumo or sumo-gui
```

OpenStreetMap is a free editable map of the whole world. It creates and provides free geographic data such as street maps, to anyone who wants them. The project was started because most maps that you think of as 'free' actually have legal or technical restrictions on their use, preventing people from using them in creative, productive or unexpected ways.

You can use *http://www.openstreetmap.org/#map=5/51.500/-0.100* to download your map.

An OpenStreetMap file contains a map with the following features related to traffic simulation:
- The nodes and their connections define the position and form of all streets and junctions.
- The type of a street specifies its size and importance (key highway).
- The speed limit of a street is usually determined implicitly by law. The implicit value may depend on the value of the highway attribute. In case the speed limit differs from the implicit legal value, it is given explicitly through the key maximum speed of a street.

- The total number of lanes (for both directions) has an implicit value depending on the highway property. If the real value differs from the default value, it can be given through the key lanes.
- The position of every traffic light is described as a node with the key-value pair *highway=traffic_signals.*
- One-way streets are marked with the key-value pair *oneway=yes.*

Figure 1 shows the map that I downloaded from *openstreetmap.org.*

You need to select the map that you want to simulate and export it. After you export the map, it will ask you to download it. Save the file. Copy the downloaded file to your working directory.

Now run the following commands, one by one. *Netconvert* imports digital road networks from different sources and generates road networks that can be used by other tools from the package. It imports the road network stored in *map.osm* and stores the SUMO-network generated from this data into *map.net.xml:*

```
netconvert --osm-files map.osm -o map.net.xml
```

OSM-data not only contains the road network but also a wide range of additional polygons such as buildings and rivers. These polygons can be imported using *polyconvert* and then added to a *sumo-gui-configuration.*

To interpret the OSM-data, an additional *typemap* file is required.

Go to *http://sumo.de/wiki/Networks/Import/OpenStreetMap,* copy the *typemap* file and save it to your working directory with the name *typemap.xml.*

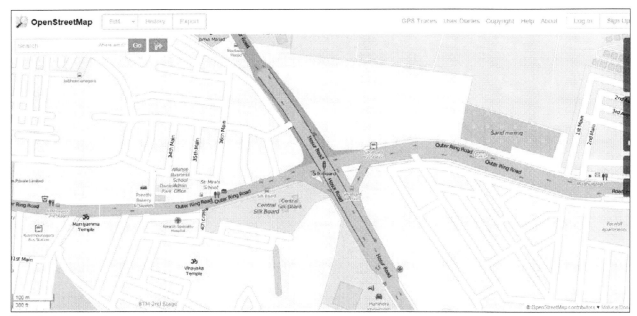

Figure 1: Map exported from *www.openstreetmap.org*

Using the file *typemap.xml*, *polyconvert* imports polygons from OSM-data and produces a SUMO-polygon file.

Polyconvert imports geometrical shapes (polygons or points of interest) from different sources and converts them to a representation that may be visualised using SUMO-GUI.

```
polyconvert --net-file map.
net.xml --osm-files map.osm
--type-file typemap.xml -o
map.poly.xml
```

Figure 2: Final map after feeding command into SUMO

randomTrips.py generates a set of random trips for a given network (option *-n*). It does so by choosing the source and destination edge either uniformly at random or weighted by length (option *-l*), by number of lanes (option *-L*) or both. The resulting trips are stored in an xml file (option *-o*, default *trips. trips.xml*) suitable for the DUAROUTER, which is called automatically if the *-r* option (with a file name for the resulting route file) is given. The trips are distributed evenly in an interval defined by the begin (option *-b*, default *0*) and end time (option *-e*, default *3600*) in seconds. The number of trips is defined by the repetition rate (option *-p*, default *1*) in seconds. Every trip has an ID consisting of a prefix (option *--prefix*, default " ") and a running number.

```
python /home/kunal/sumo-0.22.0/tools/trip/
randomTrips.py -n map.net.xml -e 100 -l
python /home/kunal/sumo-0.22.0/tools/trip/
randomTrips.py -n map.net.xml -r map.rou.xml -e
100 -l
```

Now, you need to make a *sumo.cfg* file for the configuration of the *sumo-gui*. This is what your *sumo.cfg* file looks like:

```
<configuration xmlns:xsi="http://www.w3.org/2001/
XMLSchema-instance" xsi:noNamespaceSchemaLocation=
"http://sumo.sf.net/xsd/sumoConfiguration.xsd">

    <input>
        <net-file value="map.net.xml"/>
        <route-files value="map.rou.xml"/>
        <additional-files value="map.poly.xml"/>
    </input>
```

```
    <time>
        <begin value="0"/>
        <end value="1000"/>
    <step-length value="0.1"/>
    </time>
</configuration>
```

Save the above file with a file name. I saved it as *map. sumo.cfg*

Now run the following command from the terminal:

```
sumo-gui map.sumo.cfg
```

After you enter the command, the SUMO-GUI window will pop up. Figure 2 shows what your window should look like.

If you are interested in vehicular ad hoc networks (VANETs), this article can be your starting point. It will teach you how to simulate real-time networks. You can then proceed further and add your research or project component to it.

You can refer to the complete video on YouTube; here is the link: *https://www.youtube.com/ watch?v=zm5h90H5OS8* END

References

[1] *http://www.dlr.de/ts/en/desktopdefault.aspx*

By: Nabin Pradhan

The author is studying for an M. Tech in computer science and engineering at the VIT University in Chennai. His areas of interest are networking (including wireless networks) and open source technologies like NS2, SUMO and Linux. A gadget lover, he has recently started blogging on the latest devices and the technologies they use. He is the author of *www.techerina.com*

TAKING THE FIRST BABY STEPS IN ...ııllnS-3

Ns-3 is a network simulator for computer network simulation, used mainly for research and educational purposes. This article is the third in the series as we move forward in our quest to understand and use ns-3 by looking at abstracting classes and then working with our first script.

In the past two issues, we have dealt with many tools necessary to learn ns-3, which is a system of software libraries that work together to form a wonderful simulation tool. There are a lot of system libraries that are part of ns-3, and the user programs are written so that they can be linked to the core library. Let us first discuss the different classes available with ns-3 and the way they imitate and act as an abstraction of real world network entities. It may not always be feasible or possible to imitate a real world entity completely, with computer simulation. In such situations, we need to scale down things a bit, so that computers can handle the complex and confusing real world entities, without losing the essential characteristics of the particular entity being simulated. So an abstraction is a simplified version of an entity, with its essential characteristics. In order to set up a network, we need computer systems (nodes), applications running on top of these nodes, network devices for connectivity and connecting media. The section below discusses these real world entities and a few ns-3 abstracting classes imitating them.

A few built-in classes in ns-3

Node: In computer networking, node represents a host computer. In ns-3, the term node has a slightly different meaning. A C++ class, called *Node*, is used to implement nodes in ns-3 simulation. A node is a simplified model of a computing device in ns-3 and by creating an object of the *Node* class, you are actually creating a computing device in the simulation. For example, if there are 10 objects of the *Node* class in your simulation script, then you are simulating a network with 10 nodes. This is the power of ns-3. The developers of ns-3 have already finished the code required in your scripts to imitate a node in the real world; all you need to do now is call the *Node* class to create an object that imitates a real node.

Application: The behaviour of the application programs running on a real computer in a network is imitated by the *Application* class of ns-3. Using this class, a simple application can be installed on top of a node. A real computer node can have complex software like operating systems, system software and applications, but in ns-3, we content ourselves with simple applications, which are in no way comparable to real world software. Examples of applications are *BulkSendApplication*, *OnOffApplication*, etc. The *BulkSendApplication* is a simple traffic generator which will send data as fast as possible up to a maximum limit or until the application is stopped. The *OnOffApplication* is also a traffic generator and it follows an 'On/Off' pattern for sending data. During the 'On' stage, this application maintains a constant bit rate data transfer and during the 'Off' stage, no data is transferred.

The *NetDevice* class: In order to connect a computer to a network, certain network devices like network interface cards, cables, etc, are required. Even while simulating a network of computers, we cannot ignore network devices and ns-3 has a class named *NetDevice* for this purpose. The *NetDevice* class in ns-3 provides an abstraction which, if used with the *Node* class, will imitate a real world computer with a network device installed on it. Just like an application, a network device in ns-3 is also a simplified abstraction, which in no way resembles a complex real world network device. In fact, the *NetDevice* abstraction class in ns-3 acts as a device driver as well as simulated hardware. There are several specialised variants of the *NetDevice* class called *CsmaNetDevice*, *PointToPointNetDevice*, *WifiNetDevice*, etc.

Channels: In a real network, nodes are interconnected through a medium or a channel. For example, we can connect two nodes with a twisted pair cable or a wireless channel. There is a class called *Channel* in ns-3 which acts as an abstraction of a real world channel. The *Channel* class acts as a basic framework for all the other specialised channel classes in ns-3. There are specialised channel classes like *CsmaChannel*, *PointToPointChannel*, *WifiChannel*, etc.

Our first ns-3 script

Now that we have discussed ns-3 classes imitating real world entities, it is time to deal with our first ns-3 script. The simulation script given below contains only absolutely essential code for simulating a very simple network in the real world. The simulated network contains just two nodes with a point-to-point connection between them. This is a slightly modified version of a program taken from the standard set of examples bundled with ns-3. I have removed some lines of code from the original program, which might distract from the core issues related to ns-3 simulation.

```
#include "ns3/core-module.h"
#include "ns3/network-module.h"
#include "ns3/internet-module.h"
#include "ns3/point-to-point-module.h"
#include "ns3/applications-module.h"
using namespace ns3;
NS_LOG_COMPONENT_DEFINE("SimulationOne");
int main(int argc, char *argv[ ])
{
  Time::SetResolution(Time::NS);
  LogComponentEnable("UdpEchoClientApplication", LOG_LEVEL_
INFO);
  LogComponentEnable("UdpEchoServerApplication", LOG_LEVEL_
INFO);
  NodeContainer nodes;
  nodes.Create(2);
```

```
  PointToPointHelper pointToPoint;
  pointToPoint.SetDeviceAttribute("DataRate", StringValue
("10Mbps"));
  pointToPoint.SetChannelAttribute("Delay", StringValue
("5ms"));
  NetDeviceContainer devices;
  devices = pointToPoint.Install(nodes);
  InternetStackHelper stack;
  stack.Install(nodes);
  Ipv4AddressHelper address;
  address.SetBase("192.168.100.0", "255.255.255.128");
  Ipv4InterfaceContainer interfaces = address.
Assign(devices);
  UdpEchoServerHelper echoServer(2000);
  ApplicationContainer serverApps = echoServer.Install(nodes.
Get(1));
  serverApps.Start(Seconds(1.0));
  serverApps.Stop(Seconds(10.0));
  UdpEchoClientHelper echoClient(interfaces.GetAddress(1),
2000);
  echoClient.SetAttribute("MaxPackets", UintegerValue(2));
  echoClient.SetAttribute("Interval",
TimeValue(Seconds(3.0)));
  echoClient.SetAttribute("PacketSize", UintegerValue(512));
  ApplicationContainer clientApps = echoClient.Install(nodes.
Get(0));
  clientApps.Start(Seconds(3.0));
  clientApps.Stop(Seconds(12.0));
  AsciiTraceHelper ascii;
  pointToPoint.EnableAsciiAll(ascii.
CreateFileStream("simulation1.tr"));
  Simulator::Run();
  Simulator::Destroy();
  return 0;
}
```

Before explaining the program, here's a word about the indent style used in ns-3 source files. ns-3 uses an indent style called the GNU style. It will be better if you follow this style with your ns-3 script files also. If you are unfamiliar with the GNU style of indenting, you could use a tool called Artistic Style which will format the program text in any style you prefer. Finally, a word of caution to die-hard fans of Vi and Vim; ns-3 prefers Emacs over Vi. Most often, ns-3 source files start with an Emacs mode line specifying the formatting style. Now let us break the script into small pieces and analyse it.

A few explanations

Even though the syntax of the program resembles C++, it is ns-3. I will explain only terms specific to ns-3 in the above example by making an assumption that the C++ constructs in the script are already known to the reader.

The script starts with five *include* statements. But these are not the only header files included in your script.

These five header files will, in turn, include a large number of header files required for the proper working of the ns-3 simulation script. This may not be an optimal solution to our problem of including the required header files alone. But this approach definitely reduces the burden on the ns-3 script writer; instead, the burden is passed on to the system running the simulation with many unnecessary header files included. The next line 'using namespace ns3;' makes every class, function and variable declared inside the ns-3 namespace available for direct usage without using the qualifier 'ns3::'. Remember, we haven't used the standard namespace 'std' of C++. So we need the qualifier 'std::' to get standard C++ constructs, e.g., 'std::cout<< "Hello ns-3";' will work but 'cout<<"Hello ns-3";' will result in an error.

The next line 'NS_LOG_COMPONENT_DEFINE("SimulationOne");' declares a logging component named *SimulationOne*. By referring to this logging object console, message logging can be enabled and disabled. Logging is one of the three methods used in ns-3 to provide simulation data to the user. The other two methods are trace analysis and network topology animation. Even though logging is a very useful way to obtain data from the simulation, the preferred method is trace analysis. With logging, the data is displayed on the terminal. There are seven different log types used in logging. These are: LOG_ERROR, LOG_WARN, LOG_DEBUG, LOG_INFO, LOG_FUNCTION, LOG_LOGIC and LOG_ALL. The amount of information provided increases with each level, with LOG_ERROR providing the least information and LOG_ALL providing the most.

The next line 'Time::SetResolution(Time::NS);' sets the least amount of time by which two events can be separated. The default minimum time is one nanosecond. Now consider the following two lines of code.

```
LogComponentEnable("UdpEchoClientApplication", LOG_LEVEL_
INFO);
LogComponentEnable("UdpEchoServerApplication", LOG_LEVEL_
INFO);
```

For each log type there is a corresponding log level type, which enables logging of all the levels below it in addition to its level. So the above lines enable logging on the UDP echo client and UDP echo server with log level type LOG_LEVEL_INFO, which will display information from the log types LOG_ERROR, LOG_WARN, LOG_DEBUG and LOG_INFO. If you find this line confusing, don't worry. This line does not affect the topology of the network we are simulating; it only restricts the amount of data given to the user from the terminal. So, if you want, you can use LOG_LEVEL_ALL, which will provide you with all the available information, even that which is unnecessary for your analysis.

From the following line of code onwards, we are dealing with the actual network being simulated. Earlier, we discussed the different abstract network entities used in ns-3 simulation. All these entities are created and maintained with the help of corresponding topology helper classes.

```
NodeContainer nodes;
nodes.Create(2);
```

The class *NodeContainer* in the above code is a topology helper. It helps us deal with the *Node* objects, which are created to simulate real nodes. Here we are creating two nodes by using the *Create* function of the object called *nodes*.

In the following lines of code, a topology helper class called *PointToPontHelper* is called to configure the channel and the network device:

```
PointToPointHelper pointToPoint;
pointToPoint.SetDeviceAttribute("DataRate", StringValue
("10Mbps"));
pointToPoint.SetChannelAttribute("Delay", StringValue
("5ms"));
```

You can observe that the data rate of the network device is set as 10Mbps and the transmission delay of the channel is set as 5ms. If you are unfamiliar with network simulation altogether, then this is how things are done in a simulation. You can specify different values in a simulated network without making any marginal changes. For example, you can change the delay to 1ms or 1000ms. Thus, you can create fundamentally different networks by changing a few lines of code here and there. And that is the beauty of simulation.

The two lines of code shown below will finish configuring the network and the channel. Here, a topology helper called *NetDeviceContainer* is used to create *NetDevice* objects. This is similar to a *NodeContainer* handling *Node* objects.

```
NetDeviceContainer devices;
devices = pointToPoint.Install(nodes);
```

So now, we have nodes and devices configured. Next, we should install protocol stacks on the nodes. The lines 'InternetStackHelper stack;' and 'stack.Install(nodes);' will install the Internet stack on the two nodes. Internet stack will enable protocols like TCP, UDP, IP, etc, on the two nodes.

The next three lines of code shown below deal with node addressing. Each node is given a specific IP address. Those familiar with ns-2 should note the difference. In ns-3, abstract IP addresses used in the simulation are similar to actual IP addresses.

```
Ipv4AddressHelper address;
address.SetBase("192.168.100.0", "255.255.255.128");
Ipv4InterfaceContainer interfaces = address.Assign(devices);
```

The subnet mask is 255.255.255.128; therefore, the possible IP addresses are from 192.168.100.1 to 192.168.100.126. Since there are just two nodes, the addresses are 192.168.100.1 and 192.168.100.2.

During our discussion on ns-3 abstractions, I mentioned abstract applications running on ns-3 nodes. Now it is time for us to set up abstract applications on top of the two nodes. The lines from 'UdpEchoServerHelper echoServer(2000);' to 'clientApps.Stop(Seconds(12.0));' in the script simulation1. cc are used to create abstract applications on the two nodes. The node with address 192.168.100.1 is designated as the client, and the node with address 192.168.100.2 is designated as the server.

Initially, we create an echo server application on the server node. The port used by the echo server is 2000. The line 'ApplicationContainer serverApps = echoServer. Install(nodes.Get(1));' installs a UDP echo server application on the node with ID 1. The server application starts at the first second and stops at the tenth second. Then we create a UDP echo client on the node with ID 0, and it connects to the server with the line 'UdpEchoClientHelper echoClient(interfaces.GetAddress(1), 2000);'. Remember the connection mechanisms we learned in socket programming? With the next three lines of code, the maximum number of packets sent is set as two, the interval is set as 3 seconds and the packet size is fixed as 512 bytes. The client application starts at the third second and stops at the twelfth second. So with the simulation script given above we have created nodes, installed applications on the nodes, attached network devices on the nodes, and connected the nodes to a communication channel. Thus our topology is complete and we are ready to begin the simulation. And finally, the lines 'Simulator::Run();' and 'Simulator::Destroy();' start and stop the actual ns-3 simulator.

Trace files in ns-3

I have explained every line of code in the script simulation1. cc except the following two lines:

```
AsciiTraceHelper ascii;
pointToPoint.EnableAsciiAll(ascii.
CreateFileStream("simulation1.tr"));
```

These two lines are included in the script for trace file generation. Trace file analysis is the main source of information in ns-3 simulation. There are two different types of trace files in ns-3. They are ASCII based trace files and *pcap* based trace files. *pcap* is an application programming interface (API) for capturing network traffic. A packet analyser tool called Wireshark is used to process the *pcap* files to elicit information. Initially, we will only discuss the relatively simple ASCII based tracing method. The code given above will generate an ASCII trace file named *simulation1.tr*. The text below shows only the first line of the trace file.

```
+ 3 /NodeList/0/DeviceList/0/$ns3::PointToPointNetDevice/
TxQueue/Enqueue ns3::PppHeader (Point-to-Point Protocol: IP
(0x0021)) ns3::Ipv4Header (tos 0x0 DSCP Default ECN Not-ECT
ttl 64 id 0 protocol 17 offset (bytes) 0 flags [none] length:
540 192.168.100.1 > 192.168.100.2) ns3::UdpHeader (length:
520 49153 > 2000) Payload (size=512)
```

You can download the simulation script simulation1.cc and the corresponding trace file simulation1.tr from *opensourceforu. efytimes.com/article_source_code/july2015/ns3.zip*. The ASCII trace files in ns-3 are similar in structure to ns-2 trace files. There is abundant data available in the form of a trace file in ns-3. A detailed description of the different fields in the trace file and ways to elicit information from this file will be discussed in the next issue.

Executing the script

Now that we are familiar with the code, let's move on to the execution of the code. If you have installed ns-3 inside a directory called *ns* as discussed in the last article of this series, you will have the following directory *ns/ns-allinone-3.22/ns-3.22/scratch*. Copy the file simulation1.cc into the directory called *scratch*. You have to copy ns-3 scripts into this directory so that the build automation tool, Waf, can identify and compile them. Now open a terminal in the directory *ns/ns-allinone-3.22* and type the following command:

```
./waf
```

If your script is incorrect, you will see error messages displayed on the terminal. If the simulation script is correct, you will see a message regarding a list of modules built and a few modules not built. If you see such a message, then type the following command in the terminal:

```
./waf - - run scratch/simulation1
```

This command will execute the simulation script *simulation1.cc*. Figure 1 shows the terminal with logged information displayed. From the figure, we can see that the client sends 512 bytes of data to the server at the third second. The server responds with 512 bytes of data to the client. After a waiting period of 3 seconds, at the sixth second, the client again sends 512 bytes to the server and the server in turn responds by sending 512 bytes of data to the client.

Graphical animation in ns-3

We have briefly discussed the NAM graphical animator used with ns-2 in the first part of this series. We are now going to deal with network animation in ns-3. Unlike ns-2, there is no single default animator for ns-3. But we have two tools called NetAnim and PyViz for network animation in ns-3. PyViz is a live simulation visualiser, which means it doesn't use trace files. NetAnim is a trace based network animator. I will

```
File  Edit  View  Bookmarks  Settings  Help
#
# ./waf --run scratch/simulation1
Waf: Entering directory `/root/NS3/ns-allinone-3.22/ns-3.22/build'
Waf: Leaving directory `/root/NS3/ns-allinone-3.22/ns-3.22/build'
'build' finished successfully (4.894s)
At time 3s client sent 512 bytes to 192.168.100.2 port 2000
At time 3.00543s server received 512 bytes from 192.168.100.1 port 49153
At time 3.00543s server sent 512 bytes to 192.168.100.1 port 49153
At time 3.01087s client received 512 bytes from 192.168.100.2 port 2000
At time 6s client sent 512 bytes to 192.168.100.2 port 2000
At time 6.00543s server received 512 bytes from 192.168.100.1 port 49153
At time 6.00543s server sent 512 bytes to 192.168.100.1 port 49153
At time 6.01087s client received 512 bytes from 192.168.100.2 port 2000
#
```

Figure 1: Output of simulation1

stick to NetAnim, because those who are familiar with ns-2 will find NetAnim similar to NAM. NetAnim is an offline animator based on the Qt toolkit, and uses XML based trace files generated by ns-3 scripts to display the animation. The latest version is NetAnim 3.106. But the version bundled with the ns-3.22 tarball installation file is NetAnim 3.105. If you have installed ns-3 inside a directory called *ns*, then you will have the directory *ns/ns-allinone-3.22/netanim-3.105*. Open a terminal in this directory and type the following command:

```
./NetAnim
```

Figure 2 shows the NetAnim window you are supposed to see. But there's an error message because the executable file called NetAnim is not there. What has happened is that with the tarball installation of ns-3, NetAnim did not get installed.

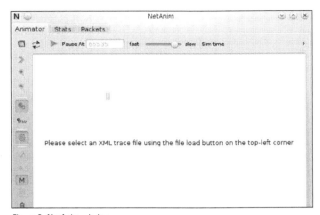

Figure 2: NetAnim window

So we need to install NetAnim separately. But that's for another day. So in the next part of this series, we will learn how to install and use NetAnim. Thereafter, we will also deal with ns-3 trace files in detail. END

By: Deepu Benson

With nearly 15 years of programming experience, the author currently works as an assistant professor at Amal Jyothi College of Engineering, Kanjirappally, Kerala. He maintains a technical blog at *www.computingforbeginners.blogspot.in* and can be reached at *deepumb@hotmail.com*

Testing
Video Transmission
in Ns-2 Using
the EvalVid Framework

Ns-2 is a discrete event simulator targeted at networking research. It provides support for simulation of TCP, routing and multicast protocols over wired and wireless (local and satellite) networks.

Conventionally, the Internet has been used for data applications like email, chat, Web surfing, etc. Multimedia technology has been around for quite some time, but with the pace of development that it has enjoyed in the last few years, it has become an integral part of almost every Web endeavour. It finds application in fields ranging from video lectures to catalogues and games to video clips. The combination of multimedia technology and the Internet is currently attracting a considerable amount of attention from researchers, developers and end users.

Video transmission nowadays has become a necessity for almost every Internet user, irrespective of the device used to access the Internet. Typically, video transmission demands high bandwidth. Without compression, it is very difficult to transmit video over wired or wireless networks.

With the increasing use of multimedia-capturing devices and the improved quality of capture, the demand for high quality multimedia has gone up. The traditional protocols used to carry such volumes of multimedia data have started showing some limitations. Hence, enhanced protocols are the need of the hour. Researchers working on developing such protocols need platforms to test the performance of these newly designed protocols. The performance of the suite of protocols should ideally be measured on a real network. But due to several limitations of real networks, simulation platforms are commonly used to test prototypes.

This article is aimed at demonstrating the widely used and open source simulation platform, ns-2, for measuring the performance of protocols when multimedia content is transmitted over the network.

Architecture of ns-2 and EvalVid

Among researchers, network simulator 2 (ns-2) is one of the most widely used, maintained and trusted simulators. It is useful for simulating a wide variety of networks, ranging from

Ethernet and wireless LANs, to ad hoc networks and wide area networks. The architecture of ns-2 is shown in Figure 1.

Conventionally, ns-2 supports constant bit rate and traffic in bursts, which resembles most of the data applications on the Internet. Multimedia traffic has characteristics that are different from data traffic. Data traffic is mostly immune to jitter and less sensitive to delay, whereas multimedia applications demand a high quality of service. Generating traffic representing multimedia data is very important when evaluating the performance of any network.

EvalVid is a framework and tool-set for evaluating the quality of video transmitted over a physical or simulated communication network. In addition to measuring the QoS (Quality of Service) parameters of the underlying network, like delays, loss rates and jitter, it also provides support for subjective video quality evaluation of the received video, based on frame-by-frame PSNR (Peak Signal to Noise Ratio)

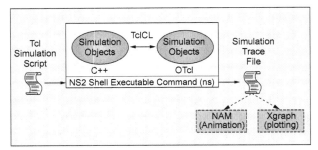

Figure 1: Basic architecture of ns-2 *(Courtesy: tutorialsweb.com)*

calculation. It can regenerate received video, which can be compared with the originally transmitted video in terms of many other useful metrics like video quality measure (VQM), structural similarity (SSIM), mean opinion score (MOS), etc. The framework of EvalVid is shown in Figure 2.

Integration of ns-2 and EvalVid

Raw video can be encoded by the required codec using tools provided by EvalVid. Video traces that contain information about video frames, like the frame type, time stamp, etc, are generated by using EvalVid. These trace files are used as a traffic source in ns-2. The integrated architecture of ns-2 and EvalVid is shown in Figure 3.

Scripting an agent in ns-2

Agents created in ns-2 need to read the generated video trace file. This agent code is easily available on the Internet. The following steps must be taken for integrating the agent code in ns-2.

Step 1: Put a *frametype_* and *sendtime_ field* in the *hdr_cmn* header. The *frametype_ field* is to indicate which frame type the packet belongs to. The 'I' frame type is defined to 1, 'P' is defined to 2, and 'B' is defined to 3. The *sendtime_ field* records the time the packet was sent. It can be used to measure end-to-end delay.

You can modify the file *packet.h* in the common folder as follows:

```
struct hdr_cmn {
  enum dir_t { DOWN= -1, NONE= 0, UP= 1 };
  packet_t ptype_;        // packet type (see above)
  int    size_;           // simulated packet size
  int    uid_;            // unique id
  int    error_;          // error flag
  int    errbitcnt_;      //
  int    fecsize_;
  double    ts_;          // timestamp: for q-delay
measurement
  int    iface_;          // receiving interface (label)
  dir_t direction_;       // direction: 0=none, 1=up,
-1=down
  // source routing
  char src_rt_valid;
  double ts_arr_; // Required by Marker of JOBS
//add the following three lines
```

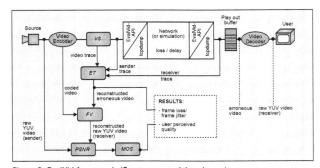

Figure 2: EvalVid framework *(Courtesy: tutorialsweb.com)*

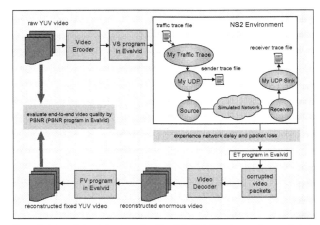

Figure 3: Integrated architecture of ns-2 and EvalVid *(Courtesy: csie.nqu.edu.tw)*

```
  int frametype_;            // frame type for MPEG video
transmission
  double sendtime_;     // send time
unsigned long int frame_pkt_id_;
```

Step 2: You can modify the file *agent.h* in the common folder as follows:

```
class Agent : public Connector {
public:
  Agent(packet_t pktType);
  virtual ~Agent();
  void recv(Packet*, Handler*);
..........
inline packet_t get_pkttype() { return type_; }
// add the following two lines
  inline void set_frametype(int type) { frametype_ = type; }
  inline void set_prio(int prio) { prio_ = prio; }

protected:
  int command(int argc, const char*const*argv);
..........
  int defttl_;        // default ttl for outgoing pkts
                 // add the following line
  int frametype_;                 // frame type for
MPEG video transmission
```

www.opensourceforu.com
An EFY GROUP PUBLICATION
Open Source Is Hot In The IT World
Hadoop
Apache
Postgres
Android
MySQL
OpenStack
Joomla
PHP
THE COMPLETE MAGAZINE ON OPEN SOURCE
OpenSource For You
5 Amazing How-Tos For SysAdmins
» To find dealers to buy copy from news-stand, visit: www.ezine.lfymag.com
» To subscribe, visit: pay.efyindia.com
» To buy an ezine edition, visit: www.magzter.com choose Open Source For You

```
........
private:
  void flushAVar(TracedVar *v);
};
```

Step 3: To modify the file *agent.cc* in the common folder, write the following code:

```
Agent::Agent(packet_t pkttype) :
  size_(0), type_(pkttype), frametype_(0),
  channel_(0), traceName_(NULL),
  oldValueList_(NULL), app_(0), et_(0)
{
}
........
Agent::initpkt(Packet* p) const
{
  hdr_cmn* ch = hdr_cmn::access(p);
  ch->uid() = uidcnt_++;
  ch->ptype() = type_;
  ch->size() = size_;
  ch->timestamp() = Scheduler::instance().clock();
  ch->iface() = UNKN_IFACE.value(); // from packet.h (agent
is local)
  ch->direction() = hdr_cmn::NONE;

  ch->error() = 0;          /* pkt not corrupt to start with */
// add the following line
  ch->frametype_ = frametype_;
. . . . . .
```

Step 4: Copy the *myevalvid* folder (which contains *myevalvid.cc, myudp.cc, myudp.h, myevalvid_sink.cc* and *myevalvid_sink.h)* into ns2.35; for example, *ns-allinone-2.35/ns-2.35/myevalvid*.

Step 5: To modify *ns-allinone-2.35/ns-2.35/tcl/lib/ns-default.tcl*, add the following two lines...

```
Agent/myUDP set packetSize_ 1000
Tracefile set debug_ 0
```

Step 6: To modify *ns-allinone-2.35/ns-2.35/Makefile. in*, put *myevalvid/myudp.o, myevalvid/myevalvid_sink.o* and *myevalvid/myevalvid.o* in the *OBJ_CC* list.

Step 7: Recompile ns-2 as follows:

```
./configure ; make clean ; make
```

Formulating video traces from raw video and simulation

Assume that EvalVid and ns-2 are installed on Ubuntu. Similar steps will work on other Linux distros too.

Download a raw *yuv* video sequence (you can use known *yuv* videos from *http://trace.eas.asu.edu/yuv/)*. Here is an

1	I	15876	16	0.002
2	P	1223	2	0.049
3	P	1116	2	0.084
4	P	937	1	0.103
5	P	1163	2	0.140
6	P	1168	2	0.178
7	P	1079	2	0.215
8	P	1234	2	0.234
9	P	1290	2	0.272
10	P	1388	2	0.310
11	P	1230	2	0.347
12	P	1383	2	0.384
13	P	1727	2	0.403
14	P	2016	2	0.440
15	P	2387	3	0.478

Figure 4: Snap of source video trace

example where *bus_cif.yuv* is used as raw video.
1. Encode the raw *yuv* file to *m4v* as follows:

```
$ffmpeg -s cif -r 30 -b 64000 -bt 3200 -g 30 -i bus_cif.yuv
-vcodec mpeg4 bus_cif.m4v
```

2. Convert the *m4v* file to *mp4:*

```
$MP4Box -hint -mtu 1024 -fps 30 -add bus_cif.m4v bus_cif2.mp4
```

As an option, you can create a reference *yuv* file. This video can be used for encoding loss estimation:

```
ffmpeg -i bus_cif2.mp4 bus_cif_ref.yuv
```

3. Send an *mp4* file per RTP/UDP to a specified destination host. The output of the mp4trace will be needed later, so it should be redirected to a file. The *Source_Video_Trace* file is the video trace file which has the information about each frame of the video and will be used by ns-2 as a traffic source.

```
$mp4trace -f -s 224.1.2.3 12346 bus_cif2.mp4 >
Source_Video_Trace
```

(A section of *Source_Video_Trace* is shown in Figure 4.)
4. Create a network topology representing the network to be simulated in *Evalvid.tcl* and run the simulation as follows:

```
$ns Evalvid.tcl
```

5. After simulation, ns-2 will create two files, *Send_time_file* and *Recv_time_file* (the filename as used in the *tcl* file), which record the sending time and received time of each packet, respectively.
6. To reconstruct the transmitted video as it is seen by the receiver, the video and trace files are processed by etmp4 (Evaluate Traces of MP4-file transmission):

To be continue on page... 89

ERPNext: An Open Source ERP for Entrepreneurs

Enterprises never had it better! ERPNext is a system of integrated applications that can manage the entire business and automate back-end office functions. This free and open source platform offers everything from product planning and manufacture to accounting and inventory control.

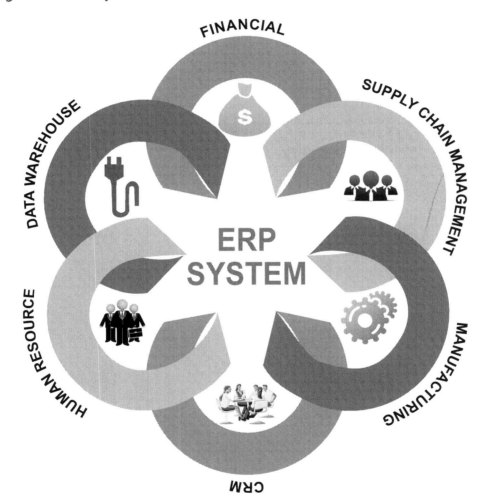

In the late 80s, everyone wanted government jobs, and in the 90s, it was engineering and medicine that people were attracted to. Today, everyone is trying to turn into an entrepreneur. Every other day we find a group of highly ambitious, talented youngsters toiling hard to make their dreams come true—becoming job providers rather than seekers. Even venture capitalists are showering them with funds. And now, a few open source enthusiasts have developed an enterprise resource planning (ERP) tool for entrepreneurs, called ERPNext.

ERP, as the name suggests, is business management software. It allows an organisation to use a system of integrated applications to manage the business and automate many back-office functions related to technology, services and human resources. It is an integrated platform which helps the company to collect, store, manage and interpret data from its business activities like product planning, manufacturing, marketing, inventory management, shipping, payment, etc.

ERPNext is a modern tool that covers accounting, HR, inventory, billing, quotes, leads, payroll, etc. It can be downloaded and installed from *https://erpnext.com/download*. The image can be downloaded from *https://erpnext.com/downloads/ERPNext-020415.ova*. After installing and creating a project, the home screen that appears will look like what's shown in Figure 1.

We all know that accounts are the backbone of any institution; so let's start with what ERPNext has to offer in this field. The accounts part of the package contains Journal Entry, Sales Invoice, Chart of Accounts, Making Payments, Accounting Reports, Item-wise Tax, Point of Sales invoices, and many more features. All types of entries other than sales invoices and purchase invoices are done using Journal Entry. To create a Journal Entry one has to go to *Accounts ->Documents->Journal Entry ->New* (Figure 2).

Payments made against Sales Invoices or Purchase Invoices can be entered by clicking on the 'Make Payment Entry' button on 'Submitted' invoices. The credit limit is also built into this. The credit limit is the maximum amount of credit that a financial institution will extend to a debtor for a specific line of credit. This can be achieved by going to *Selling->Document->Customer*.

Stock maintenance is also very important in ERP, and this has been thoroughly dealt with in this tool. If we want to request for material, then we must go to *Stock->Documents->Material request-> New*. The material request is categorised into three types—*Purchase* (if the requested material is to be purchased), *Transfer* (if the material is to be transferred from one warehouse to another) and *Issue* (if the material is to be issued)—to ease the process. The Stock entry is used to record the transfer of an item from one warehouse to another. When shipment is made from the warehouse, a delivery note is generated. The warehouse, being the most important part of 'Stock', must be under constant scrutiny and for this, one can go to *Stock->Warehouse*. In ERPNext, every warehouse must belong to a specific company, in order to maintain company-wise stock balances. Warehouses are saved with their respective company's abbreviations. This helps to identify which warehouse belongs to which company, at a glance.

Moving on to customer relations management, ERPNext's CRM module contains leads, customers, opportunities, campaigns and many other features. Leads are important because they help a company to make a sale. Since there are multiple contacts and addresses for a customer or supplier, these leads are stored separately in ERPNext. Even the campaign is managed in the *Campaign* tab and tracked via the *Leads* UI.

The buying and selling of goods is also managed, and here the user can generate quotations for clients as well as keep a track of supplier's quotations. The Sales Order confirms your sales and triggers purchase (Material Request), shipment (Delivery Note), billing (Sales Invoice) and manufacturing (Production Plan).

Figure 1: Home ERPNext

Figure 2: Journal

Figure 3: Customer

Another important aspect in the ERP is human resource management. Right from the planning of resources to the attendance and the leave report, everything is well integrated into this system. New employees can be added from *Human Resource-> Employee ->New* as shown in Figure 4.

When employees spend some money from their own pocket for official purposes, they can claim these by raising a new expense claim. The salary and payroll is also well integrated in this ERP. The Salary Structure represents how Salaries are calculated based on Earnings and Deductions. To process Payroll in ERPNext, one has to first create Salary Structures for all Employees, then generate salary slips via the salary management tool, and then book the salary in the respective accounts. By creating

Figure 4: HR

a new Job opening in the portal, we can also share the information about the job.

The ERPNext Web portal gives one's customers quick access to their Orders, Invoices and Shipments. Customers can check the status of their orders, invoices and shipping status by logging on to the Web. To log into their account and check the order status, customers have to use their email ID and the password sent by ERPNext, generated through

the sign-up process. The best part is that ERPNext provides Web support, i.e., static content like Home page, About Us and Contacts can be created using the Web page by going to *Website-> Web Page->New*.

ERPNext also offers customisation. One can simplify the forms by hiding features not needed, by using *Disable Features, Module Setup, Add Custom Fields*. One can also change form properties, like adding more options to drop-down boxes or hiding fields using *Customize Form View*, and make one's own Print Formats by using HTML Templates.

ERPNext is a very well integrated tool, which caters to almost all the requirements of a company and especially a start-up. I would recommend it for all those young entrepreneurs who have set up a company and will be working hard to fulfill their dreams. END🐧

By: Ashish Kumar Sinha

The author is a software engineer based in Bengaluru. A software enthusiast by heart, he is passionate about using open source technology and sharing it with the world. He can be reached at *ashi.sinha.87@gmail.com*

Continued from page... 86

```
$etmp4 -f -0 -c Send_time_file Recv_time_file Source_Video_
Trace bus_cif2.mp4 bus_cif_recv.mp4
```

This generates a (possibly corrupted) video file, in which all frames that got lost or were corrupted are deleted from the original video track. The reconstructed video will also demonstrate the effect of jitter introduced during packet transmission.

etmp4 also creates some other files, which are listed below:

loss_bus_cif_recv.txt contains I, P, B and overall frame loss in percentage.

delay_bus_cif_recv.txt contains frame-nr., lost-flag, end-to-end delay, inter-frame gap sender, inter-frame gap receiver, and cumulative jitter in seconds.

rate_s_bus_cif_recv.txt contains time, bytes per second (current time interval), and bytes per second (cumulative) measured at the sender and receiver.

The PSNR by itself does not mean much; other quality metrics that calculate the difference between the quality of the encoded video and the received video (which could be corrupted) can be used. Using a specialised tool like MSU, video quality in terms of VQM, SSIM can be measured, as transmitted and received videos are available.

7. Now, decode the received video to *yuv* format:

```
$ffmpeg -i bus_cif_recv.mp4 bus_cif_recv.yuv
```

8. Compute the PSNR:

```
psnr x y <YUV format> <src.yuv> <dst.yuv> [multiplex] [ssim]
```

```
$psnr 352 288 420 bus_cif2.yuv bus_cif_recv.yuv > ref_psnr.txt
```

Simulating an experimental set-up

All relevant files for simulation can be downloaded from *http://opensourceforu.efytimes.com/article_source_code/july15/vt_ns2.zip*.

Performance evaluation

We can plot the graph PSNR as mentioned in Step 8. We can also plot other quality metrics like VQM and SSIM. END🐧

References

[1] Klaue, Jirka, Berthold Rathke, and Adam Wolisz;'Evalvid–A framework for video transmission and quality evaluation. Computer Performance Evaluation. Modelling Techniques and Tools". Springer Berlin Heidelberg, 2003. 255-272.
[2] *http://www2.tkn.tu-berlin.de/research/evalvid/EvalVid/docevalvid.html* source file.

By: Vijay Ukani and Jitendra Bhatia

Vijay Ukani is associate professor at Institute of Technology, Nirma University, Ahmedabad. He enjoys teaching and exploring network protocols and multimedia transmission. Connect with him at *vijayukani@yahoo.com*.

Bhatia is senior assistant professor at the Department of Computer Science and Engineering, Institute of Technology, Nirma University, Ahmedabad. His research interests are in the area of computer networks and software defined networking. Connect with him at *jitendrabbhatia@gmail.com*.

Why Open Source Software
is NOT Free

A common misconception among customers, who are not necessarily clued in to the open source philosophy, is about the 'free' attribute of open source. Here is how author explains to them what OSS is all about.

Image courtesy http://northforker.com

Many of my sales guys go into the field and face the following question put to them by customers, "We heard that open source is free. So why is your company charging us for it?"

At this point, I tell them a small story, which they can effectively use during their next sales call. Here is what I tell them.

Tom takes his girlfriend Jenny for a date to the beautiful seaside restaurant 'Jimbaran Bay' in Bali (Indonesia) and orders fresh lobsters—the costliest dish the restaurant offers. The sea breeze and the alcohol served in coconut shells makes them relax. The lobster arrives in exactly 30 minutes, as promised in the menu card. Jenny has never tasted a lobster before and is not sure how to eat it. Being the experienced traveller that he is, Tom helps her out with the techniques of handling the lobster. Jenny loves the lobster and enjoys the entire experience of learning how to eat it.

The waiter brings the finger bowls for the couple to wash their hands, and the bill shortly afterwards. Tom picks up the bill, stares at it and exclaims, "What is this?"

"Sir, the bill for the lobster," the waiter replies.

"What do you mean by a bill for the lobster?" asks Tom.

"Sir, you and your friend just ate the lobster now. This is our bill for it," the waiter continues politely.

"But...I thought the lobster is freely available," Tom retorts, pointing towards the sea.

The waiter faints.

Once you narrate this incident to customers, the

irrationality of their question about why they need to pay for 'free software' becomes clear to them.

Are we not almost always paying for free things? We go to restaurants and pay for fish, which is available for free in nature. What about the gold in the ring, which you bought last week? What about the diamonds in the necklace you presented to your daughter for her birthday? What about the water in the bottle you just bought? As you can see, we mostly pay for free things. Sounds illogical? Irrational, maybe?

To understand just how illogical some people's expectations are with regard to 'free software', we need to understand the supply chain involved in any product. Let us take fish, for instance. Somebody has to buy a boat, fill its tank with diesel, hire employees and send them to sea to catch fish. He then needs to price the fish in such a way that he can recover the cost of the boat, diesel, employee salaries, and make a profit for himself. Now, the next element in the supply chain would be the person who buys the fresh fish, transports it in ice and then stores it in a freezer. Obviously, this person, too, needs to add the cost of ice, employee salaries, etc, apart from his profit margin to the original cost of fresh fish. Depending on the location, there could be yet more elements in the supply chain before it reaches a fish store where you can buy the fish as an end customer.

So what does the supply chain look like in the open source scenario? Assume that a generous programmer and his community developed a piece of software for remote controls. It is not practical for the end customer to just download the software and start using it as a remote control. This is where a company can play a role in bridging the gap between the raw software and a functioning remote control in the hands of the customer. This company X understands that there is such software available, chooses a suitable hardware platform to run this software, and also scouts for manufacturers for the plastic parts encasing the hardware—such as buttons for the user to issue commands. It pays some amount to the hardware manufacturer, to the plastic manufacturer and so on. Finally, the company has a beautiful product in hand.

Now, the customers should become aware that there is such a product that they can hugely benefit from. Again, money has to be spent on marketing and a sales channel. The company, even if it is a non-profitable organisation, has to spend for all these activities and recover its expenses from the final product price. Also, those at company X need to set aside funds for the cost of warranties, infrastructure for support, etc. This is how free software becomes a priced product in the customers' hands.

Adam Smith defines capitalism as follows: "It is not from the benevolence of the butcher, the brewer, or the baker, that we expect our dinner, but from their regard to their own interest." Similarily, our company X finds the software, hardware and plastics, puts it together and sells it to make profits. Also, the customer, who buys the product, at say US$ 25, feels that paying this price once is better than getting up and going to the TV to change channels 10 times in a day. Each works in their own interest to bring about overall economic gain.

It is important that companies that provide open source software understand the economics behind their existence, and educate their sales force to not feel embarassed in front of 'intelligent customers'. Instead, the sales force must be trained to communicate and explain the economics of open source software. **END**

By: Dr Devasia Kurian

The author is the CEO and founder of *astTECS, an open source telecom products company supplying IP PBX, call centre diallers, voice loggers, IVRs, etc. He can be contacted at *d.kurian@asttecs.com*.

Protect Your Eyes with Redshift

Redshift will help you to reduce the strain on your eyes when working with computers and laptops, particularly in the dark or in low-light conditions. This amazing tool makes working with computers less strenuous and is available in Linux and Windows versions.

The problem with working on computers is that one experiences a certain type of physical strain because of constantly sitting in front of the keyboard, while the eyes suffer due to excess exposure to the monitor's light. This is worse when using a laptop, especially at night when working in bed without the lights on. This article looks at the latter scenario and recommends the use of Redshift to protect your eyes. The position one sits in can be adjusted based on comfort, and coloured light from the monitor can be reduced by using computer glasses or following the common 20-20-20 rule, which states that you need to rest your eyes after every 20 minutes for a period of 20 seconds by looking at objects which are at least 20 metres away. If you do not take enough care, you will suffer from red eyes, blurred vision, headaches, etc. If this continues over a

long period of time, you might even suffer from computer vision syndrome (CVS). The disadvantage of using computer glasses is that they are costly (the basic versions start from about ₹ 5000 (US$ 85) in India. There may be other problems associated with these glasses like not being comfortable, leaving marks on the face and negatively altering a person's appearance. I suggest that you use them, even if you are using Redshift, and maybe you can increase the time limit for constantly working on a screen to 30 minutes or an hour from the earlier twenty minutes.

How Redshift works

Jon Lund Steffensen (the creator of Redshift) says that he created his own tool, as *f.lux* didn't work well for him. He made it open source (GPLv3) and it is under constant

Figure 1: Redshift with reduced temperature only

Figure 2: Redshift with reduced brightness only

Figure 3: Redshift with both reduced temperature and brightness

development. You can contribute to its development at *https://github.com/jonls/redshift*. The working of Redshift is simple—it adjusts the temperature of the monitor based on the time and the surroundings. In the background, it makes use of the RandR (resize and rotate) communication protocol extension for X11 and Wayland (which is supposed to replace the X11) protocol for the display servers to adjust the colour. An alternative to RandR is the VidMode extension. Redshift can also be configured to change the

```
→  ~  sudo apt-get install redshift redshift-gtk
[sudo] password for ravinder:
Reading package lists... Done
Building dependency tree
Reading state information... Done
The following extra packages will be installed:
  geoclue-hostip python-appindicator
The following NEW packages will be installed:
  geoclue-hostip python-appindicator redshift redshift-gtk
0 upgraded, 4 newly installed, 0 to remove and 0 not upgra
Need to get 83.7 kB of archives.
After this operation, 1,020 kB of additional disk space wi
Do you want to continue? [Y/n] y
Get:1 http://in.archive.ubuntu.com/ubuntu/ trusty/universe
Get:2 http://in.archive.ubuntu.com/ubuntu/ trusty-updates/
Get:3 http://in.archive.ubuntu.com/ubuntu/ trusty/universe
Get:4 http://in.archive.ubuntu.com/ubuntu/ trusty/universe
```

Figure 4: Installing Redshift in Ubuntu/Debian

colours individually and to reduce the brightness in a different manner. It actually doesn't reduce the light from the monitor but it applies a black filter to the screen, which creates a similar effect. Adjusting both the temperature and the brightness makes the monitor very eye friendly. Figures 1, 2 and 3 give three screenshots of *opensourceforu.com* with Redshift in various configurations.

Installing Redshift

Ubuntu/Debian: Installing Redshift in Debian/Ubuntu can be done by issuing the following command in a terminal:

```
sudo apt-get install redshift redshift-gtk
```

After installing the *redshift-gtk* you get the status icon in the tray with which you can control Redshift very easily. You can toggle between 'On', 'Off' and 'Pause Redshift' for certain periods if you are doing colour sensitive work such as editing pictures or videos.

Fedora/Red Hat: In these systems, you can use the Yum package manager to install Redshift, as follows:

```
sudo yum install redshift redshift-gtk
```

Note: In the recent version of Fedora 22, Yum is replaced by *dnf*, which is better. So *dnf* should be used in place of *yum* in the above command.

SUSE based systems: If you are using a system based on SUSE you can use *zypper* as below:

```
sudo zypper install redshift redshift-gtk
```

Arch based systems: The command for Arch linux will be:

```
sudo pacman -S redshift redshift-gtk
```

If you are using some other Linux distro in which the package manager doesn't have the package Redshift, you can install it from the source using the following commands:

Figure 5: Redshift status icon in the taskbar

Figure 6: *dnf* install

```
    wget -c https://github.com/jonls/redshift/releases/
download/v1.10/redshift-1.10.tar.xz

    tar xf redshift-1.10.tar.xz

    cd redshift-1.10/

    ./configure --prefix=$HOME/redshift/root \
--with-systemduserunitdir=$HOME/.config/systemd/user

    make

    make install
```

Note: Earlier, version 1.8 *redshift-gtk* was known as *gtk-redshift* so you might need to change the name while installing. Also, there is *redshift-qt* for the KDE desktop.

Configuring Redshift

By default, Redshift configures itself based on the user's location. The location is obtained using GeoClue which may or may not work out-of-the-box, in all cases. It can be configured manually. Uninstall the *Redshift-gtk* and **not** Redshift, and follow the steps below to use Redshift without the GUI.

Location: The location for Redshift can be set manually by using the *-l(location)* flag:

```
redshift -l 22.5:88.3
```

The above is the latitude and longitude of Kolkata, which works for most of India. Feel free to change the above value to that of the city which is nearest to you.

Temperature: The temperature of the screen can be set by using the *-t(temperature)* flag:

```
redshift -t 4500:3000
```

…where 4500 is the daytime temperature and 3000 is the night temperature.

Brightness: The brightness of the screen can be set by using the *-b (brightness)* flag. And the value for it can be between 0.1 and 1.0.

```
redshift -b 0.8
```

Note: As I have mentioned above, brightness doesn't reduce the light from the screen but it applies a grey filter, which creates a similar effect. And you can combine the above commands according to your needs.

Configuration file: You can also use a configuration file instead of the above commands. Here is the configuration file example given by Jon Lund Steffensen in the Redshift website. You can create the new file in your favourite editor and put it at *~/.config/redshift.conf*:

```
; Global settings for redshift
[redshift]
; Set the day and night screen temperatures
temp-day=5700
temp-night=3500

; Enable/Disable a smooth transition between day and night
; 0 will cause a direct change from day to night screen
temperature.
; 1 will gradually increase or decrease the screen
temperature.
transition=1

; Set the screen brightness. Default is 1.0.
;brightness=0.9
; It is also possible to use different settings for day and
night
; since version 1.8.
;brightness-day=0.7
;brightness-night=0.4
; Set the screen gamma (for all colors, or each color channel
; individually)
gamma=0.8
;gamma=0.8:0.7:0.8
; This can also be set individually for day and night since
; version 1.10.
;gamma-day=0.8:0.7:0.8
;gamma-night=0.6

; Set the location-provider: 'geoclue', 'geoclue2', 'manual'
```

```
; type 'redshift -l list' to see possible values.
; The location provider settings are in a different section.
location-provider=manual

; Set the adjustment-method: 'randr', 'vidmode'
; type 'redshift -m list' to see all possible values.
; 'randr' is the preferred method, 'vidmode' is an older API.
; but works in some cases when 'randr' does not.
; The adjustment method settings are in a different section.
adjustment-method=randr

; Configuration of the location-provider:
; type 'redshift -l PROVIDER:help' to see the settings.
; ex: 'redshift -l manual:help'
; Keep in mind that longitudes west of Greenwich (e.g. the
Americas)
; are negative numbers.
[manual]
lat=22.5
lon=88.3

; Configuration of the adjustment-method
; type 'redshift -m METHOD:help' to see the settings.
; ex: 'redshift -m randr:help'
; In this example, randr is configured to adjust screen 1.
; Note that the numbering starts from 0, so this is actually
the
; second screen. If this option is not specified, Redshift
will try
; to adjust _all_ screens.
[randr]
screen=0
```

Note: I suggest that you do not use the screen option in the configuration file to adjust all screens, like external monitors too.

Making Redshift a start-up application: You can make Redshift start at boot using the status icon in Ubuntu. If you have any difficulty with the status icon, you can add Redshift to the start-up application, manually.

If you can't find the start-up application in your Linux distribution desktop environment, you can also add this file at

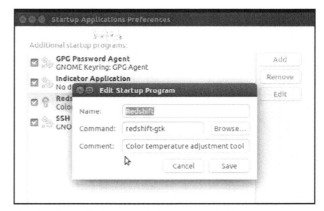

Figure 7: Adding applications manually to start-up applications

~/.config/autostart/redshift.desktop.

```
[Desktop Entry]
Type=Application
Exec=redshift -O 3000
Hidden=false
NoDisplay=false
X-GNOME-Autostart-enabled=true
Name[en_IN]=Redshift
Name=Redshift
```

Redshift vs *f.lux*

The most important reason to use Redshift rather than *f.lux* is the freedom that comes with it. It is licensed under GPLv3 and works very well with GNU/Linux (it can be used for Windows too). The only disadvantage is that it can't be installed on OSX. If you face any difficulties with Redshift, you can report them at *https://github.com/jonls/redshift/issues/new.*

References
[1] *http://jonls.dk/redshift/*
[2] *https://github.com/jonls/redshift*

By: Tummala Dhanvi
The author is a security enthusiast who loves FREEdom software. He can be contacted at *dhanvicse_AT_ gmail_ DOT_ com.*

An Introduction to GNU Emacs

GNU Emacs, created by Richard Stallman, is an extensible, customisable text editor. While Emacs has many variants, GNU Emacs is the most widely used. This article spawns a series on learning to use it.

GNU Emacs is a very popular text editor written in C and Emacs Lisp. It can be run on many platforms, and can be easily customised and extended for user needs. It was created by Richard Stallman, the founder of the GNU project. This article is the first in a series on how to use it. There are a number of tutorials available for GNU Emacs; this series of articles provides one approach to understanding and learning the software. You are encouraged to refer to the official GNU Emacs reference manual for more information, and it supersedes everything.

Here are a few interesting quotes on Emacs.

"I use Emacs, which might be thought of as a thermonuclear word processor." - *Neal Stephenson (from 'In the Beginning... Was the Command Line')*

"Emacs is undoubtedly the most powerful programmer's editor in existence. It's a big, feature-laden program with a great deal of flexibility and customisability. ... Emacs has an entire programming language inside it that can be used to write arbitrarily powerful editor functions." – *Eric S. Raymond (from 'The Art of UNIX Programming')*

"Personally, I feel inspired whenever I open Emacs. Like a craftsman entering his workshop, I feel a realm of possibility open before me. I feel the comfort of an environment that has evolved over time to fit me perfectly - an assortment of packages and keybindings which help me

bring ideas to life day after day." – *Daniel Higginbotham (in 'Clojure for the Brave and True')*

"Emacs could not have been reached by a process of careful design, because such processes arrive only at goals which are visible at the outset, and whose desirability is established on the bottom line at the outset. Neither I nor anyone else visualised an extensible editor until I had made one, nor appreciated its value until he had experienced it. EMACS exists because I felt free to make individually useful small improvements on a path whose end was not in sight." – *Richard Stallman*

Installation

You can use your favourite GNU/Linux distribution package manager to install GNU Emacs. On Debian/Ubuntu, you can install it with the following command:

```
$ sudo apt-get install emacs
```

On Fedora, you can use the Yum package manager as shown below:

```
$ sudo yum install emacs
```

The *emerge* tool can install GNU Emacs on Gentoo, as follows:

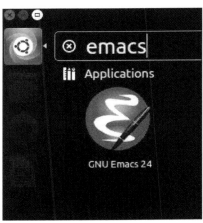

Figure 1: Unity Emacs search image

Figure 2: Metacity Emacs

```
# emerge --ask app-editors/emacs
```

On Arch, the Pacman software can help you in installing GNU Emacs:

```
$ sudo pacman -S emacs
```

Use the Zypper package manager in SUSE as shown below:

```
$ sudo zypper install emacs
```

Start-up

If you use the Unity interface, you can search for Emacs in the Dash, and it will show the Emacs icon that you can click to open the editor. This is illustrated in Figure 1.

On the Metacity interface or any other desktop environment with a panel, you can open GNU Emacs from *Applications -> Accessories -> Emacs,* as shown in Figure 2.

You can also open the editor from the terminal by simply typing 'emacs' and hitting the return key.

```
$ emacs
```

The version that I have used for this article is GNU Emacs 24.3.1.

Exit

To exit from GNU Emacs, you need to use *C-c C-q*, where 'C' stands for the Control key. You can also use your mouse and close the editor by clicking on the 'x', but GNU Emacs was designed to be completely usable with a keyboard, and I am going to encourage you to only use the keyboard shortcuts.

Concepts

While you can work using GUI editors, I am going to teach you to work entirely on the keyboard to experience the power of shortcuts in GNU Emacs. You can disconnect the mouse and your touchpad when working on GNU Emacs. Just as an exercise, I'd encourage you to remove your mouse completely and see how you can work with a computer for one day. You will realise that a lot of user interfaces are heavily dependent and designed for mouse interactions! By only using the keyboard, you can be blazingly fast and productive.

The keyboard shortcuts in GNU Emacs may seem to involve many keys. But please bear with me on this, because the way the shortcuts are designed, you will be able to remember them easily. As you practice, you will gain an insight into how consistently they have been defined.

GNU Emacs is a 'stateless' editor for the most part. By 'stateless', I mean that there are no specific state transitions that need to happen before you can use the commands. There does exist the concept of modes. When you open GNU Emacs, you will see menus, buffer and a mode line as illustrated in Figure 3.

As mentioned earlier, we will not be clicking on the menus or icons with a mouse, but only use keyboard shortcuts. Everything is a buffer in GNU Emacs. Each buffer can have one major mode and one or more minor modes. The mode determines the keyboard shortcuts that are applicable primarily on the buffer. Examples of major modes are given in Table 1.

Table 1

Mode	Description
Text mode	Writing text
HTML mode	Writing HTML
cc mode	Writing C, C++ and C-like programs
Dired mode	Handling files and directories
Shell mode	Working with shell
LaTeX mode	Formatting TeX and LaTeX files
Picture mode	Creating ASCII art
Outline mode	Writing outlines
SQL mode	Interacting with SQL databases
Lisp mode	Writing Lisp programs

The mode line exists below the buffer and it gives you a lot of information on the status of the buffer, such as what modes are active and other useful information. Below the mode line is the mini-buffer, where any commands you issue are indicated and prompts for user input are shown. This is the overall view of the default GNU Emacs interface.

In today's user interface applications, an application is treated as a window on a desktop. But, when you open GNU Emacs, you are actually opening a frame. A frame can be split into many windows. Everything is a buffer in GNU Emacs. So, you can

To be continued on page 99....

Penetration Testing Tools for Android

Since Android devices have become all-pervasive, they need to be monitored and secured for obvious reasons. Numerous Android apps are available in the market for a range of purposes. Read about which of these could make your Android experience safe, secure and anonymous!

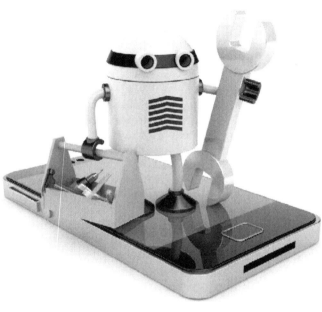

We are nearing the age of the Internet of Things. Almost all our devices are connected to the Internet, through which we send so much of sensitive data. Therefore, monitoring and securing these networks is crucial. Android devices provide a convenient and flexible solution for basic penetration testing. As they are Linux devices, rooted Android devices can run almost all the basic commands used in the Linux command line. This helps to perform most of the penetration testing techniques.

Network monitoring

The following applications require a rooted Android device with Busybox installed.

1) **Fing**: Fing is a professional app for network analysis. It lets you monitor networks completely with a simple and intuitive interface that helps you evaluate security levels, detect intruders and resolve network issues. It displays the list of devices connected to a particular network with their MAC addresses. It also offers ping and *traceroute* to test network performance.
   Similar apps: Network Discovery and Net Scan

2) **Port Scanner**: A port is where information goes into and out of the computer. Scanning ports can identify the 'open doors' to a computer. Therefore scanning ports is vital in managing networks. This app lets you scan ports on a remote host via its IP or domain name so that you can know which ports are open on the host. It supports 3G, protocol recognition, and many other features.
   Similar apps: Port Detective and PortDroid for network analysis

3) **Interceptor-NG:** Packet sniffing is to computer networks what wire tapping is to a telephone network. All network data travels across the Internet, in the form of various data packets. Since the typical user never 'sees' any of this raw data, many spyware systems covertly send sensitive information (like passwords or IP addresses) out of users' computers without their knowledge. Interceptor-NG is a multi-function network toolkit that helps you analyse these packets being sent. It offers a good and unique alternative to Wireshark for Android.
   Similar apps: Packet Capture and Shark for Root

Penetration testing

The following applications were developed as penetration testing tools and are not intended to be used in public networks.

1) **ANTI:** ANTI (Android Network Toolkit) from Zimperium Mobile Security is perhaps one of the best penetration testing tools for security professionals; at the same time, it is a handy tool for hackers! It offers you the power of Backtrack (Kali) in the palms of your hands. This app can simulate various attacks like MITM (Man-in-the-middle), DoS (Denial-of-service), password cracking and Metasploit. It also has the popular Nmap utility integrated into it.

2) **DroidSQLi:** On a typical user authentication Web form, when the user name and password are entered into the textbox provided, the values are inserted into a select query. Attackers can use these input boxes to send their own requests to the database and obtain vital information. This is called SQL injection. DroidSQLi is the first automated MySQL injection tool for Android. It allows you to test your MySQL based Web application against SQL injection attacks.
   Similar apps: sqlmapchik

3) **DroidSheep:** On a user's first visit to any dynamic website, a session ID is granted, which is basically used to keep track of the user's data when the user bounces to different pages in the same website. DroidSheep reads all the packets through a network. It looks at their contents and identifies the user's SessionID and uses this as its own SessionID, thus hijacking the user's website in a logged-in state.

Anonymity

The following applications help users to stay anonymous on the Internet.

1) **Orbot:** We've all used TOR to access blocked social media websites in our college and office Web filters. Orbot is an Android application from the official TOR project that does exactly that. It is the safest way to stay completely anonymous on the Internet, instead of connecting to VPNs and proxies. The app lets you choose which apps need to use TOR. ORWEB is a dedicated TOR browser for Android, also from the TOR project.

2) **OpenVPN:** OpenVPN is the best VPN client for Android. As the name suggests, it is completely open source. It can be easily configured to run on any port. It only uses a 128-bit encryption key which makes it faster but still, to all intents and purposes, remains uncrackable through brute force, and will remain so for the foreseeable future. END

By: Chandramohan Sudar

The author is an Android enthusiast/developer, a member of the XDA community and also the lead-guitarist in a band. He blogs about his experiences at *https://chandruscm.wordpress.com/*

Continued from page 97....

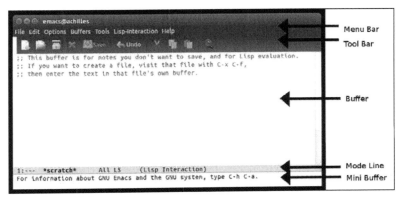

Figure 3: Emacs default screenshot

have many frames of GNU Emacs, and inside each you can have one or more windows containing buffers (or files).

Features

Although GNU Emacs was designed primarily for text editing, it can do a lot more. 'A lot' is probably a highly simplified term. It has got support for syntax highlighting for a large number of programming languages. You can also generate code snippets from templates using the *yasnippet* package. You can also enter markup or markdown text. There is support for indentation of text and programs depending on the programming languages and modes. Internationalisation support is available, and you can use it to even enter text in Indian languages.

A number of configurations are available for setting it up for your development work, including automating tasks for compiling, executing, testing and deployment. When you become familiar with Emacs Lisp, you can implement your own modules. Since it is Lisp, it is also easily extensible. You can write your own macros to perform repeated tasks. You can also query an inbuilt help system for information, shortcuts, tutorials and other documentation. You are not at all dependent on the Internet for information, and thus you can work offline too. Version control support is available for many centralised (cvs, svn) and decentralised systems (Git, Hg).

org-mode is a very popular mode for managing your notes. You can use it for planning your day-to-day activities.

GNU Emacs can be used as publishing software. You can create wikis, blogs and publish books using it. This article is written using org-mode. Spell-checking modules are also available for your documentation needs. It is also possible to export plain text into a number of formats (PDF, HTML, etc).

A number of Emacs Lisp packages are available for networking. You can use Gnus for checking your e-mails, and reading and writing to newsgroups. Emacs Relay Chat (ERC) can be used for connecting to Internet Relay Chat (IRC) channels. There are modules that support the Jabber protocol for communicating with chat servers. There is also support for viewing Web pages inside Emacs. There are a large number of Emacs modules available through package repositories such as MELPA (*melpa.org*) and Marmalade (*marmalade-repo.org*).

History

The first version of Emacs (macros) was written by Richard Stallman and Guy L. Steele, Jr in 1976 for the TECO editor in MIT. It was written in a low-level language for the PDP-10 assembler. People were able to freely hack the code, make improvements and share their changes. This was the original hacker culture that existed in MIT. Unfortunately, business entities started to make software proprietary and this hacker culture ceased to exist, especially in the MIT AI labs. Richard Stallman wanted to revive the hacker culture and started the GNU project. He wrote the second implementation of the editor entirely in C in 1984, and released it as the first program of the GNU project. Today, it is a very popular editor that is widely used, and has more than 570 contributors. The official website for GNU Emacs is *http://www.gnu.org/software/emacs/*. END

By: Shakthi Kannan

The author is a free software enthusiast and blogs at *shakthimaan.com*.

THINGS TO DO AFTER INSTALLING
FEDORA 22

Having installed Fedora 22, a newbie is often at a loss for what to do next. This article guides the reader through the process of installing Fedora 22, explains the use of the DNF install tool and then suggests some applications to be installed.

Fedora 22 is one of the most commonly used operating systems in the open source world. It is popular among GNOME developers because most of the GNOME development tools are by default in Fedora 22. It is even more popular for its stability, when compared to other Linux distros.

Fedora 22, which comes along with GNOME 3.16, was launched last month. The latest release features some major changes such as the change in command line from Yum to DNF. The other new feature in Fedora 22 is boxes, which comes as a default with the system. It comprises virtualisation tools like Virtual Box, VMware, etc. Some plugin packages, such as gstreamer, which are required for playing.mp3, have been removed.

Figure 1: Fedora 22 desktop

Installation of Fedora 22 alongside Windows

Many notebooks these days come with Windows 8 or Windows 8.1, by default, which has UEFI enabled in the boot options. If any Linux distro is installed alongside Windows, the UEFI creates a problem by not allowing Linux to boot. But from about a year ago, all Linux based distros support UEFI. Fedora 22 is way ahead in this game. It supports UEFI based machines without any problems.

The installation of Fedora 22 alongside Windows in UEFI is slightly tricky for beginners because if you try to boot it in live mode from a bootable pen drive, it just won't work. So, to create a live disk of Fedora 22, the use of LiveUSB Creator is recommended. LiveUSB Creator is a tool specially used to create live disks which support UEFI.

Steps to be followed during the dual boot of Fedora 22 and Windows

1. Turn off *Secure boot* from the boot options in the BIOS settings.
2. Insert the live disk and then proceed with the installation process.
3. In the partitioning stage, make sure that you select manual partitioning instead of automatic partitioning.
4. In manual partitioning, there will be an option to automatically allocate the free space to the operating system or you can also do it manually.
5. If you are doing it manually, make sure to allocate a partition of around 500MB for the */boot/efi* partition where Grub will be installed.
6. Then create a new user and proceed to install and reboot the system.

You have now successfully installed Fedora 22 in your notebook/laptop with UEFI enabled.

Yum to DNF in Fedora 22

After the installation of Fedora 22, when you try to do an update of all the packages from the terminal, you will see something like what's shown in Figure 2, on the terminal screen.

Previously, the Yum (Yellowdog Updater Modified) package installer for Fedora managed the packages in RPM format, so it became the package manager of choice for several RPM-based distributions. But Yum is fairly slow in performance and has high memory usage; code *cruft* has increased the overall time as well. So, from the release of Fedora 22 onwards the Fedora community has decided to use DNF (Dandified Yum) as the default package manager.

The reason for initiating the DNF project was because of the three big drawbacks of Yum: undocumented API, broken dependency solving algorithm, and the inability to refactor internal functions. The last issue is connected with the lack of documentation.

DNF (Dandified Yum)

DNF is a forked version of Yum that uses the *libsolv* library via Hawkey. There are a few more packages included in DNF, which increase its performance. These packages are based on Python. DNF offers some backward compatibilities with Yum.

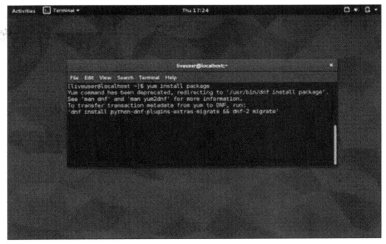

Figure 2: Using yum to install software

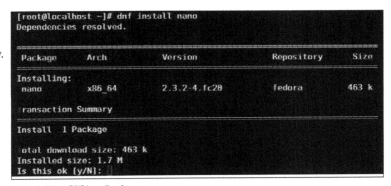

Figure 3: Using DNF install software

Figure 4: Using DNF to search package

Desktop users using graphical package management tools like the software application won't feel a difference.

If you're using the Yum command in a terminal, you will be reminded that Yum is deprecated and that you should use the DNF command instead. DNF mostly works about the same as Yum. Most of the commands in DNF are similar to Yum commands.

The Hawkey *depsolving* library on which DNF is built is well designed, optimised and is itself built on a successful, low-level SAT library that SUSE has been using for years at production level workloads. The downloading and metadata parsing component used by DNF, *librepo*, is also well designed and complements the Hawkey API nicely.

Rather than use the DNF framework directly, *packagekit* (*PK*) uses *librepo* and Hawkey to share 80 per cent of the mechanism between PK and DNF. DNF is well organised with unit tests and lots of older compatibility *cruft* removed, and the only reason it's not used in *packagekit (PK)* is that the daemon is written in C and isn't changed to marshal everything via Python for latency reasons.

DNF was designed to avoid mistakes made in Yum. From the start, all exposed API functions were properly documented. Tests were included with almost every new commit. So no quick and dirty hacks are allowed. The project is directed by agile development – the features that have the greatest impact on users are operatively implemented with higher priority.

Commands in DNF

The command line is the same when compared to Yum, and most of the commands are similar. Here is a list of a few basic commands used regularly in Fedora.

To install a package like *nano*, you would use the following command (as root):

```
sudo dnf install nano
```

To *search* for a package, use the search sub-command:

```
sudo dnf search nano
```

To upgrade the system as well as the packages, use the command below (as root):

```
sudo dnf upgrade
```

During the install and remove processes, some temporary files will be created. To make sure that these files are deleted once they are no longer needed, use the *clean all* sub-command, as follows:

```
sudo dnf clean all
```

The *clean all* command will get DNF to remove the cache files generated from the repository metadata, remove the local cookie files and any cache repository metadata, as well as any cached packages from the system. If you want to just remove one type of temporary file rather than all of them, then use either *dbcache, expire-cache, metadata* or *packages* instead of *all*.

For example, to remove the cached packages from the system, use:

```
sudo dnf clean packages
```

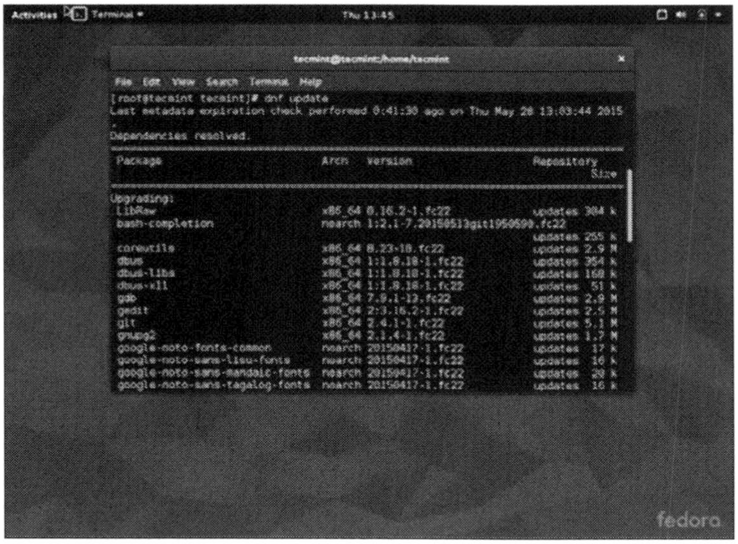

Things to consider after installing Fedora 22

1. Update the Fedora 22 distribution

Though you have just installed/updated Fedora (version 22),

Figure 5: Using DNF to update

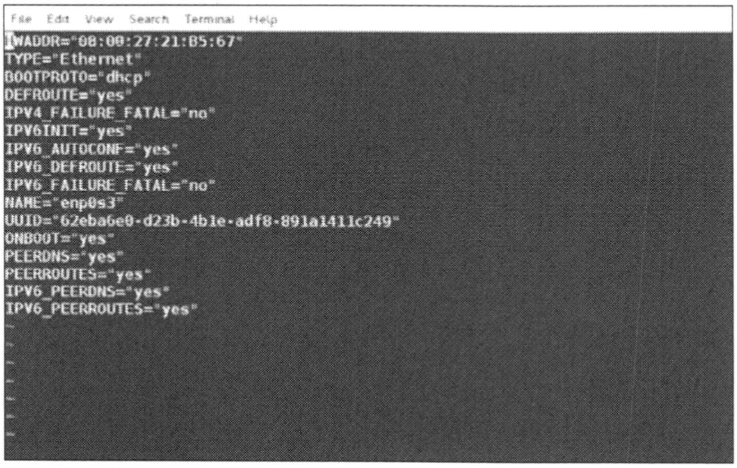

Figure 6: Details of ifcfg-en0 file

you cannot deny the fact that Fedora is at the bleeding edge, and when you try updating all the system packages you may find that lots of applications and utilities need to be updated.

To update Fedora 22, we use the DNF command as shown below:

```
sudo dnf update
```

2. Set the static IP address in Fedora 22

Set the static IP and DNS for your Fedora 22 install as follows.

Edit the */etc/sysconfig/network-scripts/ifcfg-en0* using your favourite editor or the default Vim editor.

```
Vim /etc/sysconfig/network-scripts/ifcfg-en0
```

Your *ifcfg-en0* file should look something like what's shown in Figure 6.

Now open and edit a few things. Note that you should enter 'IPADDR', 'NETMASK', 'GATEWAY', 'DNS1' and 'DNS2' as per your ISP, as shown in Figure 7.

3. Install the GNOME Tweak Tool

GNOME Tweak Tool is a utility that lets you tweak and alter the default settings of the GNOME Desktop Environment with ease. You can easily customise your Fedora workstation in the GUI using the GNOME Tweak Tool. Most of the options in it are self-explanatory.

To install it, use the following command in the terminal:

```
sudo dnf install gnome-tweak-tool
```

4. Install the VLC media player

The VLC player is most frequently used in both Linux as well as Windows and is a must-have. To install it, use the following commands:

```
sudo su
rpm -ivh http://download1.rrpmfusion.org/free/fedora/
rpmfusion-free-release-stable.noarch.rpm
sudo dnf install vlc
```

5. Install the RPM fusion repository

Fedora comes with a limited amount of software and you will surely want to install more packages in the future. The RPM fusion repository contains add-on packages that Fedora and Red Hat do not ship by default, but you will surely need. To enable the RPM fusion repository use the following commands:

```
sudo dnf install --nogpgcheck http://download1.rpmfusion.org/
free/fedora/rpmfusion-free-release-$(rpm -E %fedora).noarch.
rpm http://download1.rpmfusion.org/nonfree/fedora/rpmfusion-
nonfree-release-$(rpm -E %fedora).noarch.rpm
```

6. Install Nano and Vim

If you like editing files using the command line, you are using text editors such as Nano or Vim (Vi improved). To install Nano, run the following command:

```
sudo dnf install nano vim
```

7. Install Google Chrome

In Fedora 22, the default Web browser is Mozilla Firefox, which has benefits of its own, but many prefer Google Chrome. Here's how to install the latter. Open a terminal and issue the following command:

```
sudo vim /etc/dnf.repos.d/google-chrome.repo
```

```
File  Edit  View  Search  Terminal  Help
HWADDR="08:00:27:21:B5:67"
TYPE="Ethernet"
BOOTPROTO="static"
DEFROUTE="yes"
IPV4_FAILURE_FATAL="no"
IPV6INIT="yes"
IPV6_AUTOCONF="yes"
IPV6_DEFROUTE="yes"
IPV6_FAILURE_FATAL="no"
NAME="enp0s3"
UUID="62eba6e0-d23b-4b1e-adf8-891a1411c249"
ONBOOT="yes"
PEERDNS="yes"
PEERROUTES="yes"
IPV6_PEERDNS="yes"
IPV6_PEERROUTES="yes"
IPADDR=192.168.0.19
NETMASK=255.255.255.0
GATEWAY=192.168.0.1
DNS1=202.88.131.90
DNS2=202.88.131.89

-- INSERT --
```

Figure 7: Details of ifcfg-en0 file after modification

Then paste the following in that file:

```
[google-chrome]
name=google-chrome
baseurl=http://dl.google.com/linux/chrome/rpm/
stable/$basearch
enabled=1
gpgcheck=1
gpgkey=https://dl-ssl.google.com/linux/linux_signing_key.pub
```

Now install Google Chrome from the command line:

```
sudo dnf install google-chrome-stable
```

8. Install the GIMP for photo editing

The GIMP is an image manager similar to Photoshop and comes with a bunch of handy tools. It is preinstalled in many Linux distros, but it is not part of the default Fedora install. To install it, simply run the following:

```
sudo dnf install gimp
```

9. Install Pidgin – an IRC client

Pidgin is a chat client that can be used for multiple IM platforms. To install it, run the following command in the terminal:

```
sudo dnf install pidgin
```

By: Anup Allamsetty

The author is a long time contributor to the Mozilla community. You can reach him through mail at *allamsetty.anup@gmail.com*. He regularly blogs at *http://anup07.wwordpress.com*

Abort unwanted AJAX requests

We do many AJAX requests in our Web applications. Sometimes, many of these AJAX requests become invalid before they receive the data. For example, on auto complete, if we type each character, an AJAX request is raised to get the suggestion. But only the last AJAX request with the complete word will be considered as a suggestion, and all other AJAX requests just receive the data, which they drop.

To avoid this, we can abort the previous AJAX handler before making the next AJAX request by using the following code:

```
$( document ).ajaxSend(function(event, jqxhr, settings) {

  var url = settings.url;

  if (url.indexOf("search") > -1 ) { //select the
request by URL content

    if(typeof _lastAjaxReq != 'undefined') {

    _lastAjaxReq.abort();

 }

    _lastAjaxReq = jqxhr;

 }

});
```

—Balavignesh Kasinathan,
kbalavignesh@gmail.com

Manipulating NIC parameters

Many of us do not know that we can manipulate the parameters associated with network interface cards (NIC). *ethtool* is a tool that can help you change settings.

To display network statistics, use the following command:

```
#ethtool -S eth0
```

For auto-negotiation *on/off*, use the following commands:

```
#ethtool  -s eth0 autoneg off
#ethtool  -s eth0 autoneg on
```

To change the speed of the Ethernet device, use this command:

```
#ethtool -s eth0 speed 100 autoneg off
```

To see the current NIC ring buffer settings, type:

```
#ethtool –g eth0
```

To change the *tx* and *rx* ring buffer size of the NIC, use this command:

```
#ethtool –G –set-ring eth0 rx N1 rx-min N2 tx N3
```

—Gaurav Datir,
gauravsdatir@gmail.com

Delete files older than a particular period

Files that are older than a particular day can be deleted easily with a one line command. For example, the following command will delete files older than 30 days in the path */tftpboot/*:

```
#find /tftpboot/* -mtime +30 -exec rm {} \;
```

—Suraj Tamilselvan,
surajluvz@gmail.com

How to find opened files used by someone at a particular time

When running *top -c* and typing *SHIFT P* (to display the descending order of processor usage), if you find that a user is taking up too much of the resources, you can find the opened files used by that person by executing the following command:

```
for i in `ps aux | grep <username> | awk {'print $2'}`; do
lsof -p $i ; done
```

In the above command *<username>* is the name of the user.

This will be helpful in troubleshooting, in case a suspicious file is opened by a user.

Script to find the site speed

Here is a simple script that uses CURL to check the speed of a website. You need to log in as the root user and create a file as follows:

```
# touch speedcheck.sh
```

Now, open the file in any text editor and add the following lines:

```
#!/bin/bash
CURL="/usr/bin/curl"
GAWK="/usr/bin/gawk"
echo -n "Please pass the url you want to measure: "
read url
URL="$url"
result=`$CURL -o /dev/null -s -w %{time_connect}:%{time_
starttransfer}:%{time_total} $URL`
echo " Time_Connect Time_startTransfer Time_total "
echo $result | $GAWK -F: '{ print $1" "$2" "$3}'
```

Save and exit.
Run the script and wait for some time to get the output:

```
# sh speedcheck.sh
```

The output will be in the format given below:

```
time_connect:time_starttransfer:time_total
```

pauljanygodwin@gmail.com

Customise your shell prompt

The shell can be customised according to your requirements. All you need to do is to edit *~/.bashrc* and add your customisation.

The default value of PS1 on RHEL 5.X systems looks like what follows:

```
PS1='\u@\H:\w\$ '
```

…which results in a shell prompt like what is shown below:

```
user@hostname[FQDN]:/Current/Working/Directory$
```

If you want to add some colours to your prompt, you can try the following command:

```
PS1='\[\033[02;32m\]\u@\H:\[\033[02;31m\]\w\$\[\033[33m\]
'
```

For some more variants of colour codes, you can try out the following options:

```
clear
echo -e "\033[1m* Open Source For You *\033[0m"
echo -e "\033[5m* Open Source For You *\033[0m"
echo -e "\033[7m* Open Source For You *\033[0m"
echo -e "\033[30m* Open Source For You *\033[0m"
echo -e "\033[31m* Open Source For You *\033[0m"
echo -e "\033[32m* Open Source For You *\033[0m"
echo -e "\033[33m* Open Source For You *\033[0m"
echo -e "\033[34m* Open Source For You *\033[0m"
echo -e "\033[35m* Open Source For You *\033[0m"
echo -e "\033[36m* Open Source For You *\033[0m"
echo -e "\033[41m* Open Source For You *\033[0m"
echo -e "\033[42m* Open Source For You *\033[0m"
echo -e "\033[43m* Open Source For You *\033[0m"
echo -e "\033[44m* Open Source For You *\033[0m"
echo -e "\033[45m* Open Source For You *\033[0m"
echo -e "\033[46m* Open Source For You *\033[0m"
echo -e "\033[47m* Open Source For You *\033[0m"
```

If you want to make the changes for all users of the system, then do these in the */etc/bashrc* file. Comment out the default settings and add your customisation as below:

```
# [ "$PS1" = "\\s-\\v\\\$ " ] && PS1="[\u@\h \w]\\$ "
PS1='\u@\H:\w\$ '
```

—Rahul Pahade,
rahul.pahade@gmail.com

Share Your Linux Recipes!

The joy of using Linux is in finding ways to get around problems—take them head on, defeat them! We invite you to share your tips and tricks with us for publication in *OSFY* so that they can reach a wider audience. Your tips could be related to administration, programming, troubleshooting or general tweaking. Submit them at *www.opensourceforu.com*. The sender of each published tip will get a T-shirt.

www.OpenSourceForU.com | OPEN SOURCE FOR YOU | JULY 2015 | **105**

DVD OF THE MONTH

This DVD has something for everyone.

Fedora 22 Workstation: Fedora Workstation is a reliable, user-friendly and powerful operating system for your laptop or desktop computer. It comes with the GNOME 3 desktop environment. This sleek user interface allows you to concentrate on what's important while using your computer. It has built-in Docker support, which allows you to containerise your own apps, or deploy containerised apps out-of-the-box on Fedora, using Docker. The OSFY DVD has a live image of the Fedora 22 Workstation. You can use it to boot your computer and even install it on your hard disk.

Fedora SoaS: Sugar on a Stick (SoaS) is a Fedora based operating system featuring the award-winning Sugar Learning Platform and designed to fit on an ordinary USB thumb drive. The bundled image of Fedora SoaS Desktop is a live operating system. You can find the ISO image in the folder *other_isos* on the root of the DVD. It has everything you need to try out Fedora's SoaS Desktop— you don't have to erase anything on your current system to try it out. You can get the complete documentation on how to use the ISO image at *http://docs.fedoraproject.org/en-US/Fedora/20/html/Burning_ISO_images_to_disc/*

Sabayon 15.06: This is a Linux distribution that aims to deliver the best out-of-the-box user experience by providing the latest open source technologies in an elegant format. The bundled image in the OSFY DVD is the 64-bit edition of the KDE Desktop Environment. You can find the ISO image in the folder *other_isos* on the root of the DVD. You can get the complete documentation on how to install and use Sabayon at *https://wiki.sabayon.org/index.php?title=En:Beginners_Guide*

What is a live DVD?

A live CD/DVD or live disk contains a bootable operating system, the core program of any computer, which is designed to run all your programs and manage all your hardware and software.

Live CDs/DVDs have the ability to run a complete, modern OS on a computer even without secondary storage, such as a hard disk drive. The CD/DVD directly runs the OS and other applications from the DVD drive itself. Thus, a live disk allows you to try the OS before you install it without erasing or installing anything on your current system. Such disks are used to demonstrate features or try out a release. They are also used for testing hardware functionality, before actual installation. To run a live DVD, you need to boot your computer using the disk in the ROM drive. To know how to set a boot device in BIOS, please refer to the hardware documentation for your computer/laptop.

R N I No. DELENG/2012/49440, Mailed on 27/28th of Advance month Delhi Postal Regd. No. DL(S)-01/3443/2013-15
Published on 27th of Advance month

DO MORE WITH POSTGRES

IT HERO:
YOU
FIND BUDGET
FOR NEW PROJECTS

EnterpriseDB - a Magic Quadrant Leader for Operational Database Management Systems*

Advanced Technology
Reduce risk and boost performance

Handle More Workloads
Tackle more projects

Huge Savings
Cut budget by 80% or more

EnterpriseDB Software India Private Limited Unit #3, Ground Floor Godrej Castlemaine Next to Ruby Hall, Sassoon Road Pune - 411 001 India | Tel + 91-20-30589500/01 | Fax + 91-20-30589502 | EnterpriseDB.com

* The Gartner report, Magic Quadrant for Operational Database Management Systems, by Donald Feinberg, Merv Adrian and Nick Heudecker, was published October 16, 2014.

Printed in Germany
by Amazon Distribution
GmbH, Leipzig